CW00919407

MORAL ATMOSPHERES

Religion, Culture, and Public Life

RELIGION, CULTURE, AND PUBLIC LIFE
Series Editor: Matthew Engelke

The Religion, Culture, and Public Life series is devoted to the study of religion in relation to social, cultural, and political dynamics, both contemporary and historical. It features work by scholars from a variety of disciplinary and methodological perspectives, including religious studies, anthropology, history, philosophy, political science, and sociology. The series is committed to deepening our critical understandings of the empirical and conceptual dimensions of religious thought and practice, as well as such related topics as secularism, pluralism, and political theology. The Religion, Culture, and Public Life series is sponsored by Columbia University's Institute for Religion, Culture, and Public Life.

Perilous Intimacies: Debating Hindu-Muslim Friendship After Empire, SherAli Tareen

Samson Occom: Radical Hospitality in the Native Northeast, Ryan Carr

Baptizing Burma: Religious Change in the Last Buddhist Kingdom, Alexandra Kaloyanides

At Home and Abroad: The Politics of American Religion, edited by Elizabeth Shakman Hurd and Winnifred Fallers Sullivan

The Arab and Jewish Questions: Geographies of Engagement in Palestine and Beyond, edited by Bashir Bashir and Leila Farsakh

Modern Sufis and the State: The Politics of Islam in South Asia and Beyond, edited by Katherine Pratt Ewing and Rosemary R. Corbett

German, Jew, Muslim, Gay: The Life and Times of Hugo Marcus, Marc David Baer

The Limits of Tolerance: Enlightenment Values and Religious Fanaticism, Denis Lacorne

The Holocaust and the Nakba, edited by Bashir Bashir and Amos Goldberg

Democratic Transition in the Muslim World: A Global Perspective, edited by Alfred Stepan

The Politics of Secularism: Religion, Diversity, and Institutional Change in France and Turkey, Murat Akan

Holy Wars and Holy Alliance: The Return of Religion to the Global Political Stage, Manlio Graziano

Faithful to Secularism: The Religious Politics of Democracy in Ireland, Senegal, and the Philippines, David T. Buckley

Pakistan at the Crossroads: Domestic Dynamics and External Pressures, edited by Christophe Jaffrelot

Beyond the Secular West, edited by Akeel Bilgrami

For a complete list of books in the series, please see the Columbia University Press website.

Moral Atmospheres

ISLAM AND MEDIA
IN A PAKISTANI MARKETPLACE

Timothy P. A. Cooper

Columbia University Press
New York

Winner of the 2022 Claremont Prize
Institute for Religion, Culture, and Public Life at Columbia University

Publication of this book was made possible in part by funding from the
Institute for Religion, Culture, and Public Life at Columbia University.

Columbia University Press
Publishers Since 1893
New York   Chichester, West Sussex
cup.columbia.edu
Copyright © 2024 Columbia University Press
All rights reserved

Library of Congress Cataloging-in-Publication Data
Names: Cooper, Timothy P. A., author.
Title: Moral atmospheres : Islam and media in a Pakistani marketplace /
Timothy P. A. Cooper.
Description: New York : Columbia University Press, 2024. | Series:
Religion, culture, and public life | Includes bibliographical references and index.
Identifiers: LCCN 2023037190 (print) | LCCN 2023037191 (ebook) |
ISBN 9780231210409 (hardback) | ISBN 9780231210416 (trade paperback) |
ISBN 9780231558402 (ebook)
Subjects: LCSH: Mass media—Religious aspects—Islam. | Communication—
Religious aspects—Islam. | Mass media—Pakistan. | Islam in mass media.
Classification: LCC BP185.7 .C667 2024 (print) | LCC BP185.7 (ebook) |
DDC 297.2/7—dc23/eng/20230914
LC record available at https://lccn.loc.gov/2023037190
LC ebook record available at https://lccn.loc.gov/2023037191

Printed and bound by CPI Group (UK) Ltd, Croydon, CR0 4YY

Cover design: Elliott S. Cairns
Cover image: Yaseen Street, Lahore, Pakistan. Photo by author.

For and with Abeera

Contents

Notes on the Text

In Lahore, the language of my interlocutors was primarily Urdu and Punjabi. Several terms that I heard widely used and that came to inform this research, such as "demand," were expressed to me in English, while others were idiomatic terms in Urdu that derived either from Quranic or modern Arabic. Elsewhere, all translations of Urdu conversations or written materials are my own. These are written in italics and followed by a brief translation in parentheses. To widen the book's accessibility and readability, I employ a highly simplified system of transliteration that omits diacritical marks and hamzas and, when appropriate, uses the commonly used English spelling if such a term already exists (such as *ulama*).

While only a small number of my interlocutors requested anonymity, I anonymize names throughout to ensure that the placement of their comments and labors alongside material unknown to them (or me) at the time of research or writing does not put them in any danger or reflect negatively upon them in their private life or place of work.

Due to the unsuitability of the ethnographic present tense and the awkwardness of writing in the subjunctive, I have chosen to write the ethnographic sections of this book in the past tense.

Acknowledgments

Lahore is a city of mediators, of saints and bureaucrats, traders, and repairpersons. Through its association with literature, music, and filmmaking, it is also a city of connoisseurs. Humbled as I was by this continuous movement of knowledge and expertise, nothing could prepare me for the generosity of those who would help me conduct the research that this book documents. These friends and interlocutors appear in anonymized form, but I hope they will recognize themselves and the impact they made on my life in Lahore. There are also those who do not appear in this book but whose kindness and hospitality stayed with me. There was the uncle who called himself *Shaitaan* [Satan] who ran a photography studio in the Walled City. And there was the Multani expatriate in the Emirate of Sharjah whose wisdom, openness, and enthusiasm represented the kind of everyday support that I received in conducting this research, both in Pakistan and in the diaspora.

The pressures of fieldwork, of being here, of being there, of being productive to oneself and useful to others, create periods of euphoria as well as inert anxiety. This book is a product of all of this. It is also the fruit of the support and involvement of my wife, Abeera. While the excitement of fieldwork is so immediate, no quantity of fieldnotes, recordings, or photographs can stop the freshness of these experiences melting into air. That I got to share these with her, archives them forever in our shared experience. This book is dedicated to her companionship, intellect, and independence.

In the ensuing years, we have been joined by our daughter, Noor Anaya, whose fascination with the world around her has come to blissfully suffuse our lives with mystery and intrigue.

I would also like to acknowledge the input of my family and friends, firstly my sister-in-law Aysha Khan, who shared the city that she loves and loathes with us. My parents, Karen and Andrew, raised me in an atmosphere conducive to life-long learning, a result of the same interest in the world fostered by their parents and my grandparents, Pamela and Ernest Cooper, and Margaret and Donald Watson. I thank my brother Paul for introducing me to the possibilities of writing and of immersive research, and my nephew Johnny for humbling all of us with his emotional intelligence. I also thank our dear friends Rachele, her partner Chris, and their daughters Robyn and Erin, as well as our friends in Lahore, Usman and Mehek, Ali and Alizey, and the late Ferida Apa.

During the writing of this book, we lost several cherished family members and friends, my grandmother Pamela, best friend and matriarch, my grandfather Donald, and a dear friend of my wife, Barbara Harrell-Bond. Most cruelly, we also lost my sister-in-law Natasha. Even as the years pass those words seem scarcely believable. Her incomparable spirit, sense of humor, and taste in music lives on in her son Johnny. I also thank my parents' partners, Helen and Sharon, for being great allies in times of both celebration and mourning.

This book has also accumulated many debts through its slow gestation in British universities. As a young film scholar, my mentors at King's College London, Michele Pierson and Mark Betz, encouraged me to proceed further with doctoral research. At the Department of Anthropology at University College London, I undertook a PhD and conducted the research that informs this book. This was funded by the UK Arts and Humanities Research Council (Grant No. AH/L503873/1). I would like to thank my supervisor Christopher Pinney. His support fostered a sense of creative freedom, provided a forum through which to refine ideas, and his capacious intellect helped me to take my research in new directions. I thank my second supervisor Haidy Geismar, whose feedback to our cohort group was an inspiration to us all, for giving such supportive and incisive guidance. The constructive criticism and feedback from the external examiners of my PhD, Brian Larkin and Lotte Hoek, provided a wealth of ideas for me to reflect upon. As an anthropologist trained in film and media studies, I hope this book shows some of the benefits of thinking across these two disciplines.

Other faculty members at UCL were generous with their time over the three years spent at the department, particularly Ashraf Hoque, Victor Buchli, Ammara Maqsood, and Charles Stewart. I also benefited greatly from the input of my doctoral cohort and friends at UCL, particularly Francisco Vergara Murua, Vindhya Buthpitiya, Thomas Fry, Toyin Agbetu, Adam Runacres, Gwen Burnyeat, and Andrea Lathrop. Outside of the department Nasreen Rehman, Paul Rollier, Stephen Hughes, Tariq Rahman, and Till Trojer have kindly offered support and guidance. Special mention goes to Ali Nobil Ahmad and Chris Moffat, who have been immense sources of advice, guidance, and encouragement throughout. When I returned to London briefly from the field in 2018, it was an honour to work with filmmaker Jamil Dehlavi on a retrospective of his films at the British Film Institute.

Related aspects of the research that informs this book can be found in *Comparative Studies in Society and History*, the *Journal of the Royal Anthropological Institute*, the *Journal of Material Culture*, *Ethnomusicology*, and *Material Religion: The Journal of Objects, Art and Belief.* I thank the editors and reviewers at each of these journals for helping me to refine ideas associated with this project. Karen Ruffle and Babak Rahimi and their Sensing Shiʿism Working Group have also helped me to develop ongoing research into Pakistani Shiʿism.

It was as a postdoctoral fellow, at the Department of Social Anthropology at the University of Cambridge, that I expanded my PhD thesis into a book manuscript. This research was funded by the UK Economic and Social Research Council (Grant No. ES/V011669/1) and an Early Career Fellowship was funded by the Leverhulme Trust and the Isaac Newton Trust (Grant No. ECF-2021-008). I was able to join this exciting research environment through the support of Joel Robbins, for whose unwavering encouragement, kindness, and friendship I am ever grateful. Other members of the department have been generous interlocutors and sources of guidance; thanks go to Yael Navaro, James Laidlaw, Sian Lazar, Rupert Stasch, Andrew Sanchez, Perveez Mody, Matei Candea, Liana Chua, Natalia Buitron, Daniel White, Juan del Nido, Kelly Fagan Robinson, and Michael Edwards. During this time, I was also an affiliated researcher at the Max Planck-Cambridge Centre for Ethics, Economy, and Social

Change. Thanks go to Chris Hann, Johannes Lenhard, and my colleagues at the center for providing this film scholar with a crash course in foundational ideas in anthropology. King's College, Cambridge, also generously supported my research during the publication of this book and provided me with an unparalleled opportunity to learn from those from outside my immediate discipline. Special thanks here go to David Good, Ann Davis, Edgard Camarós, and Max Ritts.

Finally, my sincere thanks go to Matthew Engelke at the Institute for Religion, Culture, and Public Life at Columbia University, and everyone involved in the Claremont Prize for the Study of Religion, especially Katherine Ewing, Isabel Huacuja Alonso, and the anonymous reviewers. At Columbia University Press I was gifted with Madeleine Hamey-Thomas's perceptive copyediting, the most wonderful editors in Wendy Lochner and Lowell Frye, and the wider production and marketing team, through whose endeavors academic publishing remains a flourishing domain.

Prologue

I t was the middle of the afternoon on Hall Road in the Pakistani city of Lahore and the traders who worked on this vast and diverse electronics marketplace were slowly strolling back to work after Friday congregational prayers. From somewhere in this crowd of thousands, I heard the rising melody of "Chalte Chalte" composed by Ghulam Mohammad for the Indian Bollywood film *Pakeezah* (1972). Despite its association with the film trade, I rarely heard music on Hall Road. In place of the sublime rasp of Ram Narayan's sarangi and Lata Mangeshkar's vocals, I heard a voice heavy with reverb and backed up by rhythmic, low-register breathing, reminiscent of *dhikr* meditation through which some Muslims draw closer to Allah. Despite the percussive quality of the layered voices, there was no instrumental accompaniment. I looked around to see where the sound was coming from. The crowd was too thick for it to be emanating from a car stereo system. I listened out for the Urdu poet Kaifi Azmi's familiar lyrics. "*While walking . . . I happened to meet someone.*" As it grew louder, I recognized the ragged sonic edges of the kind of low-voltage amplifier used by small prayer gatherings in mosques and shrines and began to make out quite different lines. "*I have become complete . . . I go to your city where they recite your* na'at." While I rarely heard music on Lahore's streets, I often heard recitations on the threshold of song.

This famous film song had been turned into a *na'at*, a poem of praise for the Prophet Muhammad. The crowd began to part, as if the moving sound of the recitation had created its own discrete volumetric space. Respectfully, but without reverence, the traders and customers moved aside, and an elderly, visually impaired man passed slowly and assuredly through. Fastened to his chest was a double shoulder-holster with a hand-held megaphone in one side and the cassette player to which it was wired in the other. Whenever he felt the gentle, guiding hands of people close to him, he stretched out his palm and received small-denomination notes.

His sonic aesthetic was appreciated by many of Hall Road's traders. Faisal, a late middle-aged man who ran a basement store, sent his nephew and shop assistant Idris to furnish the man with a larger denomination note. Back at his store I asked him about the service the man with the megaphone provided. "The *mahaul* of this street is not good," Idris said, using the Urdu word for *atmosphere*, and referring to its longstanding association with the film and video trade. "This man helps to make it pure."

During over a year of ethnographic fieldwork in the Pakistani city of Lahore conducted between 2017 and 2020, spent studying the relationship between media aesthetics and the ethics of mediation, I found the conditions of mahaul an issue of great interest to my interlocutors. While it has come to be used in ways akin to the English word for *atmosphere* or *environment*, the term describes a sense of immersion formed through the subjective adjudication of the moral and social qualities of a particular setting. Unlike other possible synonyms, *context* or *character*, for example, mahaul is an avowedly social formation, referring closely to the cultural dynamics of stratification and public morality.

Idris was one of at least twenty-five thousand traders who made their living on Hall Road. When I first met him, he had just come back from fourteen years spent working in Dubai and was struggling to adapt to his new life. He left Pakistan when he was just seventeen, and with their ancestral home some distance west of the city of Peshawar towards the Afghanistan border, his family were happy that he was abroad during the worst of the countrywide insurgency that had caused untold suffering in the region. While work in Dubai was hard, and he came back no wealthier than when he left, there Idris had no elders to answer to and found it easy to make friends outside of the Pakistani expatriate community. As he struggled to adapt to Hall Road's hierarchical merchant community, Idris liked to distinguish himself from his peers by recalling his old friends in Dubai who hailed from far-flung countries or observed faiths other than Islam. Although many men spend periods of time working in the Middle East,

Idris felt that his experiences set him apart from his immediate colleagues and close kin. This cosmopolitanism made him feel individual and distinct. But the pluralism he cultivated in Dubai stayed in Dubai. Once back in Lahore, Idris was keen to rediscover the appropriate distance between himself and those affiliated with other religions and *mazhabs* [jurisprudential schools of thought].

Idris was increasingly exasperated with his job, and his reluctance to work often drew the ire of Faisal, his uncle and manager of the business. There was work to be done and Idris was more interested in rediscovering the city and its people than dealing with customers. During the time he had been away, Faisal's store, Durrani Electronics, had moved from selling Pakistani films on recorded videotapes or copied onto discs to dealing in imported televisions, smartphones, spare parts, and internet data. This mirrored the pace of change which had seen the rapid adoption of smartphone and internet access transform the economic and political map of Pakistan. Hall Road itself had gone from being a global center for the trade in local and pirated film to a labyrinth of sole traders offering everything from memory cards to sacks of obsolete hardware sold by weight, and from USB cables to high-end smartphones.

Faisal had changed too in his advancing years; he had strengthened his faith and turned more fervently to Allah. He was not nostalgic about the old days and the bad mahaul that he felt still clung to the street. He missed the money rather than the morality of the film trade. During the years his nephew Idris was away, the fortunes of the Lahore-based film industry known as Lollywood had faded and taken with it its high-octane energy, lascivious sexuality, and distinct aesthetics. Even though this once popular, even populist, filmmaking idiom once closely allied with the Punjabi *awaam* [the people, public] had waned, Faisal still did a little related work on the side. He drew on his large collection of Pakistani Lollywood films from his days in the trade to create compilations of popular song and dance segments to sell as master copies to the traders in the basement film market adjacent to them. These were all curated around individual themes, with titles like, "Hippy Item Numbers," "Wronged Women," "Old is Gold: Punjabi Item Numbers Volumes 1–25." This helped him to remember his youth and to rekindle something of the vibrant scene he used to play some small part in sustaining. Most of all, it kept fixed in his customers' minds the former stature of their business in the film trade. Their longevity in the marketplace made them the first port of call for many customers unfamiliar with Hall Road.

While for his uncle this all made perfect sense, to Idris something did not add up. Whenever asked, Faisal was quick to express his belief that, once all is said and done, film is impermissible in Islam and that secular music and singing are morally repugnant. I had come to Lahore to find out about the marketplace circulation and distribution of film in Pakistan but soon found the mutual coexistence of conflicted, often opposed viewpoints evinced a disjuncture between how my interlocutors felt about popular media and how they acted. Whatever name its defenders give to film—entertainment, culture, or *time-pass*—Faisal could no longer give his approval to an industry, art form, or object of attention that he considered resistant to moral order. He was particularly incensed by films about the life of the Prophet Muhammad, or his family and companions, made in Shi'a-majority Iran and guided by different sensibilities over depicting important figures in Islam than those widely accepted in Pakistan. As many find when they delve deeply enough, the Quran and the sunnah, the body of literature that compiles the sayings and doings of the Prophet Muhammad and the prototypical Islamic community, invite multiple interpretations over the permissibility of moving-image media, image-making, and music. When established modes of scriptural discourse are unable to tackle changing media situations, or their critics are not well-versed in theology or jurisprudence, many speculate on the mahaul that radiates from people and things. Explicating the problems of Iranian films circulating in Pakistan, Faisal explained to me, "In this mahaul of filmmaking, some people acting the role[s] of Prophets might be drunks or lechers in real life; how can they be allowed to work on such a pious topic?" His refusal of film a place in his ethical life referred to the moral atmosphere that surrounds it. The paradox of atmosphere is that while it has the power to obstruct or cloud the piety of a given place, as evinced by the man with his loudspeaker, another atmosphere through which one can find membership can be marshalled to purify that place. Atmospheres are mutable and closely related to affective and moral thresholds, in this instance between recitation and song, that allow the suggestions that film and music provoke to be rerouted to different ends.

Over the months I got to know him, Idris began to read up on the contradictions he saw in Faisal's opinions so that he could debate them more successfully. One morning, a copy of *Alat-e Jadida ke Shari'i Ahkam* [The Orders of the Shari'a on Modern Inventions] was waiting for me beneath the counter when I went to visit Durrani Electronics. This is a book on the religious permissibility of technological apparatuses and media forms, written and compiled by Maulana Mufti Muhammad Shafi, an influential Pakistani Islamic scholar and Sunni Deobandi authority on Quranic exegesis. I was surprised when Idris, ever a man to strike a hard bargain, presented this to me as a gift, remarking on the ways in which it might add to my research. Echoing his uncle's words of some months earlier, Idris told me that this book taught him one must first grasp the environment or *mahauliyat* of media technologies before understanding the communication of its content.

In this book I ask, is it possible to take Idris's suggestion at face value and locate moral orientation in the atmospheres that emanate from media environments? My interest is also a disciplinary one. With a conceptual vocabulary already rich in moods, spirits, sounds, and emotions, what can atmosphere do for anthropology? Can its conceptualization, through the identification of its thresholds and interfaces, provide ways of drawing equivalence with our interlocutors' encounters with the affective intensity of social change?

MORAL ATMOSPHERES

Introduction

Viewing film as a subject of social debate allows us to conceive of morality as a series of thresholds rather than fixed ethical stances. In a vast electronics market in the Pakistani city of Lahore, I observed traders of film, music, and Islamic media try to reconcile their own ethical selfhood with the objects they sold. In so doing, they were also attempting to come to grips with the material, visual, and sonic culture of public feeling and those indeterminate others always just outside the bounds of description or immediate experience. In these contexts, ambient interruptions, offending images, and competing soundscapes shaped the character of shared space. For my interlocutors, speculating on the ambient and the airborne helped them to make sense of the difficult relationship between an emotional, internal life of knowledge and feeling and an external world of surfaces and sensations. Atmospheres show how ethical life can be sensed and felt.

In Pakistan, forms of popular entertainment such as film are one of the sources from which emanates a *mahaul*, a term that describes an atmosphere, an environment, a sense of proximity, but also an ambient aura of right and wrong. One might speak of the ambiguous atmosphere of diaspora life, the salacious atmosphere of a film studio, or the inspiring milieu of a religious shrine. The tactile earthiness of the term is reminiscent of the agricultural concept of *terroir* which describes the unique sense of place embodied in a crop yield, that shapes the product from which it is made.

Figure 0.1 One of many loudspeakers affixed to Hall Road's plazas, calling a working population of over twenty-five thousand to prayer at one of more than a dozen mosques. (Photo by author.)

To define terroir is also to suggest that these elements can be harnessed and influenced by humans. Likewise, mahaul is the product of human cultivation and disturbance; it carries a weight that transforms space and time and pervades everyday life. In studies of contemporary Pakistan and North India, mahaul has been understood to communicate a sense of "disquiet" about a place and the people who form its "social atmosphere."[1] Nida Kirmani has extensively analyzed the term, defining it as a social boundary that involves both the act of exclusion and being excluded. Working with Indian Muslims facing insecurity and marginalization, Kirmani studies the "mental maps" people make of their neighborhoods and how these maps are read at a scale removed.[2] She found that identifying and binding oneself to an Islamically resonant atmosphere provided a sense of belonging to her mostly female interlocutors. Although grounded in a male-dominated market, the research presented in this book closely aligns with Kirmani's understanding of mahaul. Yet, Idris's suggestion that I engage with the mahaul of Hall Road was both a moral one and a product of the patriarchal public sphere to which he, as a young Sunni Muslim man, and I, a male researcher, had privileged access.

The Hindustani word mahaul originates in an Arabic term for *what is around or about in near proximity*. It is formed from the consonant root *h-w-l* which also gives us words that denote a mood, an attitude, or something which ushers in a change or a transformation. I translate mahaul in English as a *moral atmosphere* rather than "surroundings" or "character" to evoke the airborne qualities of breath, pollution, scent, and floating sounds so richly described by the metalinguistic use of the term. In English, the semantic emergence of terms of close correlation, such as climate, ambience, atmosphere, milieu, to describe a social environment, can be traced to the influence of Romanticist ideas, and the concurrent pursuit of "all-embracing" concepts in Euro-American philosophy, science, and aesthetics.[3] Initially, it was this commitment to anthropological holism that shaped my interest in moral atmosphere.[4] Yet I soon realized Idris was gesturing at something more nuanced, to how atmosphere can be generative of modes of judgement and decision-making. Unlike other words for social environment, on Hall Road, a longstanding hub of film reproduction, mahaul can also be stirred, reproduced, and mediated by artistic and technological objects.[5]

While an atmosphere can be identified as authoritative and present, its constitution is often mired in ambiguity. As with many others who made their name in the marketplace trade in the local Pakistani film industry, Faisal found his self-image as a Muslim devoted to prayer and dedicated to his faith easy to reconcile with his enthusiasm for song numbers from the heady days of 1970s Lollywood filmmaking. In the parlance of Euro-American film spectatorship, it would be fair to call Faisal a cinephile. Many of those at his local mosque found his affection for film disturbing. The DVD compilations he made were illustrated with homemade covers featuring scantily clad women towering over leering men, wielding a Kalashnikov or a bloody knife, while their contents featured suggestive dance numbers and sequences of "Western" hippies parading around crates of whiskey. But Faisal did not feel the need to bifurcate his trade and his faith; his confidence in the hybridity of religious and entrepreneurial worlds trumped rational explanation. While he felt comfortable dealing in things that he considered immoral, his objection to film concentrated on its mahaul, on a moral atmosphere that neither clung to his store nor emanated from him.

Faisal's opinions were based on deep intimacy with his surroundings. For the last thirty-five years he had spent eleven hours a day, six days a week, working on Hall Road. The market had established its reputation following the birth of Pakistan amid the Partition of the Indian subcontinent in 1947, when several outlets offering the sale and repair of radio sets were joined by importers and wholesalers dealing in its constituent parts. The local model of the commodity zone—in which traders dealing in similar produce congregate in densely occupied bazaars—proved well suited to the boom in the sale of consumer electronics in the 1970s and 1980s, when the extant radio stores were joined by those dealing in audio- and videocassette hardware.

It was here that the disparate objects explored in this book—film, video, ritual and procession footage, film music, and devotional images—became united by one seismic change, the widespread availability of a new generation of electronic media. Most influential were magnetic tape-recording formats suitable for audio and video recording and playback, but photocopiers, personal computers, and digital storage devices also played an important role. These allowed small, independent traders to develop a market in recording, retrieval, and reproduction. In the normative narrative that celebrates audio- and videocassette cultures, the introduction of commercial tape formats in the late 1970s provided an Eastern Bloc under Soviet control, eager for Western music and film, with the tools to subvert state censorship. Home-recording technology was seen to be emancipative, the inverse of state broadcasting, in that it could foster an "unofficial culture" and expose the porosity of regimes once believed to be fixed and impenetrable.[6] In Europe and the United States home recording drove the creation of musical undergrounds, particularly in closely connected urban genres like punk and hip-hop. By the early 1980s there were countless local and international cassette networks. Home compiled or recorded tapes were given as gifts between friends, families, and lovers, shared with fellow enthusiasts, or sold to a public who would come to be defined by their circulation. Sometimes cassette networks actively attempted to transgress large recording corporations' copyright and the laws that enforced it.

Pakistan's own social histories of recording were shaped by a pervasive appetite for Bollywood films from across the Indian border. Less than a decade after the Partition of British India into the Dominions of India and Pakistan in 1947, the leading directors, producers, and film personalities of the Lollywood industry gathered in front of the Regent Cinema on Lahore's McLeod Road for the premiere of an Indian film, *Jaal* (1952). The area was still known as Charing Cross after its central London namesake. Only the previous year had the bronze statue of Queen Victoria been removed. The stars of the nascent Pakistani film industry were not there to celebrate the release but to protest the film having broken the import quota on Indian films via a loophole in national commercial trade policy, by shipping the film from East Pakistan, where it had already received permission to run, to West Pakistan. After many of the stars of the Lahore film industry were arrested and imprisoned, what became known at the "Jaal Agitation" resulted in a film-for-film trade agreement with India. This ended with the 1965 Indo-Pakistani War when military general Ayub Khan, who had assumed power in a coup d'état in October 1958, cancelled the censor certificates of Indian films imported earlier into the country and banned future imports.[7] It took another military ruler, Pervez Musharraf, to formally overturn the ban on the import of Indian films in the early 2000s, which continues to be sporadically re-imposed during heightened tensions with India, particularly regarding the disputed status of Kashmir.

These forty years of cultural embargo coincided closely with the availability of commercial recording and playback formats and, later, cable and satellite television on both sides of the border. By the late 1960s filmmaker and activist Alamgir Kabir observed that an early form of magnetic tape recording was used by "agents of local producers in India [who] tape-record the entire dialogues and songs of films from cinema halls and smuggle [them] out for Pakistani 'film-makers' to imitate to their heart's content."[8] Rather than fostering support for a national industry, the Jaal Agitation and Ayub's embargo on Indian film turned Pakistani consumers towards alternative distribution channels. As a commodity zone that included spare parts, audio and visual hardware old and new, local entrepreneurs, and established businessmen with operations in the Gulf, Britain, the United States, Canada, and beyond, by the 1980s Hall Road began to generate its own signature produce. Drawing on the availability of production and distribution materials and manpower, the street became one of the central junctures of the trade in pirated film and music in South Asia. Its distribution networks were both intimately local and widely dispersed. For example, a London-based videocassette distributor would secure celluloid reels from the producers of the local Lahore-based Lollywood film industry and have them professionally converted to videocassette in London for rental shops around the UK. Hall Road traders, only a few hundred meters from the offices of Lahore's film distributors, would pay vast amounts to secure one of these videocassettes from the UK, from which it would produce hundreds of copies in the top-floor duplication factories of the vertical

Figure 0.2 On Hall Road, an advertisement for event photography and filming features a taxonomic line of icons depicting different video mediums. (Photo by author.)

plazas. These copies would then be sold as master copies to traders in the Gulf, who made their own duplicates for sale to the Pakistani expatriate labor population residing there. Small fortunes were made in the plazas of Hall Road during the videocassette era, providing an incentive for countless imitations.[9] Following the growth of Hall Road, the Rainbow Centre in Saddar, Karachi, became an arguably even larger center for the trade in informal media. These markets share much with that in Delhi studied by Ravi Sundaram in his 2009 monograph *Pirate Modernity*, which traces how dynamics of access are adapted to local systems of labor and trade capital.[10] The result is a "bleeding culture," marked by blurred edges and ambiguous boundaries that provide fertile ground for subaltern media infrastructures.[11]

The sale of Indian films, as well as Pakistani, religious, and Euro-American media, also fed the trade in their constituent parts and hardware, allowing Hall Road to grow in tandem with the appearance of plazas across the city. As a vernacular architectural form, plazas are cheaply constructed vertical bazaars formed of modular units housing numerous small businesses. By the end of the 1980s, many of the owners of properties assigned to them following the post-Partition migration to India of their original, often Hindu or Sikh, owners, had bypassed laws concerning such "evacuee property" and sold their land to developers. Plazas were built in their place, providing small units for traders' salesrooms, repair workshops, or offices. As access to cable television, then to the internet and digital video-enabled smartphones, grew, by the mid-2010s, hundreds of traders switched from film copies to mobile accessories, televisions, drones, and even virtual reality headsets, with the old stalwarts of the videocassette and videodisc era pushed to the basement of the two oldest plazas where they once ran street-facing shops. These *DVDwallas*—a descriptor that may change with formats for access—are store-holders, usually only one or two individuals, who work from a dispersed repertoire to produce cheaply made reproductions of films in copy. They usually use cheaper VCDs (Video-Compact Discs) and load content directly onto USBs and smartphones. Unlike in other countries, Pakistan's *DVDwallas* have rarely fallen afoul of intellectual property laws but have been targeted by hardline religious groups given the public visibility of their trade. Violent raids

Figure 0.3 Lahore's Hall Road: a mud-splattered standee of a Pakistani film star advertises a new Chinese-made smartphone on which consumers can stream films, communicate cheaply with relatives abroad, and benefit from increasingly sophisticated photographic "selfie technology" and "beautification filters." (Photo by author.)

on videocassette and disc stores in Islamabad in 2007 were a favored tactic of the militant groups that centered around the Lal Masjid and Jamia Hafsa madrasah, who would boast of their anti-vice activities with large, public bonfires of media they deemed immoral or obscene.

On Hall Road, the promises and dangers of film coexist. The aspirations pinned to consumer electronics, the ambiguous ethics of entertainment media, the patriarchal politics of a primarily male marketplace, and the lascivious aesthetics of Lollywood film come together to give the street a moral atmosphere that is well-known across the country, even by those who have not experienced it firsthand. As Faisal described to me, this atmosphere is not experienced only in proximity to film actors or to film experience, but is contagious and omnipresent, mediated by individuals, collectives, by hardware and by software, and fastened to the media associated with the market.

The Aesthetics and Ethics of Atmospheres

The recitation on the threshold of song with which I began the prologue illustrates several key facets of mahaul as I experienced it. First, that the moral atmosphere that surrounds film in Pakistan is multisensory and multimodal. Songs are often more recognizable elements of a film's social presence than the narrative itself; the atmosphere of film is sonic as well as visual and, in the body's ability to sense its resonances in public space, also proprioceptive. Second, that many of these ideas around atmosphere were shaped by Hall Road traders' devotional orientation, which is associated with natural agents like the divine light of Allah's guidance, fragrance, in the *attar* perfume oils applied after regular prayer ablutions, and airborne effects like sound, associated with the amplified volume of poems and chants for the Prophet Muhammad. What was it, then, that made my interlocutors use atmosphere as a medium for expressing their disquiet over public morality? Inayat Khan, a musicologist and Indian Sufi sage who wrote widely on the philosophical import of the airborne, provided a possible answer.[12] In his work on sound, mostly dating from the 1920s during time spent performing and lecturing across Europe, he wrote,

> Space itself does not have an atmosphere. Space is negative in that it allows its pulse to beat to the rhythm it is charged with, and at the

same time it is positive in that it absorbs and assimilates all, sooner or later. When a person says that the atmosphere of a place is quiet or exciting, this only means that the impression of someone who has charged the atmosphere of that place lingers there. This shows that every individual is a tone, a rhythm; a tone that draws the tone of every other person to its own pitch, a rhythm that compels every other person to follow the same rhythm.[13]

Atmospheres are not like language forms but possess the elasticity of musical notes. And like musical notes, atmospheres need a medium to travel through the air. These vibrations in matter are provided by the presence and lingering absence of other people. Khan went on to question what it is that holds atmospheres together. Consider wireless telegraphy and mirages, he wrote, "why does not the air scatter the sounds and words spoken many miles away? . . . It is the same with the phenomenon of mirage. One sees in the desert a picture that is nothing but a reflection on the waves of light of something really existing."[14] He believed that what "holds this picture intact" and holds signals together is the experience of containment rather than a perceptible container technology.[15] This subtle shift in focus raises a question that this book attempts to answer. What is it that atmospheres hold together? The epochal shift with which Khan's observations coincided remains fresh. This was a time when new technologies transformed the meaning of communication from face-to-face contact to airborne forms carried by signals, electricity, and radio waves.[16]

German philosopher Herman Schmitz, whose work is most closely associated with the contemporary study of atmosphere, might agree with Khan. In Schmitz's words, "emotions are atmospheres poured out spatially."[17] As a self-proclaimed herald of "new phenomenology," Schmitz considers atmospheres to be conditioned by local and historical frameworks even at the same time as being understood by the perceiver to be intersubjective facts. For Schmitz, the philosophical subdivision between a person's inner being and an outer sphere of sensation—also known as the mind–body dualism—is anathema for the way the body as an autonomous, feeling entity inhabits and shapes itself to its surroundings. Crucial to Schmitz's distinctive view of the felt body is its encounter with spaces that do not possess surfaces. Sonic experience is an example of this, as are weather, wind, and bodies of water. One's affective response to these spaces provides a kind of feedback that fills them with something of the felt body of the perceiver. Another German philosopher of atmospheres, Gernot Böhme, whose work has influenced recent anthropological interest in the subject, is concerned with their manufacturing, design, and mediation beyond the perceiving self. His object-oriented approach finds atmospheres pose a profound uncertainty over whether their constitution should be attributed to the things and spaces from which they are felt to emanate, or from those who experience their resonance. Like Schmitz's felt body, objects can also resonate beyond themselves, filling space with "tensions and suggestions of movement."[18] These Böhme calls "tuned spaces," finding that they play a pivotal role in the social experience of harmony or dissonance.[19] Yet by focusing on their "production" or staging, Böhme's atmospheres become awkwardly wedded to agency and intention, while Schmitz's belief in the autonomy of the felt body denies the value of individual reflection that might locate atmospheres in the realm of the ethical or the moral. It is here, at the disjuncture between the ethical and the aesthetic, that these recent philosophies of atmosphere are ill-suited to the study of mahaul as the result of a sense of moral unease.[20] While mahaul contains within it the seeds of submission, passivity, and authoritarianism, it finds ways to celebrate or critique forms of attachment without wading into debates on affect or materiality. In so doing, it can communicate a sense of disquiet without recourse to more overt forms of appreciation or critique.

Anthropologists studying religion and media have explored how the atmospheric and ambient can become a powerful social force. Studying the ways consumers of Islamic media in Mauritius identify efficacy and attachment in "sonic presence," Patrick Eisenlohr finds atmosphere a useful tool for thinking beyond religious mediation as a question of point-to-point transmission.[21] Drawing on the work of Schmitz, Eisenlohr considers sounds "atmospheric half-things" that are not immanent to religious practice but whose thresholds emerge from multiple sources of feedback.[22] In his work with Indian Shi'a Muslims in Mumbai, he finds that the social boundaries that this feedback transcends or reinforces can be constitutive of "atmospheric citizenship," illustrating how individuals coexist in the presence of others with whom they may or may not share a bond.[23] The ways Eisenlohr's notion differs from cultural theorist Lauren Berlant's notion of "ambient citizenship" illustrates the difference between atmosphere and ambience. Ambient citizenship is about whose presence dominates a political situation and who has the "right to take up soundspace."[24]

Atmospheric and ambient citizenship are both about sound and about the right to occupy and reside. But if ambience revolves around reclaiming a political space, atmospheric citizenship is about mutual recognition.

In Matthew Engelke's ethnography of Christians in England advocating for Biblical publicity, the contours of "ambient faith" are a potentially powerful agent for change.[25] Engelke's interlocutors saw their religion suffering from the bifurcation of faith into normative public and private realms. Advocating for a new way of being Christian in England, they looked to the agential possibilities of ambience to publicize religious feelings that are not necessarily tethered to institutions or organized practices. The difference between the atmospheric and the ambient can be found in the demands it makes of its perceiver. Engelke was hesitant to ask people about the public installations his interlocutors hoped would blend into the character of the town. "Calling attention to an ambient effect is a sure-fire way of dispelling it," he writes, and "ambience is most successful in this context through its unconscious affection."[26] Ambience resides in place and is more conducive to inviting reflection, but rarely coexists with other ambiences. Alone, it provides a total background that powerfully animates the foreground. In contrast, atmospheres emanate from and come to envelop people and things. While they can be multiple and coexistent, they make more immediate demands.[27]

Understanding atmospheres ethnographically requires finding an approach that makes them more than discursive strategies or allusions, while capturing the overlap and interaction between the aesthetic and the ethical. After Inayat Khan, I feel that the solution is to look at atmosphere as a quality of containment, to examine what it is that they contain, and look for the interfaces that make them perceptible to others. The Hindustani concept of mahaul takes shape as a human response to the demands made by airborne events, encounters, and disruptions, particularly those that leave debris. Pollution leaves its oily residue on a framed Muslim prayer, smog closes schools and fills hospitals, an amplified sermon helps one to remember Allah or drives another to file a noise complaint against their neighbor, air-conditioning divides and binds economic classes, and broadcast media signals the coming of religious commemorations with a solemn or austere change of tone. Atmospheres are not symbols or metaphors; they are containers which, like earthenware jars, retain the temperature of their contents.

And what is it that they contain? Ideas, reflections, judgments, and affin-ities, yes, but most of all they contain values. Despite the perceived gulf that divides them, aesthetics and ethics share this concern. If the latter pro-vides the impetus to recognize or manifest values, the former provides the means of hierarchizing them. In European philosophy, the disjuncture between the aesthetic and the ethical provided the basis of Søren Kierke-gaard's 1843 *Either/Or*, where he outlined two opposing viewpoints of how one might live a good life. In the first section, the aesthetic mode of life triumphs.[28] Kierkegaard was not posing a choice between these two modes of existence. For him, religious belief protects the self from total immersion in either the aesthetic or the ethical, a surrender to the senses that would result in existential despair or a renunciation of the world as it is lived and felt. The kinds of literature Idris was beginning to read and share with me gave a bleaker picture. Islam was permanently "in danger" of being polluted by secularity, minority faiths, and immoral media. When the moral is felt in and through the presence of an emergent challenge to its fixity and legibility, the Enlightenment distinction between the ethical and the aesthetic loses its vanishing mediator.

In their journey to the marketplace, film, popular music, and, more recently, social and electronic media have had to traverse moral anxieties around hygiene, purity, and the contagious danger of unknown influences. The early history of one of the earliest Pakistani consumer items illustrates this journey well. Pakola, a soft drink named after its North American counterpart, was created by the Teli Brothers after migrating to Pakistan after Partition. With an emphasis on purity and cleanliness in production, they developed and imported manufacturing equipment that did not require bottles to be manually washed and filled. As Mariam Ali Baig explains, this technology helped the firm to devise their early slogan: "Untouched by human hands."[29] Evoking *acheiropoieta*, the Christian icons said to have miraculously appeared rather than having been painted by (human) hands, Pakola strived for an unmediated relationship between company and consumer. Yet the company's abandonment of the slogan tells of a broader realization. Rather than erasing them, technologies of reproduction mul-tiply the hands of laborers, mediators, and repairpersons.[30] These hands might instead become bearers of an ethos commensurable with that of the consumer. In deciding to buy a product as with judging the behavior of others, ethics are a "matter of taste" or a "question of style."[31] In such a sphere, where good behavior and positive reputations are closely correlated with appearances, the aesthetics of the public good are tirelessly wrought and hard fought.

Film and Public Morality

While these scholarly trajectories helped me to locate mahaul in a broad history of ideas and sensations, I did not bring them to bear on my fieldwork. I did not go looking for atmosphere; it found me, becoming readily apparent as a local sensibility and category of moral experience. My own positionality also played a substantial role in shaping my identification of atmospheres in film culture and experience. Having studied film before coming to anthropology, I was always puzzled by the heightened affective response I felt sitting in a cinema and listening to music. From sensory overload to sudden lows and emotional highs, for many years I avoided watching films altogether, understanding myself to be a cinephile averse to film, or even a kind of *cinephobe*. Later, I enjoyed studying experimental, structural film, and artists' moving image media for the ways in which it demanded a different kind of attention. I bring these experiences to the study of film and public morality in Pakistan, and they have shaped the data I have gathered in several ways. First, in the understanding that an aversion to film experience can take many forms. Second, in the belief that the experience of film is something that cannot always be decoded, and that the aesthetic judgment of taste is just one of many possible ways in which moving-image media is adjudicated.

Until recently, Pakistani film and media had been a long neglected field of study before a wealth of new scholarship from Ali Nobil Ahmad, Gwendolyn Kirk, and Iftikhar Dadi, among others, situated it in the complex tide of social change and vernacular audio and visual culture.[32] Before a new wave of moviemaking spearheaded by a new generation of filmmakers hailing from elite economic and educational backgrounds, public discourse on film in Pakistan associated male and female actors, dancers, musicians, and songwriters with the Hira Mandi, the red-light district of the Walled City of Lahore. The mixed origins of performative trades, in an area known as much for its musical traditions as for sex work, are amplified in the *masala* [mixed, variety] elements of Lollywood film such as song and dance. For many, the Hira Mandi is an indivisible part of the mahaul of film culture, one that government heritage bodies like the Walled City of

Lahore Authority (WCLA) have been eager to sanitize at the same time as retaining something of its heritage value. This urban atmosphere remained palpable through the presence of the last functioning cinema in the area. Initially built in 1903 as the Aziz Theatre, it started showing silent films as early as the 1910s under the name Taj Mahal. Following the adoption of sound technology and the Partition of the Indian subcontinent in 1947, the cinema changed its name to Pakistan Talkies. A group of scholars told the caretaker it was one of the oldest continuously running cinemas in the world. "Great," said the caretaker flatly, before adding, as many of my other interlocutors did when talking about film, "but because of my faith, I feel that film is un-Islamic."

During my visits to the WCLA I was told that this last functioning cinema in the Walled City was controlled by some shadowy development firm, known as the "plaza mafia," who had also been held responsible for destroying the nearby Tarannum Cinema to build a cheaply constructed shopping plaza. Although no one in the office admitted to having watched a film at the cinema, I was told that the Pakistan Talkies fostered a bad mahaul that hampered their attempts to "clean up" the Hira Mandi area which lies just south of the majestic Badshahi Mosque. Over the past few years, the WCLA have destroyed encroaching buildings from the Delhi Gate to the Kashmiri Bazaar and organized rickshaw tours for foreign visitors, domestic tourists, and Lahoris living in gated housing districts in the south of the city. Having enjoyed numerous visits to this remarkable cinema, often accompanied by my wife, Abeera, I was unsure of what to make of articles in the English-language press that reported that "vulgar films" are shown and "females are not allowed inside."[33] Certainly, the films screened were likely to offend the morals of many, but they had passed the national Central Board of Film Censors and were screened in accordance with rules underlined by the local Punjab Film Censor Board. It was hard not to feel that the audience of widowed women, working-class and elderly men, and transgender individuals were soon to be dispossessed of their cinema. "Pakistani cinema is finished," a young professional at the WCLA told me. "New films are being made now, for educated people like you and I." Sure enough, by 2020, Pakistan Talkies had stopped operating. It is hard not to believe that the atmosphere associated with it played a role in its closure, even though many of its critics had never actually visited it. As with anthropologist Jason Throop's suggestion that moods can "reveal moral concerns in flux," within atmospheres are sedimented moral

judgements formed of imagining its movement into a lived past and possible future, such as the feeling on the part of the WCLA that the mahaul
of a working-class cinema cannot coexist with heritage tourism.[34]

Surveying the last two decades of anthropological studies of ethical
life—one of the milieux that this book emerges from—one would not be
mistaken for feeling that the most troublesome theme is the problem of
subjective experience. Is it possible to experience an atmosphere second-
hand, as mediated by the sentiments of others? Is it possible to experience
moral values that are not yet consolidated as manifest norms? Are social
atmospheres immanent in all human action, or are they an intrinsic part of
the freedom to fashion oneself into a certain kind of subject? Or is it that
ethics themselves are atmospheric or transcendent, lying just outside of
immediate perception? This book, an ethnography of media and morality
in Pakistan, tackles these questions, and attempts to come to grips with
the wider environment that emanates from film as a particularly distributed and dispersed object of attention. In my case, I build on scholarly
interest in the phenomenology of film and film's social imagination and
historicity in South Asia to examine how they expand beyond the screen
and suffuse the moral undercurrents of public life.[35] Despite a long and difficult relationship between cinema and public morality, film experience has
been curiously absent from the ethical turn in anthropology that gathered
momentum in the twenty-first century. And despite the prevalence of emotional, affective, and phenomenological approaches to the study of ethical
life, atmosphere and ambiance, with much of their conceptual and philosophical traditions resting in the arts and humanities, also appear to have
been less smoothly aggregated into anthropological debate. There are a
number of ways of bridging these gulfs. Many of the factors that shape the
identification and reception of atmosphere in Pakistan, such as the mutual
entanglement of social life and theology, or the close relationship between
collective enthusiasm and values, have been brought to the center of anthropological debate over the last two decades by the work of Joel Robbins in the
quite different context of Melanesian Christianity. For Robbins, if anthropology wishes to meet its own obligations to account for social change, it
must consider how social parts work as a whole, even if that includes moral
irritants like film.[36]

Early twentieth-century reports into film were keenly aware of its
potential to find expression in public life, brokering a sense of intimacy
that is compelling and binding, that often forms discrete, less-than-public

spaces. These commissions examined the role film played in communal living rather than individual conscience, such as the 1917 investigation into film in Britain by the National Council of Public Morals, or that by the 1927–1928 Indian Cinematograph Committee. Under colonial rule, the uncertain, unfixed, and unfinished ontology of film culture was seen as a potential challenge to social order. The late-colonial emphasis on examining and mastering film experience in India was cloaked in fervent anxieties over the possible emancipation of subject peoples.

Despite their potential mutability, the atmospheres that surround film have proven remarkably stubborn, as I examine in chapters 1 and 2. In the 1990s, to help budding actors and their anxious families from whom societal pressures forced them to run away, a Pakistani film professional by the name of S. M. Shahid wrote a guidebook, "dedicated to those young people who have a deep interest in acting and have been separated from their parents."[37] Specifically focused on runaway children and the social stigma attributed to acting, it warned against networks of fraudsters, pimps, and cheats waiting to exploit budding film laborers, a term I use to address attitudes towards film work rather than to specific hierarchies of fame. These touts and traffickers fixed in the public mindset the film studio as a social contaminant. To offer another interpretation, the film studio, along with the cinema hall, provided a container for the atmosphere that emanates from film experience. As atmospheres can themselves be containers, in sites such as these layered and conflicting values coexist. This is why there is so much at stake with a bad mahaul. Once exposed to it, it moves with you. It is not what you bring to the atmosphere, it is what you bring back with you from the encounter that stimulates the kind of familial and kin anxiety that Shahid's guidebook examined.

Anthropologist Naveeda Khan has skillfully handled how anxieties can shape public culture and mediate relationships between the state and everyday lives. In her ethnography Khan describes battles between local mosques in Lahore over defining "the rightful atmosphere for prayer."[38] This competition thrived on a pervasive feeling of dissensus over the appropriate place of Islam in Pakistan. Khan anchors her examination of these feelings of disquiet in Muslim traditions of disputation, arguments, and debate, and a tendency towards skepticism. She reads this through anthropologist Veena Das's work on how "moral striving" can be seen to lead to a form of "ordinary ethics."[39] According to Das, ordinary ethics are resistant to ethical projects brokered by religious or political authorities and rely upon cultivating a sensibility to act within the everyday, living through adversity, and being receptive to the "concrete specificity of the other."[40] The sense of dissensus that Khan encountered in Lahore was constitutive of this moral striving, instantiating a future-facing Pakistan, open to experimentation and debate. By characterizing the ethical and aspirational mood of striving, Khan also shows that Pakistani public culture is permeated with forms of anxiety that complicate the shape of aspiration. This focus on "striving" factors in affective encounters, outrages, and intensities in ways that a focus on individual reflection or ethical self-cultivation cannot. Yet, the specificity of the other on which Das's ordinary ethics is predicated must always be "concrete" but never transcendent.[41] This "other" is presumed to be knowable and ethical life flows steadily and smoothly from this transparent encounter.

Earlier I asserted that by speculating on atmospheres my interlocutors were attempting to come to grips with indeterminate others that lie just outside their immediate experience.[42] What I meant by this is that these kinds of moral sentiments are often about things that are transcendent to them, that is, beyond the range of their everyday lives. Atmosphere is an example of a transcendent encounter that pervades everyday life, in which myriad external forces act upon people and make demands on them that contribute to shaping a shared environment. We can see another example of this in Amira Mittermaier's ethnography of Egyptian Sufi or mystical communities and the dreams that visit upon these Muslims effects which they are not able to bring about themselves. What Mittermaier calls being *acted upon*, such as by dreams or visitations, rather than *acting* as an ethical subject, can serve to "*constitute* her or him as a moral being and witness."[43] Dreams occupy an intermediate space known to many Muslims as the *barzakh*, where dreams, the dead, and the imagination reside. To understand this world of the imagination, Mittermaier calls for an "*ethics of in-betweenness*" that drives an empathy and openness to the transcendent nature of others.[44]

Whether atmosphere can be said to possess an ethics is disputable, but I did indeed find it occupies an intermediate space of a kind, between the shrinking industrial activity of local Lollywood filmmaking and a new wave of films being produced by those with little association with the old industry. To learn about this bifurcation, Idris recommended I go to Lahore's Evernew Studios to meet another of his matrilineal uncles, Akhtar, a senior choreographer whose career dated from the 1960s when he interned as a schoolboy in the studios. Several of my interlocutors in Hall Road's DVD markets also told me tall tales about the studios, all indicative of the lack of care producers felt towards the films they oversaw, such as how celluloid reels were left to rot in the abandoned processing laboratory onsite, and that films that lay uncollected or unclaimed were burned by staff. A long rectangular courtyard with brightly overpainted facades housed a well-tended garden and fountains, flanked by the offices of film producers. The courtyard was designed to double as an idealized backdrop for song sequences, its elegant surroundings easily the equal of the finest hotels and mansions in the city. While we spoke about Idris's return from Dubai, Akhtar took me to see the recording studio where the playback singer Noor Jehan arrived to rapturous applause and where he would sit listening and devising dance sequences, later to be performed for the cameras in one of the studios' aircraft-hangar-like studio floors. This was neither a place of decline nor decay, nor was it anymore a hub of industrial activity. Akhtar was waiting, patiently, for that "mahaul to return," as he put it, "that I struggle to believe I experienced, that time that seems now to me like a dream."

Asking me to suspend my disbelief, sensing perhaps that I had been unable to perceive the bad atmosphere so many attributed to these studios, Akhtar invited me to imagine a time of busy people and creative activity. When not immediately perceived in what Das calls the "concrete specificity of the other," atmospheres become more speculative when felt in the process of evaporation. In her book on how it is possible to feel the affective presence of other persons, Teresa Brennan asked, "Is there anyone who has not, at least once, walked into a room and 'felt the atmosphere'?"[45] The literature and theory of affect to which Brennan's work contributed in the humanities and social sciences proved instructive and influential in the genesis of this book, particularly when people spoke of atmosphere as born of the kind of conflicted sensation Berlant calls "cruel optimism."[46] Rather than reify the epistemic boundaries between the "concrete specificity of the other" or seek to prove the more abstract ideas proposed by German philosophies of atmosphere, this book uses affect to support Inayat Khan's suggestion that atmospheres emerge from a past that lingers in space or lies latent in public life. An atmosphere's reputation can precede it. In many instances in the fieldwork for this book it might have been possible to nuance Brennan's question and ask, what did the perceiver know of the room before walking into the atmosphere? It is my contention that mahaul helps to articulate what atmosphere can do for anthropology. That is, to provide an open-ended way of drawing equivalence with our interlocutors' attempts to perceive different thresholds of intensity and change, particularly in media environments where the binaries of right and wrong, or good and bad, are diffuse and multi-sited.

Morality and Thresholds Are One

I often wondered what it was about the mahaul of Lollywood filmmaking and cinema halls that grabbed the attention of government departments, the English-language press, and even kickstarted an entire so-called "New Wave" of filmmaking defined in opposition to it.

As the projector rolled in the Pakistani Talkies, the yellowed screen was filled, from end to end, with an aged, saturated, and faded celluloid image. Its patina made it seem like a rough diamond from the archives, much travelled, enjoyed, and consumed, a film with a past and a public. But the cars and the mobile phones told you that this was a film only a decade old. Despite its recent production, the presence of such aged celluloid gave it an aura of presence and decay that seemed to cling affectionately to the rotten wood, broken chairs, and darkness of the cinema hall. The experience is much the same for those consuming Lollywood film on videocassettes, VCDs, and digital data files, which add to it the glitches and fragmented pixels of digital transfer. The Punjabi-language film industry had struggled to switch to digital technologies since the closure of the last domestic celluloid processing lab at Evernew Studios in 2013. The laboratory was responsible for the distinct aesthetic of Lollywood films. Always hampered by a lack of funding and government subsidies, the high rate of import duties on processing meant that chemicals required for developing one reel were stretched for eight, ten, often twenty reels, leading to overexposure, saturated colors, and an improperly fixed image. By the 1990s, expired film stock was being bought from Iran for as little as a fifth of the price of new stock. When Paolo Cherchi Usai said that the history of film is "the art of destroying images," he could very well have been describing Lollywood film in Pakistan.[47]

It was there in the Pakistan Talkies, and while studying Pakistani films sold in the marketplace that were too heavily glitched or poorly encoded to be watched, that I asked myself, when does an image cease to be an

Figure 0.4 Discarded celluloid in Evernew Studios, Lahore's last functioning film studio. These strips of negative film were part of a pile of debris left over by the studio's celluloid processing laboratory which closed in 2013. With it ended the distinct surface aesthetic of domestic Lollywood film production. (Photo by author.)

image? What is its threshold? Once they reached the marketplace, the circuitous routes of films—across carriers, formats, and interfaces—sediment the traces of their received public on the surface of the image to such an extent that they obscure much of what lies beneath. For the researcher, the object of attention must become the gauze, the patina encrusted over the image, and the ever accelerating threshold of deterioration. Contrary to Walter Benjamin's famous argument that mass reproduction entails the decay of the aura of an artistic object, the circulation of media can leave atmospheres in its wake that are plural and polysemic.[48]

Thresholds are not only aesthetic, but also appear as moral irritants that complicate the epistemic binaries that structure their reception. Recent scholarship on Pakistani film, for example, has had to challenge dyadic narratives of industry decline and rebirth, or secular–religious friction, that all too neatly center on the question of whether Pakistan should be a politically secular nation or one in which the workings of the state should be indivisible from Islamic piety.[49] This dialectic has particularly deep roots. In 1971, writer, filmmaker, and later government minister Javed Jabbar described what he saw as the ideological binaries of the cinema in Pakistan as the reflection of "a society stretched tight and taut between the mulla," a term used pejoratively here to refer to a pious individual learned in religious law, "and the movies . . . between these two edges of darkness, the black void of the mulla's mind, and the comforting night of the theatre interior . . ."[50] In contrast, I found the perceived gulf between the "mulla and the movies" to be a fertile sphere of debate over forms of responsibility and censorship that center on individual moral limits.

On bookshelves, internet forums, and television talk shows in Pakistan, technologies for audiovisual communications and social media are the subject of questions over permissibility and comportment. For many, entertainment and broadcast media are expected to be aggregated and conditioned in relation to prevailing attitudes towards the public performance of an Islamic self. Debates of this kind have provided mill and grist for a rich body of literature on the role of Islamic jurisprudence in relation to the social life of Shari'ah-inspired legal systems and the place of new media and technologies within them.[51] A question that many of my interlocutors asked of one another, or of sources of juridical authority, was whether cinema is permissible in Islam. Idris looked to Maulana Mufti Muhammad Shafi's chronological handbook on the permissibility of technologies for an answer to how to act piously in relation to a value-neutral "*aala bayjan* [inanimate (technological) device]" like a television, a DVD player, or a cinema projector.[52] A medium should be judged according to its content, it taught him, and the environment that surrounds it. If that is not clear cut, one should judge one's actions on motive or purpose at the point of use. As well as being the felt force of belonging or otherness, the *mahauliyat* or environment with which Idris invited me to come to grips referred to a sphere of debate in which technologies enter as catalysts into an already existing sphere of consensus and dissensus.

Lahore has an ethnically and religiously diverse population that includes a large *Ithna 'Ashariyyah*, or Twelver Shi'a Muslim, minority and some small but significant Ahmadi, Christian, and Hindu minorities. While these communities may live in close proximity, the ambient frontiers that divide them are hard to penetrate. Why this matters to this study is that each of these religiously diverse communities and jurisprudential schools of thought have their own nuanced take on the appropriate place of film and media in the enactment and endurance of faith. To these approaches, the elemental conditions of media through which popular culture transmits and transforms itself proffer an expanded environmental space riven with challenges and possibilities for action with little clear precedent in received rules governing moral conduct. The religious discourse and popular sentiment that arises in relation to Pakistani film encourages us to conceive of thresholds as more than simply things you cross to arrive at a new state of being or equilibrium. Thresholds can be where incommensurable values reside, and as far as public media is concerned, morality and thresholds are one.[53] One feels these tipping points and bleeding edges through the omnipresence of dualistic concepts. These might be the legal or the non-legal, the religious or the secular, or the "mullah and the movies." These dualisms are mostly overtaken by the shifting nature of public affect, in which circulating ideas around desire, temperance, mutual obligation, and competition play out. While one cannot give a name or a shape to *moral thresholds* perceived from within, their radiation beyond the self and between others can come to form something atmospheric, as I examine in chapter 3, in relation to other shared airborne phenomena. If morals and thresholds are one, their ethics and aesthetics do not invite disjuncture but combine to produce a kind of opacity that can defuse conflict and cultivate ambiguity. This allows a moral threshold to exist on its own terms as an unresolved object of ethical life.[54] In chapter 4 I show how this holds true for perhaps the annual event in Pakistani public life whose atmospheres and thresholds precariously hold together the most varied stakes. During the first ten days of Muharram, the Twelver Shiʻa refrain from consuming film or music while mourning the martyrdom of Imam Hussain and the tragedy that befell other members of the *Ahl-e Bait* [the family of the Prophet Muhammad] at the Battle of Karbala in 680 CE. At this time, the Hall Road repertoire undergoes a perceptual shift, introducing into the market documentaries on local saints, imported Iranian films, recordings of *majlis* orations, and devotional recitations.

The Shiʻa form the largest religious minority in Pakistan, where they occupy a precarious position in relation to a Sunni-Islamic majority state. The differences between Sunni Islam, as followed by the majority of the world's Muslims, and Twelver Shiʻism can be traced to the issue of the Prophet Muhammad's succession. Sunnis believe that the Prophet assigned authority over the Muslim community to his faithful companions, beginning with Abu Bakr, while Twelver Shi'a believe that this authority should be held by the family of the Prophet Muhammad, the Ahl-e Bait, and their heirs, the Twelve Imams. Commemorative mourning is arguably the practice most closely associated with Shi'i faith, where they remember the martyrdom of Imam Hussain and the perceived theft of the divine rights of the Ahl-e Bait. On the climactic tenth day of Muharram, known as the Day of Ashura, Pakistani Shi'a stage public demonstrations of grief: flagellation and chest-beating, processions of model mausolea, and the shedding of tears together. Some members of the Sunni majority consider these practices excessive, even idolatrous, and along with the dispersal of religious authority in Shi'i piety, feel they undermine the doctrine of *tauhid* (the one-ness of Allah).

Pakistani Shi'a face numerous barriers to participation in public life and worship, including restrictions on religious processions, the threat of targeted violence, and discrimination in the workplace. Hall Road's trader population is comprised primarily of Barelvi Sunni Muslims, whose clerics often enflame anti-Shi'a sentiment by demanding measures such as the inclusion of religious denomination on identity cards and targeted changes to Pakistan's notorious blasphemy laws. Followers of the Barelvi movement are known for their devotion to Muslim saints, their *na'at* recitations in praise of the Prophet Muhammad, and their majoritarian and public approach to popular piety. Many pray at one of more than a dozen mosques that occupy rooms and repurposed structures in Hall Road's labyrinthine alleys. For Friday prayers, many like Faisal and Idris cross the Regal Chowk junction that connects Hall Road to the Mall and visit the Jamia Masjid-e-Shuhada where many other movements faithful to Sunni Hanafi jurisprudence gather. These include the Tablighi Jamaat, a movement based on proselytization, and Deobandis, who hold a more literalist stance towards Islamic scripture. Thinkers, preachers, and followers of the Deoband school are more likely to produce literature and sermons defining the permissibility of media and openly vilifying Shi'ism, saint veneration, and musical performance. With an estimated twenty-five thousand individual businesses with between thirty to one-hundred thousand workers by the estimation of the *Anjuman-e-Tajiran* [Tradespersons' Union], Hall Road is a not only a place to buy a cheap USB cable, but a forum to assert the ambient contours of Sunni patriarchy and power in Pakistan.

Despite being almost wholly Sunni in demography, Hall Road's traders observe Muharram as a period of moral exception through perceptible changes in the repertoire of media in circulation. On the one hand, this temporary change to the repertoire often introduces images, rhetoric, and affective elements that clash with the Barelvi affiliation of those who copy and re-distribute them on Hall Road. On the other hand, popular forms of Sunni devotion that accept saint veneration draw on their own repertoire of shared saints, Sufic themes, symbols, and sounds that occasionally overlap with Shi'i worship.[55] Beyond Hall Road, most media stores of a religious nature I came across in Lahore served Shi'i communities. What they traded, by circulating religious media—which most of my interlocutors felt should not share space with film and music—constantly redefined the thresholds between film and not-film; music and recitation; permissibility and impermissibility. Becoming aware of these thresholds marked the turning point in the fieldwork that informed this book. Up until that point I had strived to understand my own fascination with the palimpsestic surfaces and visual noise of the mass-copied Pakistani media found on Hall Road. While looking for a site associated with the inaugural Lahore Biennale, a festival of contemporary art, I met a trader in Shi'i religious media, whose recordings of ritual processions taking place on his street made a sharp differentiation between the ethical qualities of media recorded live and studio recordings. I was told that only live recordings, their rough grain, shaky sound, blurry visuals, and proximate and participatory bodies, possess the added quality of mahaul. After hearing it described for so long as a negative attribute, I was fascinated by the idea that a video or sound recording could possess an unquestionably good mahaul. I also learned that it was from these independent videographers that Hall Road traders would appropriate content during periods of Shi'i commemorations like Muharram. Other Shi'i "cassette and video houses," as these videographers' stores are still known, operate beside shrines widely visited by Shi'i Muslims or in Shi'a-majority neighborhoods. The purpose for their existence is either to proselytize or to spread *azadari*, a term which refers to the public and communal mourning for Imam Hussain and the Ahl-e Bait.

In these ways, atmosphere can also serve to carve out a niche in ways recognizable to the initiated yet not provocative to majoritarian pieties. These atmospheres always remain vulnerable to majoritarian public affect as reified in state power and military force and commodified by traders capitalizing on annual religious commemorations. What atmospheres and thresholds are most concerned with is alterity.[56] Recalling Inayat Khan's ideas around containment, in the words of Simone Dennis, atmospheres have "the capacity to hold within them opposed things."[57] When disagreement does arise in relation to media forms, it is to assert that something or someone has "crossed the line." This line is often expressed by the Quranic term, used in Urdu, *hadd* (plural: *hudood*) that describes the social location of divine boundaries. The term has evolved through its application in Islamic jurisprudence and state legal systems to describe means of punishing perceived transgressions.

The term is also familiar in relation to a set of controversial laws known as the Hudood Ordinances, perhaps the most seismic change installed by the theocratic regime of General Zia-ul-Haq that existed between 1977–1988. Constituting a set of legal reforms to incorporate elements of Islamic jurisprudence into Pakistani law, the Hudood Ordinances included various forms of capital punishment, some of which were never enforced but remained symbolic of a newly Islamized legal system. More vigorously enforced were the draconian Zina Ordinances, which instituted legal changes regarding rape and premarital sex. While the context in which I heard *hadd* or *hudood* mentioned was in reference to the threshold between recitation and song, the term relates to broader thresholds that can be disciplined into coercive legal strictures.

If hadd is a divine threshold whose values are not yet consolidated as manifest norms, its identification in everyday life often emerges at the disjuncture between aesthetics and ethics. In anthropological theory, the analytic figure of the threshold means something quite different. It is the conflation of a frontier and the magnitude of intensity that looms at its boundary. In the early history of anthropology, the figure of the threshold was a long-running theme. Thresholds provided a location and processual narrative to varied kinds of ritual that correlated with their predominance in both non-Western and Judeo-Christian faiths as points of transition and as altars. Following a period of dormancy, in recent work from across the humanities and social sciences the analytic of the threshold is reappearing in various guises as a state of unresolved tension rather than as the location of an act of crossing.[58] Thresholds have also become an important part of the metalanguage of climate destruction and ecological change which manifest "where an element is on the verge of changing form."[59] Melody Jue's work on the ability for volumetric forms like the ocean to communicate information shares much with my interest in film and moral atmosphere. Jue finds that the ways deep-sea divers know the limits of their bodies and of the technological appendages that allow them to endure greater depths means experiencing the ocean not as a "flat threshold," but through a "saturated sense of the interface."[60] In the case of Hall Road, the mahaul of media is brought on by a public sphere saturated with ideas around moral performance. This is one of the calls that this book makes, for a new consideration of the interfaces through which the elemental converges with the ethical, and through which different thresholds of intensity and change radiate beyond the self and affect the lives of others.

Media, Mediation, and the Situation of the Interface

The research for this book was undertaken through ethnographic fieldwork conducted between August 2017 and October 2018 and between December 2019 and March 2020. It was also undertaken through archival research into film experience in international libraries and in the collections of producers of religious media.[61] Participant observation entailed gathering qualitative data sensitive to embodied, ambient, and rhythmic modes of participation to engage the methodological problem of how to understand my interlocutors' conception of atmosphere and their location of it in mediatic events. As I show in chapter 5, the distinct characteristics of urban experience and economic informality on Hall Road shaped how my interlocutors and I experienced atmospheres and thresholds. In studying the technical and social grounds for media circulation in a Pakistani marketplace, I found that traders associated with the powerful conservative middle class, and their attitudes towards public morality, marked the physical landscape in which their goods circulate with certain ethical qualities.

Having come to Hall Road to find out about practices of distribution and reproduction that sustain the circulation of Pakistani film, I spent my time at Durrani Electronics, a store founded in 1984 and for many years a prominent name in the videocassette and disc trade. Like thousands of other similar businesses on Hall Road, Durrani Electronics was made up of a tight-knit group of men hailing from a shared kin group, in their case the Pashtun Durrani tribe. Once known for the image quality of their film copies, they had turned to selling flat-screen LCD TVs. It had been almost a decade since they had left the film trade, but like many of their peers, their continued popularity among customers in the congested market hinged on the reputation they had built during the videocassette era.

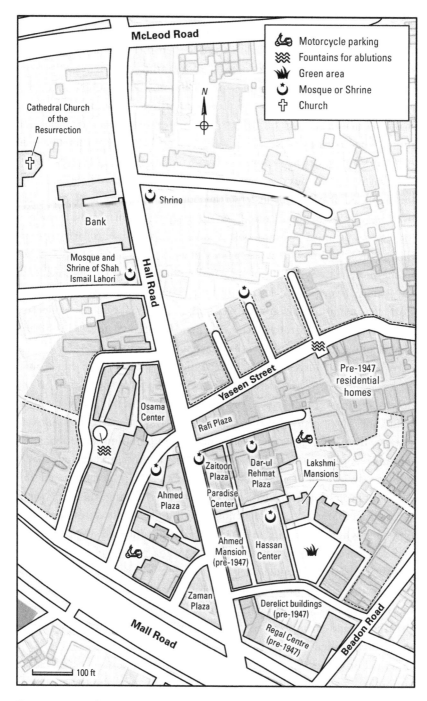

Figure 0.5 Map of Hall Road. Created by Rob Weickart/Network Graphics.

Among the white halogen lights, stacks of flat-screen TVs still in their flat rectangular boxes, and dozens of showpieces tiling the walls, cupboards skirting the enclosing walls held a trace of their former glory. Inside were thousands of their old master copies of Indian films on videocassette from which they had once made copies for sale but now were of little value due to the widespread availability of those same films on the internet. Their stock of master copies of Pakistani films—rare, scarce, disappearing things—had recently been sold in bulk to a local cable television channel. Pakistan's poorly defined copyright laws had led to it being accepted practice that when one buys or sources a master copy crisp and clear enough for broadcast or copy, one also has the right to reproduce it. When I first lived in Pakistan in 2013, I was drawn to studying the marketplace trade in local film and music when I observed that, in the absence of a national film archive, Pakistani cinema as a body of work owed much of its existence in the present to dynamics of informal circulation.[62] At that time, with few external verifiers of legal and moral norms, different roles ranging from censorship to punishment were taken up by individuals, collective decision-making, or groups acting independent of the state. In this sphere, objects of mediation formed an interface with hierarchies of value.

When Faisal, Idris, and the other employees of Durrani Electronics took me into their confidence, they recommended I spend time in the downstairs market halls where the last bastion of film traders operated. In these airless basements, I was struck by the ways traders tried to cultivate distance from the objects they sold: vintage Pakistani films, devotional recitations recorded at the shrines of local Muslim saints, and various shades of pornography, both imported and domestic. They demonstrated this through professional rivalries with their neighboring traders, voiced through acerbic attacks on their moral standing and embrace of pornography, even while they traded in the same material, and even swapped master copies when relations were more cordial. Many were eager either to discuss the mahaul of film and its negative influence on the nation or to declare outright that film is impermissible in Islam. At the same time, they were businessmen and entrepreneurs who needed to remind their customers that they could promise clean transfers from quality master copies rather than glitch-ridden discs that might prove inoperable.

This book does not simply identify when people have perceived an atmosphere to be moral, but how these atmospheres shape the economic logic and activities of a busy electronics market. It also identifies how they

Figure 0.6 Due to the rarity of older Pakistani films, small, market-based shops like this one, sitting beside a coal store in the Walled City of Lahore, have long kept personal collections of Pakistani films for later retrieval and copying should a customer or another trader request them. In some cases, these stockpiles account for one of the last available instantiations of a film, since most directors and producers have not saved copies of their works. The reserves these shops hold work like the coal supplier: money in the bank, a future surplus to wheel out when *demand* requires; as well as fuel for the kinetic energy of a circulatory system that sustains their continued existence. (Photo by author.)

are disciplined by regulation and appropriation, scaling up both on the part of the Pakistani state and back down to those who retrieve and circulate film materials. In chapter 2 and 6, I do this by following the notion of public demand, an ethical and an economic principle that determines both what is desired and what is permissible among the public at large. As an abstract economic principle, the idea of market demand describes phenomena that are felt in others but not wholly quantifiable. In the logic of "demand," disparate market logics, ethics of responsibility, and digital forms of remediation come together to shape the visual culture of contemporary Pakistani Islam. The force of public demand, and the moral choices and value-decisions that drove it, dictated what films were and were not retrievable and reproducible, and resulted in an accumulated inventory of media, aesthetic choices, and value-decisions that I call the "Hall Road repertoire." The traders I worked with were not archivists, but rather provided a social interface between the atmospheres that inform public demand and the material availability of content in the repertoire. For this shifting inventory of retrievals and reproductions, the book that Idris gave me to study seemed almost its inverse, in that it provided ethical systems to live by and rules to govern future conduct. In contrast, one locates moral decisions in the Hall Road repertoire through the ways one interfaces with it and its mediators. Integrated into the book are short interludes detailing classic films either lost to the Hall Road repertoire or available due to the kinetic force of demand. These act both as a means of grounding the ethnography in person-to-person circulation and as a fragmentary history of film in Pakistan told through marketplace systems of recording, reproduction, and retrieval.

As I have argued above, in Pakistan the relationship between Islam and media technologies plays out against a backdrop in which jurisprudence and consensus are debated as living, changing notions. In his work on customary law in Indonesia, John Bowen calls these debates "repertoires of justification."[63] Diana Taylor uses the same term in her study of the ways that performance and performance art has been preserved in practice and cultural memory. Taylor makes a differentiation between the "archive" and the "repertoire." She explains, "The repertoire requires presence: people participate in the production and reproduction of knowledge by 'being there.'"[64] Its contents impossible to reproduce without change, the repertoire of media content in electronics markets such as Hall Road includes religious media, devotional recitations, Pakistani films long out of circulation, as well as pirated computer software, local and imported pornography, and curated compilations of music loaded directly onto smartphone memory cards. This repertoire remains grounded in the technical and social conditions of person-to-person exchange.

I chose to take up Iftikhar Dadi's call, as an early inspiration for my work, for further study of the "complex relay between screen imagination, modernization, and political authoritarianism" in the history of film experience in Pakistan.[65] The study of Pakistani film owes much to Dadi's work, from his and Elizabeth Dadi's *Urdu Film* series (1994–2009) that depicted the mutual exchanges between cultural memory and electronic media, to his work as a curator and writer on contemporary art. Dadi is interested in how it might be possible to study film history through recursive forms and practices that emerge from a complex assemblage of South Asian art and ideas. These forms and practices act like repertoires, which possess various centers of consolidation and performance, such as the city of Lahore itself.[66] While a product of past traditions and practices, repertoires are remade and reanimated in the present; they require people to perform them and make them vital again. Perhaps the sense of presence that Taylor sees as essential to repertoires, and the extent to which they are tethered to a space of cultural production identified by Dadi, is what Idris meant by the *mahauliyat* of media technologies: a system of atmospheres that in their use and justification come to form different interfaces through their mediation. It is here, when changing technologies evade existing evaluating frameworks that atmospheres are marshalled to do analytical work.

By seeking to reconcile what he saw as hypocrisy in his uncle's behavior in relation to the Hall Road repertoire—making compilations of song and dance numbers while claiming that film is religiously impermissible—Idris's predicament draws attention to a key debate between the so-called "discursive" and "lived" traditions that has come to animate the anthropology of Islam. Roughly summarized, the latter examines the refinement of ethical normativity, while the former engages with the ambivalences and contradictions inherent in everyday practice.[67] Debates around media and Islam have mostly been taken up by the discursive tradition and have come to focus on the relationship between the democratization of religious authority through Foucauldian paradigms of ethical self-cultivation.[68] In *The Ethical Soundscape*, a deep and immersive ethnography of the Islamic revival movement, Charles Hirschkind found that cassette sermons offered the chance for listeners to "sediment" within themselves pious conduct.[69] As Hirschkind admits, environments for the reception of religious media can be sonically crowded—cacophonous, polyphonic, and occasionally ambivalent—but they can also be suffused with other ambient conditions that disrupt practices of ethical self-cultivation. While this discursive tradition in the anthropology of Islam is richly informed by sensory experience, its emphasis on ethical normativity often ignores the possibility that discontinuity and interruptions can be a source of pleasure and fascination. Central to film culture are the interfaces through which it is experienced, which are as likely to introduce interruptions as facilitate continuity. Lalitha Gopalan argues this in her influential conception of Indian film as a "cinema of interruptions" derived from the myriad halts prevalent in its consumption: the waterfalls and burst rain clouds that interrupt a sex scene or the intermission that jolts spectators from the diegetic world into the world of the cinema hall. For Gopalan, such jolts are a source of pleasure that provide entry into a series of filmic repertoires specific to Indian film that are notable for their "in-between-ness [and] propensity for digression and interruption."[70] As I explore in chapter 3, the experience of intermittence can act as a catalyst around which conflicting values comes to reside together on a perceptible threshold.[71]

The primary moral threshold that I found manifest through interruptions and in the space between dualisms was the coexistence of interdiction and reproduction in the practices and sentiments of my interlocutors on Hall Road. In the basic terms of mediation, this is unusual. For something to be eschewed or tainted with associations of immorality and then found in such abundance suggests that the controversies and anxieties surrounding its morality might be doing other work. Following the pathways of interdiction and practices of reproduction in Pakistan shows that they are not mutually exclusive nor is it a surprise to find them coexisting within the same public sphere or within the opinions of a single individual. By reproduction, I refer to the mechanical production of duplicate containers of media content or their digital transformations. By interdiction, I refer to a discursive and sensory realm somewhat more accessible than juridical spheres of debate, that might also be called the permissible. Returning to some of the foundational ideas in the anthropology of religion shows that the coexistence of interdiction and reproduction have been seen as essential to avoiding societal rupture. The folklorist and early anthropologist James George Frazer wrote widely on the Polynesian loanword, *taboo*, and the conceptual ramifications of it that came to animate turn-of-the-century anthropology. In contemporary parlance, we might call taboos interfaces between phases of being or moral states. Frazer called them "electrical insulators [that] preserve the spiritual force with which . . . persons are charged from suffering or inflicting harm by contact with the outer world."[72] This image of the suffering "insulator," providing an interface between opposing realms, illustrates how the professional and moral standing of Hall Road traders is contingent on their role as mediators of a film's moral atmosphere.

In his delineation of the shift from the anthropological study of media to the topic of mediation, Dominic Boyer strikes a distinction between "radial"—the massified outward divergence of broadcast media—and "lateral"—or sidelong, peer-to-peer—potentialities of electronic mediation.[73] Forms of lateral mediation are further amplified by digital platforms and social networks that allow users to distribute and share radially. The turn towards the study of mediation has also impacted the anthropology of religion with the insights that faith can be elemental and environmental, formed of complex feedback loops that include some and omit others.[74] What Brian Silverstein, in the circulation of Sufi CDs and DVDs in Turkey, calls "disciplines of presence" are fundamentally ethical practices that play a role in the formation of moral selves and communities.[75] Likewise, among media traders in Lahore, atmosphere is a way of giving presence to these sites of pious (or impious) reception. The reason I chose to conduct ethnographic research among those who mediate moving-image media, rather than those who produce it, is due to the extent to which these traders were forced to empathize with different sides of the debate over the morality or permissibility of media forms and the mahaul they possess.

By following its argument through individuals and their status as subjective moral agents this book was inspired by two Lahore ethnographies. In the first, Katherine Pratt Ewing examined the tension between moral codes prescribed by religious authorities and ethical ideals derived from more diffuse sources. Communities can thrive on ambiguity, rather than it being a source of friction. For Ewing, it is on the threshold of transition between limits tacitly agreed between differing communities that the "organizing principles" that undergird a society can be perceived.[76] As in Ewing's ethnography, one of the sites in which I locate this tension is in the local surfacing of controversy, or "everyday interpersonal arguments."[77] Secondly, I take inspiration from Naveeda Khan's aforementioned ethnography which similarly explores the struggles of individual agents and their attempts to shape, as well as reconcile themselves to, the prevailing ethical environment. These complementary approaches to the concomitant "stresses and fissures" of collective interaction are a testament to what ethnography does best.[78]

Due to the porosity of moving image and sonic media, the point at which persons and media objects fuse provides a palimpsestic surface that retains the trace of moral debates, assertions of ownership, and censorship. Understanding this palimpsest requires taking on the kind of social understanding of the interface in evidence in Jack Goody's *The Interface Between the Written and the Oral*. While Goody did not define his use of the term "interface," his exploration of it as the modes of interaction that lie between written and oral communication gives a hint to the anthropological utility of the term. His interface is a meeting point whose surface tensions reveal unexamined qualities emergent in both disparate systems. This allowed Goody to resist describing cultures dialectically as either oral or written and to focus instead on how to manage their coexistence. Surface tension is fed by context, feedback, and phasal changes, or what Goody called "the situation of the interface."[79] The persons and things that my interlocutors believed atmospheres emanate from, such as film experience, a recitation on the threshold of song, or the effervescence of a religious gathering, should be considered kinds of interfaces, for which moral contestation are their situation. I understand an interface to be a point of connection between phases of activity, or the common overlap between otherwise separate practices. While media theorists might look to the surface qualities of technical interfaces as derived from digital and screen cultures, like Melody Jue I understand interfaces as products of bodily immersion and absorption, in this case, in morally conflicted spaces and moods. In chapter 6 I argue that it is here that the problem of atmospheres and thresholds comes to relate to a wider question of the fixity of cultural forms, and the ability for these forms to communicate across the bounds of difference. In my field-site, interfaces are also heuristics, means of discovery that look for continuities, similarities, and recognizable forms through which to find common ground. If atmospheres concern the spatial mood of moral alterity and thresholds are the states of intensification that they contain, interfaces provide the objects, things, and material forms that make these sentiments perceptible to others.

Structure of the Book

This book is structured as a narrative that begins by examining how ongoing dissension and contestation over film's place in Pakistan has helped to produce ideas around moral permissibility that mingle social and theological interdictions. Each chapter arises from Hall Road, just as atmosphere emanates from persons and things, before addressing discrete challenges posed by atmosphere or the identification of the moral attributes of a social environment. It is through this anchor laid on the street that the ethnography demarcates itself in space and time. As this is the story of one small corner of Lahore, and a select number of mostly male participants and their economic activities, the atmospheres I describe are intended neither to be hegemonic nor uniform.

Chapter 1 explores how film, music, and entertainment media are intimately subject to the forces of public consensus and dissensus. In this sphere in which "the people" are taken as the arbiters of public morality, the English loanword and local system of "demand" guides and buttresses the recording, retrieval, and reproduction of media content. Among the former, demand explains the existence or absence of a rare film, while in the latter, demand speaks of the devotion, respect, and disciplinary character of the customer. In chapter 2 I ask, how is demand gaged and expressed? How does demand produce atmospheres of consensus and common ground within the reach of its circulation? The (mechanical) reproduction of media content and containers deemed immoral can be said to define a form of consensus, in that they are the accumulated body of value-decisions such as, to circulate or not to circulate; to whom to circulate? In this chapter I also explore how roles usually adopted by the state—the preservation and censorship of media—are taken up by self-appointed guardians of both material culture and morality. This purported fidelity to the contours of public demand is the result of Hall Road and its traders' unsteady relations between the state, infrastructural utilities, and the repertoires of their use. Being the most experimental, chapter 3 aims to highlight some of the ways in which the idea of moral atmosphere is understood through the figure of the threshold. This idea of the threshold is taken not as a moment of crossing—in the traditional anthropological sense—but as an interface of intensity.

For those on Hall Road and the Shi'i neighborhood recording companies engaged with in chapter 4, mahaul as a positive moral atmosphere of locality serves to shape the conditions of knowledge transmission, patronage, and power. The ways in which atmospheres become perceptible through their thresholds is brought into focus during the first ten days of the Islamic month of Muharram, in which the death of Imam Hussain is commemorated, and Lahore transforms its media, social, and emotional landscape out of respect for its Shi'i minority. The largely voluntary practice widespread across Pakistan originates in the belief that celebrations, entertainment, singing, and dancing should be avoided during periods of mourning. During this time, traders on Hall Road temporarily add another type of moving-image product to their usual stock: sermons, recitations, and procession recordings that help to produce a space conducive to public mourning. Driven by an interest in the kinds of moving-image media that are sold in replacement of film and music, chapter 4 also explores the audiovisual repertoire documented and circulated by these small, long-established stores situated beside shrines and along Shiʻi procession routes.

Chapter 5 documents how my interlocutors felt that the marketplace logic of Hall Road either aided them in navigating infrastructural precarity or contributed to the destruction of what they deemed to be Pakistan's heritage. Looking at the experience of Hall Road's urban form I argue that the circulation and reproduction of film, music, and performance requires an understanding of the expanded ethical environment against which transfer, recording, and transmission takes place, in ways that are quite separate from traditional understandings of piracy and informality. Rather than being tethered to state-centered perspectives like piracy, the circulation of film follows other forms of regulation and aesthetic hierarchies that build ethical selves through ideas of quality. Media environments like Hall Road are central to the stakes at play in the contestation over the public place of Islam in Pakistan. Such media repertoires are not just the result of value-decisions based around consumption but also diverse consent-decisions about what the shared environment of Pakistani Islam should look, sound, and feel like.

In 2008 Hall Road's official traders' union publicly burned 60,000 discs containing "pornographic" content following an anonymous bomb threat. Many worried the event would mark the beginning of the "Talibanization of Lahore." Hall Road's traders, however, saw this as an act of pragmatism rather than appeasement; they were cheap copies that were burned, not the valuable *master copies* from which duplicates are made. Ten years later, in the digital era, the *camera print* and the master copy continued to be key terms in the vernacular of the residual trade in film copies, reflecting reputations traders have long nurtured as mediators of a film's genealogy. Chapter 6 shows how Hall Road's audiovisual media trade has never been based on legality or legitimacy but on quality and provenance, particularly a product's proximity to the master copy. Through these practices traders on Hall Road describe what they do as an essentially participative, future-oriented activity, using watermarks and head and shoulders portraits as guarantees of image quality. I explore what role these incisions on the surfaces of media objects play in establishing professional reputations, particularly in a trade that relies on the integrity of flimsy discs and the navigation of the moral atmospheres of media. The materiality of persons and things becomes interfaces that complicate dualistic and binary thinking, such as between the moral and the immoral or the legal and the nonlegal, and from which atmospheres emerge.

The intention of this book is to establish a fresh perspective on moral experience, founded on empirical evidence and influenced by encounters with atmospheres. My interlocutors taught me that atmosphere can be an opaque form of power and an opaque form of resistance, and when social divisions are rife, an opaque form of intimacy.

CHAPTER I

Cinema Itself

Film and Faith in Pakistan

Owing to a large public demonstration that had taken place on a busy intersection where Hall Road meets the main thoroughfare, Mall Road, Durrani Electronics had been closed for two days. The demonstration had been staged by the Tehreek-e-Labbaik Pakistan (TLP), an Islamist political party who had risen to prominence in Pakistani Punjab in 2017, and who had become popular among sections of Hall Road's merchant middle class. Even Faisal, the manager of Durrani Electronics, was an ardent supporter. When business slowly returned to normal, stepping out of the auto-rickshaw that had dropped me at the intersection, I saw little evidence of the scale of the demonstrations that I had watched on Pakistan's rolling-news channels, which showed TLP supporters burning tires, destroying cars, and parading down the street jabbing long wooden sticks at motorists. The group had captured public attention for its demonstrations against purported changes to the required declaration of Khatm-e-Nabuwwat [the finality of the Prophethood] in oaths of office, which also provided them a platform to demand the Pakistani state further curtail the rights of its Shi'i, Christian, Hindu, and Ahmadi minorities. TLP supporters' tactics included blocking central junctions and traffic arteries, attacking vehicles, and destroying property. These tactics had been refined a few months before in their occupation of an important traffic interchange in the capital city Islamabad that led to widespread disruption and media

Figure 1.1 The Khurshid Cinema, one of the last functioning Pashto-language cinemas in Pakistan, began life before Partition as the Lakshmi Cinema. In January 1991, a timebomb was left in the stalls of the cinema, killing seven. The attack coincided with protests over the advent of the first Gulf War. (Photo by author.)

coverage and saw the TLP position themselves as enforcers of Pakistan's blasphemy laws.[1]

As I gingerly walked across the busy dual carriageway to visit Faisal and Idris, the only reminder of the chaos that had taken place just a day before was a pair of cardboard signs hung at a traffic island. Their message bore little relation to the specific demands of the TLP. Written hastily on cardboard, the first sign informed passers-by that: "Film actress pictures are *haram*" [forbidden]. Next to it another sign, half bent over on the pole to which it was affixed, read, "From film pictures to the fire of hell." On one side of the road, a short distance away, lay the near-derelict remains of one of Lahore's oldest cinemas, the Plaza, and on the other, tall billboards featuring film actors advertising the newest Chinese-made smartphone covered the facades of Hall Road's colonial-era buildings. Neither the cinema nor Hall Road—whose association with the film trade had waned in favor of smartphone paraphernalia—seemed efficacious enough to attract such resentment, particularly in relation to the demands of the TLP. Even passers-by were scarce, the sign having been erected at one of the busiest traffic lights in the city, so haphazardly policed that few pedestrians were able to stop and decipher the scrawl. In a city so difficult to traverse on foot, who was this sign for, demanding as it did such an intimate address? Despite the diminishing presence of film as a popular form of public leisure in Pakistan, its latent potential continued to be a source of outrage for groups whose political clout hinged on their ability to occupy the streets, both in bodies and in discourse. That the authors of this makeshift public service announcement wrote "From Film pictures to the fire of hell" suggested a journey towards damnation that film culture still had the power to initiate.

This chapter explores some of the ways that the interaction between film, faith, and ethical discourse has been defined and negotiated in Pakistan. These range from questions over permissibility put to sources of religious authority, to cases taken to legal courts over the compatibility of cinema exhibition with the public culture of Pakistani Islam. Despite taking a long view of these issues, this chapter and the fieldwork that informed it emerged from a time when the Lahore-based industry was seen by journalists and commentators to be in decline, its analog cinemas short of films to screen, and a new wave of filmmaking on the rise, with Pakistani films proudly showing at newly built cinemas with ticket prices beyond the reach of many. At this time scholarly interest in the cinema in Pakistan examined how it might be possible to conceive of a Pakistani (national) cinema in terms of production and representation. In this chapter I tilt the axis of enquiry to ask how the ontology of film has been understood in Pakistan and ask where its moral body has been situated and negotiated.

Good Art, Bad Art, and the Permissible

Faisal's and many other Hall Road film traders' passionate support for the TLP's violent religious protests surprised me, because up to that point I had been told a straightforward narrative that pitted film production and appreciation in Pakistan on one side and the Islamization of public life on the other, as antagonists in a story that saw the latter eclipse the former.[2] The line of flight that I had assembled from film collectors, connoisseurs, and members of the industry went something like this. The military coup that brought General Zia-ul-Haq into power in 1977 transformed the country's film scene from an industry of family melodramas and madcap cosmopolitan pastiches to a dour, violent, and sexually repressed scene that destroyed from the inside any vestiges of moral integrity or liberalism in filmmaking. Pakistan's newspaper columns told a similar story. The Zia era was found responsible for the dismantling of cinemas and the creation of shopping plazas, tyrannical censorship policies, and the transformation of audiovisual culture. The Iranian Revolution of 1979 and, perhaps most importantly, the advent of the Afghan wars in 1978, were rarely cited in articles' similar diagnostic narratives of decline and rebirth. Regime change in Iran triggered a renewed political awakening in Islamic-majority nations like Pakistan, while upheaval in Afghanistan initiated a brutal proxy war in which the United States fought the Soviet Union through various insurgent groups which brought violence and instability to neighboring Pakistan. Because Zia's planned Islamization of the country appeared such an obvious binary to the aesthetics of indigenous Pakistani Lollywood film, the "decline" narrative thrived.

The seeds of the decline narrative were sown in much older debates about culture and taste. In a short essay titled "What Would You Have?," the poet Faiz Ahmed Faiz found the anti-art and anti-culture tendencies he saw evident in Pakistan of the 1960s and 1970s not without rational basis. Contrasting the art patrons of old who cared little for popular opinion or public morality with the commercial media producers of his present day, he wrote, "There is . . . much debasement of beautiful folk legends, much flippant, perversion of national history, much bad music, bad cinema, bad painting, and bad literature. All this should be condemned. It corrupts public taste and therefore also corrupts public morals. It perverts values and debases the intellect and is, therefore, truly subversive."[3]

For Faiz, a lack of any criteria for aesthetic distinction within an overarching anti-art platform allows "bad art" to thrive, "at the expense of the good."[4] For the "anti-culture partisans," however, aesthetic taste is not the object of their critique; both a high-modernist painting and a film poster are vulnerable to their scorn.[5]

Faiz's observations coincided with government attempts to develop national cinematic output through the establishment of the National Film Development Corporation (NAFDEC). Founded during Prime Minster Zulfiqar Ali Bhutto's leadership, NAFDEC acquired funding through an agreement with American film producers.[6] It began operating as an arm of the Ministry of Culture, establishing film clubs, regional distribution centers, and a journal inspired by the British Film Institute's *Sight and Sound* magazine. It also financed a wide range of films, from big budget productions such as an adaptation of Naseem Hijazi's Partition novel *Khak Aur Khoon* (1979) to an unreleased A. J. Kardar film, *Door Hey Sukh Ka Gaon*, with a script written by Faiz. With NAFDEC proving to be short-lived, a new wave of popular Pakistani films in the 1970s and 1980s, such as *Dubai Chalo* [Let's Go to Dubai!] (1979), attempted to appeal to the cosmopolitanism of budding expatriates. Iqbal Sevea argues that the popularity of many Punjabi films of this era, with their distinct sense of masculine identity and storylines which responded to a "total absence of everyday forms of the state," coincided with a new era of populism in Pakistan.[7] The release of arguably the most famous Pakistani film, *Maula Jatt* (1979)—a bloodsplattered vigilante flick—was contemporaneous with the trial and execution of former Prime Minister Zulfiqar Ali Bhutto, who had been ousted by a coup led by General Zia-ul-Haq. Despite facing censorship, court cases, and accusations of bad taste, *Maula Jatt* came to encapsulate Lollywood filmmaking.

While a similar point could be made about many film cultures and industries, the cinema in Pakistan evinces how the aesthetic and the ethical converges to present something unruly to public morality. Scholarship on film and media in South Asia has been particularly adept at showing how the convergent forces of film experience are found in a much wider sphere than the immediate event of its exhibition.[8] In its earliest days, the emergence of cinematic space in India took shape in the shadow of the racial anxieties of the British Empire and alongside the growth of Indian middle-class anxieties that stratified film experience in contrast with the enjoyment of the urban poor. By the end of the twentieth century, scholars had begun to recognize film's latent power as a proscenium arch through which ethnographic examples of spectatorship, ideology, and order could be viewed; its capacious halls sites for the rehearsal of societal transformation.[9]

Because of the absence of shared ethical precepts that address film culture, we must begin here with the domain of speculation rather than seeking to uncover the codes that guide it. I call this domain the "permissible," as one informed by myriad approaches to living well amongst others, including theological precepts, notions around obscenity and indecency, and the embodied forms of ethical life as they have taken shape in North India. Farina Mir's work has explored this through the study of *akhlaq* [ethics] literature, an Islamic genre of popular writing in the late colonial period that aimed to be an instructive expression of "Muslim subjectivity that valued ethical striving."[10] Akhlaq literature locates ethical cultivation in the ability to tame one's impulses. In Arabic, and passed over into Urdu, *khulq*, the singular form of akhlaq, means *disposition*. Islamic ethics are suffused with the importance of bodily disposition, particularly as a medium for the cultivation of intention and future actions. As Asiya Alam has shown, in the North Indian Muslim reformism of Sayyid Ahmad Khan, ethics were about intimacy, about how one related to and comported oneself around others, and were therefore critical to educational and social reform.[11] As a less prescriptive, but equally forceful, element of moral orientation, might it be possible to locate film's mahaul as a product of speculations on permissibility and understand it as a distributed form of Muslim ethical striving?

It is important to note that this striving is not solely the domain of theological interdictions. Lotte Hoek's work on the circulation and censorship of film in Bangladesh shows that claims of obscenity emanate from the domain of secular regulation and public participation, rather than from Islamic ethics. She writes, "Obscene forms are . . . always public forms marked by an oscillation between being in and out of view."[12] To position themselves within the labor force of the industry, film actors must negotiation this oscillation, or what Hoek calls "regimes of visibility."[13] A similar phenomenon animated my ethnography. In the introduction I argued that Faisal's approach to his former career as a film trader was characterized by reproduction, the duplication and spread of film, and interdiction. By interdiction I mean a discursive realm sensitive to sensory phenomena that becomes more accessible to many than juridical spheres of debate. This might also be called the permissible, which is the domain of ethics but also of appearances, aesthetics, and taste, where ethical obligations are expressed as much in atmospheres as in outright prohibition. We might adapt the means by which Hoek's interlocutors negotiated their labor to describe dissension and contestation over film's place in Pakistan as the production of different regimes of permissibility.[14] To understand how Faisal's moral world was capacious enough to contain cinephilia and disapproval, it is important to examine how aversion to film can be appropriated by the kind of reactionary and populist religious outrage that fed the TLP protest at the entrance to Hall Road.

The Question of Cinephobia

In this section, I examine *cinephobia*, a moral impulse that shapes questions over permissibility and forms the inverse of *cinephilia*, a term that emerged in tandem with the European "new wave" traditions of filmmaking in the post–World War II era. A tension running through recent work on Pakistani film finds scholars divided between studying the cinephilia of film enthusiasm and the cinephobia of the various moral, class-based, and faith-driven anxieties that film can evoke.[15] Rather than equating Islamic belief with any kind of universal antipathy to film experience, I understand what Sarah Keller calls "anxious cinephilia" to be as much shaped by disquiet over the ontological and affective affordances of the medium as it is by enthusiasm for the content.[16] Even the most fervent anti-film demonstrations are cinephilic is one sense, in that they have been affectively moved to action by the distributed presence of film experience.

Scholarly reflection on cinephobia is almost as old as the discipline of film studies itself. Jean Giraud's *Le lexique français du cinéma* cites the frequent use of terms like cinephobe or cinephobia in cinematographic trade

Figure 1.2 Two precautions for navigating anti-cinema violence: a fire hydrant and prayer beads in the projection room of the Odeon Cinema, Lahore. (Photo by author.)

journals, growing between 1908 and 1912.[17] Ricciotto Canudo mentioned it in a growing glossary of terms to categorize the assets of film phenomenology in his seminal essay "The Birth of a Sixth Art."[18] While this scholarly trajectory serves to challenge the ways in which early cinema in Europe has been understood, cinephobia in South Asia possesses its own history. Ravi Vasudevan's work on Indian film publics in the three decades preceding the 1947 Partition reveals fears that film as an ephemeral force possessed the power to mingle with its audience and produce a third space of potential change, division, and strife.[19] While M. S. S. Pandian noted a late flowering of cinephobia among Tamil political and literary elites in the 1940s, S. V. Srinivas argued that by the 1930s these largely bourgeois anxieties about the intermingling of classes had dissipated.[20]

I first lived in Pakistan in early 2013, just a few months after countrywide riots on September 21, 2012, saw dozens of inner-city cinemas destroyed. The "Day of Love for the Prophet" saw incensed crowds demonstrate over *The Innocence of Muslims*, a crude and amateur—and, to many, blasphemous—digital video uploaded to YouTube in the United States. Amid the uproar over the video, Javed Ghamidi, a celebrity religious scholar and critic of Pakistan's blasphemy laws, appeared on television to urge calm, encouraging those incensed by the film to respond to it with proselytization rather than violence. Yet it did little to assuage public anger. After the attacks, a poster hung over the gutted remains of one cinema hall in Karachi featured before-and-after pictures of the charred remains and was captioned in English and Urdu, "Who is going to take responsibility for this catastrophe?" Despite the prevalence of disapproval over the morality and permissibility of film, there was widespread confusion over why cinemas were targeted and held responsible for the actions of a solitary individual in the United States.

There had been recent precedents, namely the 2007 attacks on CD and video shops by students of the Islamabad Lal Masjid shortly before the seminary was stormed by the armed forces, and the destruction of cassette stores by supporters of the Muttahida Majlis-e-Amal (MMA) administration in Peshawar in the early 2000s. The MMA coalition had then recently banned musical performance in the province, leading to a period of vigilante activity which saw musicians and dance performers attacked and killed. Militant attacks on cinemas were also not uncommon. In February 2014 dozens of filmgoers were murdered in grenade and bomb attacks on the Shama and Picture House cinemas in the Pakistani city of Peshawar.

The press had long cited both theaters as exhibitors of pornography, a label often given equally to sexually explicit material and to low-budget Punjabi or Pashto-language films screened in inner-city cinemas frequented primarily by working-class men. Similarly, I heard the term pornography used ambiguously in the context of Hall Road, variously describing Pakistani films that had passed the censor board, sexually suggestive *mujra* dance videos, and domestic or international material with sexually explicit content. When sources of religious authority have much to say on issues which are primarily a matter of taste, but little theological leverage on the subject, many fall back on embodied social hierarchies that inscribe order based on a system of binaries between high and low culture.

This is a question that animates William Mazzarella's ethnography of film censorship in India. Can anti-cinema demonstrations be considered "public" outrage if they are the organized efforts of a small group, many of whom did not even see the film in question? Mazzarella argues that to take a lack of textual engagement as an empty and irrelevant gesture would imply "that we can draw a clear line between what is 'in' the work and what is external to it. But from a social standpoint, the 'content' of the film includes not only the layers of interpretation and reaction that it generates over time—its interpretive patina, sometimes even its canonicity—but also its continued potency, its ability to potentiate its contexts in unpredictable ways."[21]

The expectation that people engage with a film presumes a certain kind of spectator, a cinephile who can talk about and debate narrative, form, and content. Spectatorship, Mazzarella argues, is more dispersed than this. He wants us to consider demonstrations against film, as "part of a series of gambles on the potentials that may dwell in public cultural fields."[22] Yet there is a distinction to be made here. Attacks on cinemas are indeed common in India, where outrage and agitation are rarely seen to be the sole domain of faith but also organized acts of political will, as street-power wielded for more diffuse aims. In these cases, attacks usually center on cinemas screening a particular film deemed transgressive in some way. In Pakistan, however, the *Innocence of Muslims* was not being screened anywhere; its offense radiated from its interface of access to the cinema hall. In this case, the platform for access was the digital video-sharing site YouTube which, as a response to it refusing to comply with demands to remove the video, was banned by the Pakistan Telecommunication Authority. The ban was not lifted until 2016, when YouTube developed a local version that made it easier for domestic authorities to remove content. The YouTube ban was just one of many subsequent attempts to regulate public morality by restricting the interface through which new repertoires might manifest and take shape. In 2018, the new social media application and video-sharing platform TikTok rose to popularity in Pakistan long before its adoption in Britain and America. TikTok's primarily teenage and young adult users took to the platform for its ability to record videos up to fifteen seconds long with found soundtracks, encouraging the cultivation of a repertoire of sound clips over which users gesticulate, mouth, mime, mock, and imitate. By 2020, TikTok, and dating apps such as Tinder, were being intermittently banned in Pakistan for promoting "immoral content."

The overarching figure of film is arguably the longest-standing interface through which repertoires become unruly enough to inflect public morality. Ali Haider, manager of the Gul Cinema in Lahore, was quick to give me several examples of street demonstrations by Islamist movements in the last few decades that had begun with political aims but rapidly descended into attacks on cinemas, drama theaters, or musicians' studios. Chuckling to himself through a cracked smile he told me how the contingency and exorbitance of the internet does not allow for the purified public place that these movements strive to demarcate. "You see all these clerics on television and their interviews uploaded to YouTube. Then suddenly, at the bottom, little advertisements pop up with women dancing half naked. In this country we cannot control the internet, so these activities are destined to go on side by side."

Lahore managed to avoid the worst of the anti-cinema attacks. Ali Haider remembered the moment of tense negotiation as mobs approached the cinemas of Abbott Road in 2012, "People came and threw things at the cinema. They even threw petrol bombs. We decided we had to make them understand and told them that this is their property, the property of Pakistan, and begged them not to do it. You could say those people were uneducated, some didn't even know why they were doing it, and those who knew why they were doing it didn't know this was property for public use."

Without pausing, he went on to implicate film producers and the government for causing deeper and more sustained damage than the rioters ever could have, "In our film industry people have just earned money and never invested any back in. If you look for Pakistan's biggest film, there is nothing of it remaining, neither [film] negative nor sound . . ." Amid the threat of mob destruction to his cinema, Ali Haider's act of negotiation appealed to sentiments warm to nationalism and public leisure. Reflecting on it later, however, he saw it dwarfed by wider problems facing the film trade, industry greed, and the absence of the state.

In another instance in which the public place of cinema halls was under examination, the Supreme Court of Pakistan sought a comprehensive report from the provincial Sindh government and Karachi Metropolitan Corporation (KMC) in 2016 following the repurposing of a latent Islamic cultural center, the Al-Markaz-e-Islami, into a cinema hall run by the CinePax chain of exhibitors. An article in Pakistan's *Jhang* newspaper that prompted court proceedings described how the building was constructed for the purposes of accommodating a combined Islamic academy, cultural space, and research center. Completed around 2001, the auditorium was one of the largest in Karachi, being able to seat around seven hundred and fifty persons, but it lay empty for many years when public funds dried up before the building could be put to its intended use. When the mayor of Karachi who initiated the project left office, the building was let out for concerts, dance shows, and stage dramas. In 2015 an Expression of Interest tender was released under the Public Private Partnership Act, passed a year before, as a way of expanding the private provision of infrastructural development, and later awarded to the CinePax company. Perhaps this tender of the long-postponed Islamic cultural center angered the leadership of the Islamist political party the Jamaat-e-Islami (hereafter JeI) as much as the exhibition of Indian films. These screenings prompted them to compare, through the juxtaposition of edits in a campaign video released by the JeI on social media, the inhabitation of the Al-Markaz-e-Islami to the destruction of the Babri Masjid in Ayodhya, India, in December 1992. Recalling an event in which Hindu nationalist groups destroyed a sixteenth-century mosque in the Indian state of Uttar Pradesh, the JeI's use of an incendiary image of rioters gathered on the roof of the mosque attempted to mediate their own outrage over the "cinema with domes," to which it was scathingly referred.

Following the *Jhang* article an application was filed by the Karachi leader of the JeI, requesting details of the law under which an Islamic center owned by the City Government of Karachi had been permitted to be converted into a cinema, an action the JeI claimed was un-Islamic and contrary to the ideology of Pakistan. In early deputations the chief justice expressed anger over the Sindh government's inaction over the covering of the *shahada*—the declaration of Muslim faith—with a billboard hung on the façade of the building.[23] The defendants claimed that no mosque or religious structure had existed on the property, nor had it ever been declared

Figure 1.3 A former cinema in Lahore. (Photo by author.)

Figure 1.4 One of the last remaining analog cinemas on Lahore's Abbott Road. (Photo by author.)

Figure 1.5 An advertisement on a rickshaw promotes a repertory screening of *Ghunda Tax* (2001), at the Metropole Cinema on Abbott Road. (Photo by author.)

as a religious or charitable endowment or an Amenity Plot as defined by the 2002 Karachi Building and Town Planning Regulations. What the defendants had not realized was that it was the architectonic and calligraphic features—domes and Quranic text—that made cohabitation with performance activities appear so affectively impermissible. This is not because of any delineated boundaries that had been transgressed, but an intense feeling that the powerful atmospheres of prayer and of film experience should not be allowed to coexist.[24] Indeed, while an Islamic "cultural center" might become a cinema by means of private tenancy laws, it was inconceivable for my interlocutors to imagine a cinema becoming a mosque.

Perhaps this is because of the anomalous place of cinema halls in Pakistan, situated as they are on thoroughfares, as remnants of a once more religiously diverse public sphere. Cinemas are key landmarks in South Asian cities, reminders of a former colonial ordering of infrastructure and urban space. Across Pakistan it is possible to find streets named Cinema Road, just as it is possible to find Jail Road and Canal Road. Even after such buildings stop operating as cinemas, they remain palpably former-cinemas—wedding halls, car parks, and apartment buildings—in a way that gated multiplexes, integrated into other structures, or hidden from public view, do not. With many cinemas dating from before Partition and assigned as evacuee property after the departure of their Hindu owners, cinemas halls share similar status with the gurdwaras left behind by Sikhs, temples left behind by Hindus, and churches left behind by the British. Cinemas in Pakistan have an aura of being a temple to something possible, to a duration yet to elapse; they are residual container technologies for an unfixed morality, as well as reminders of an earlier ideological ordering of urban space. When a video like *Innocence of Muslims* is said to insult the Prophet, the cinema as a capacious, urban temple becomes filled with a hypothetical image of offense and outrage. That they are on the thoroughfares, built to be attended, and property "for public use" in the words of Ali Haider, means that they are readily filled by whatever offenses are deemed possible.

The First Placard: Patriarchy and the Mahaul of Film Labor

To better address the anxieties evident in the two placards hung at the entrance to Hall Road by an insurgent far-right movement, we can take up their division of attention between the epistemology of film labor—the film actresses referred to in the first placard—and the ontology of the film image—the "film pictures" of the second. With spaces of material circulation, such as Hall Road, almost exclusively male, assertions over permissibility or the mahaul of film often come to reinforce majoritarian and patriarchal forms of public morality. One of my neighbors during my time in Lahore, a middle-aged woman named Shamaila Begum, despite being a fervent cinephile who could sing dozens of songs recorded by the playback singer Noor Jehan, had never visited a cinema or a media market. Shamaila, whose family village and cattle were situated near Kasur some fifty kilometers from Lahore, believed there to be greater prospects for her two sons and six daughters in the city. They moved to a majority-Christian area in Bara Pind, a village adjacent to Jannat Cottages, one of the sprawling, partially gated, housing communities in the south of Lahore where she took work as a cleaner at the nearby Arfa Karim Technology Park, where start-ups and young entrepreneurs worked to develop a new digital economy. Since she had moved to Lahore, her community had slowly been turned into its own enclave by the gated walls of Jannat Cottages built around it.

Noticing my curiosity, Shamaila invited my wife and I to a performance at her church for the *taj poshi* [garlanding or crowning] of the Virgin Mary, in which her teenage daughter was scheduled to perform. When Shamaila arrived to pick us up at the nearby bus stop to supervise our dash across the dual carriageway that separated the station from Bara Pind, she was downcast, spitting invectives at the federal government. Responding to outrage over the rape and murder of an infant girl in Kasur—and to assuage widespread calls for the public hanging of the accused—the Punjab Government had banned dance performances in all private and government schools. While fearful over the state of local policing, Shamaila's most pressing concern that night was that her daughter's long rehearsals and new dress would come to nothing; any sections of dance in the performance had been cancelled.

Following an outbreak of sexual violence and murders in the town of Kasur, many news outlets and public figures cited the popularity among young people for reproducing "item numbers," the extended song and dance routines in Indian and Pakistani films, as a contributing factor. The item number is an assemblage of sensations and spectatorial expectations, featuring dance, song, and film as the primary ingredients.[25] Together, many politicians and celebrities claimed those reproducing them invited sexual assault and murder. While these discussions circulated widely on social media in Pakistan and the diaspora, the Punjab Government appealed to popular sentiment. The resolution was followed shortly after by another banning "DJ nights" and "dance parties" at educational institutions to shield the young from "immorality." Few were surprised by the decision. Female dancers, singers, and performers popular on the "stage drama" circuit are often cited as figures of immorality, and the frequency with which they face violence is met with scant media coverage.

This underlines how the regimes of permissibility that address film are often heavily gendered by a pervasive and violent patriarchal morality. While a good mahaul might be predicated on the gendering of ritual or public space, a bad mahaul is often closely associated with a cultural space populated by female dancers, singers, or performers. These distinctions are not merely passive judgements. During the period of my fieldwork alone at least two female performers in Punjab were murdered in a space in which the condemnation of a particular mahaul contributed to providing their male killers with lenient sentences. Linking concerns for public morality to acts of physical violence, murder, and victim-blaming undergirded by systems of power, allows atmosphere to be used to manage the boundaries of patriarchy.

The ethnographic relationship I trace between patriarchy and atmospheres concerns the appropriation of authority. In an early ethnography of film labor, Hortense Powdermaker saw in the mid-twentieth-century Hollywood studio system a microcosm of totalitarianism. In its devaluation of individual rights and its centralization of power, she found an "atmosphere of breaks, continuous anxiety, and crises."[26] She argued that if the result of this atmosphere is a poor standard of production, inefficiency, and a "deep frustration in human relations," it is in the industry's interest to become democratic.[27] In reaching this conclusion, Powdermaker built on Erich Fromm's then-recently published *Fear of Freedom*, which itself was a response to the perceived dangers to individuality and uniqueness represented by the authoritarianisms of the 1930s. Fromm asked, "Is freedom only the absence of external pressure or is it also the *presence* of something—and if so, what?"[28] He believed that many scholars neglected the influence of "anonymous authorities like public opinion and 'common sense,' which are so powerful because of our profound readiness to conform to the expectations everybody has about ourselves and our equally profound fear of being different."[29] The idea that common sense is attractive and alluring yet undergirded by "anonymous authority" bears similarities to Matthew Engelke's notion that "ambient faith" as a palimpsest of subtle suggestions can become impactful and binding.[30]

The career trajectories of actors, dancers, and singers associated with the film industry in Pakistan also offer insights into the feelings associated with such trades.[31] In Pakistan in the early 2000s, it was common to see both female stage and film actors undertake *tauba*, an act of repentance to Allah that serves to renounce their former life in the business.[32] Most notably, film actor, dancer, and stage performer Nargis undertook tauba under the supervision of celebrity Islamic scholar Maulana Tariq Jameel, who accompanied her on the annual Hajj pilgrimage to Mecca. Her remarkable career and turbulent public persona took another turn when she later returned to the stage, thus effectively renouncing her renunciation.[33] Female actors and singers from Shi'i communities, on the other hand, rarely undertake tauba, but often transform their careers as performers to those of reciters of laments and elegiac poems in commemoration of the Shi'i Imams and the Ahl-e Bait. In the same way that tauba does the work of renunciation, female actors and singers-turned-devotional reciters transform from performance personages to that which is ostensibly not musical, simply by crossing a threshold between song and recitation. In these instances, one can navigate between the poles of film's contaminant and its salvation, underlining the pliable nature of its mahaul, in contrast to more stubborn ideas around permissibility.

The day after the ban on dance performances was announced, Shamaila Begum was eager to vent her frustration. Her daughter's rescheduled performance had been amended so, instead of dancing to an upbeat Christian song, the girls were all to dress as angels in bleached white frocks, file up the stairs of an open-air courtyard and stand rigid on the adjoining walls for the finale. Shamaila could not understand why song, dance, and performance were viewed with such distain by many of her wealthy Muslim employers who supported the ban. Her employers believed that all film stars and singers come from the *mirasi* caste, a term often used as a derogatory way to describe anyone who is involved with performances deemed immoral. Etymologically, the term derives from the Arabic word for inheritance or heritage, and describes the genealogists, bards, and minstrels of North Indian oral storytelling. It was British colonial administrator Denzil Ibbetson who declared the mirasi a caste unto themselves, reflecting the already changed dynamics of a social group once lauded—or at least patronized—by the North Indian Mughal elite. He explained, "The social position of the Mirasi, as of all the minstrel castes, is exceedingly low, but he attends at weddings and on similar occasions to recite genealogies. . . . [The Mirasi] is notorious for his exactions, which he makes under the threat of lampooning the ancestors of him from whom he demands fees."[34] This is reminiscent of rituals performed by transgender or third-gender performers—often referred to as "eunuchs"—at contemporary Pakistani weddings, in which "inspiring both reverence and fear, they play upon their own supposed impotence."[35] Thus, entrenched in anxieties about the public place of performance is a residual anxiety over the power of mediators, specifically the power to mediate genealogies.

Film laborers arguably face fewer dangers than stage performers, further removed as they are from their audiences. Yet for many their social place is often seen as equally contaminant, the beginning of a journey that ends in the fires of hell. In the book *Film Acting Guide* discussed in the introduction, S. M. Shahid argues that much of the Lahore and Mumbai film industry was built on runaways. "Watching a film was considered *haram*.

In those cases, a Muslim child's interest in working in the film industry would be an invitation to judgement day."[36] Shahid recognizes there to be a surfeit of books on how to enter and thrive within the Pakistani film industry. The book was also a guide for parents of budding film professionals. Recalling Melody Jue's call for "a new saturated sense of the interface,"[37] Shahid writes that when yearning or enthusiasm [shauq] for film wells up in a child, it cannot be dissimulated. "When the interest in film mingles with the personality then it is impossible to stop them from acting . . . Just as water makes its own routes, so can one's enthusiasm."[38] Shahid tells of predatory figures preying on this saturated enthusiasm for film. Boys and girls, lured by fraudulent advertisements in smaller towns and villages calling for new actors to audition in Lahore for an upcoming production, fell into sex work or crime, or were defrauded by touts with a low-level association with the studios. The book can be read in parallel with a rise in rural-to-urban migration in Pakistan during the last decades of the twentieth century. Considering the dishonor of a child in the film trade coupled with the fear of the depopulation of the villages, Shahid welcomes the arrival of permanent stage dramas in smaller cities and villages as a way of stopping runaways and providing local work.

As I read Shahid's book, I began to see the decline narrative, that equated the rule of General Zia ul-Haq with the spread of religious conservatism and the collapse of the Lollywood film industry, as a way of giving a political genealogy to the moral atmospheres and regimes of permissibility that surround film. The predominance of this narrative seems to be derived largely from what was until recently the only authoritative book on film in Pakistan, Mushtaq Gazdar's *Pakistan Cinema 1947–1997*. Gazdar was one of a small contingent of arthouse filmmakers who benefited from the pre-Zia era sponsorship of film production under Zulfiqar Ali Bhutto and suffered under the subsequent decade of military rule. Curbing obscenity and vulgarity was the purpose of replacing the Censorship of Films Act, 1963, with the Zia-era 1979 Motion Picture Ordinance. Despite this, the films that followed appeared as standard to be more lascivious, violent, and unruly as anything that could have been imagined under prior regimes. The more Pakistani films I watched from the late 1970s and 1980s, the more improbable the Islamist lobby appeared as the grounds for the decline narrative. It seemed that rather than fewer films being made, a great many more were produced, if to a more formulaic template and largely in the Punjabi and Pashto languages, rather than in Urdu. Both Punjabi and Pashto films, often like the language in which they are acted, are often denigrated by Urdu-language economic elites and have been seen as symptoms of the "decline" diagnosed in Pakistani film.[39] Under the rule of Zia, the propagation of top-down Islamization was only implemented a few months before his death in a plane crash. Only after the June 1988 Shariah Ordinance was passed were television authorities required to reduce the number of adverts featuring women or were cinema agents and producers required to remove film poster hoardings showing women from the public sphere.[40]

At the same time, popular theatrical traditions and performers were making their way to the government-built theaters in Lahore.[41] There they created a comedic style interpenetrative with *filmi* Punjabi styles of social and political satire. Both Punjabi-language theater and film exposed the porosity of Zia's supposedly rigid codes of gender and morality through the materialization and performance of gender relations. This fluid assemblage of different performative traditions prompted a discursive sphere to arise in the Zia era that portrayed a national culture vulnerable to obscenity and vulgarity, and that mapped these threats onto women's bodies, trades, and performances. The result was a greater sexualization of women's bodies across media forms and formats. The Women's Action Forum (WAF), whose "action-based research" attempted to harness the outrage and the anger of the 1980s, conducted a pioneering study titled "Re-Inventing Women." It explored attempts to reduce the visibility of women in the public and political sphere at the same time as the state and many of its supporting ulama worked to further institutionalize the female body as site and symbol of male honor.[42] In turn, such antagonistic discourse provided fuel for many media assemblages to thrive. As Sanjay Srivastava argues in a more optimistic reading, discourses of transgression can also make the unstable nature of thresholds of taste, sexuality, or class a site for self-making.[43] Yet, one of the consequences of Zia's anti-women reforms was a public sphere not only shot through with patriarchy and machismo but one in which the threshold through which women could be considered to transgress was far narrower than for men.

The Zia era also saw the figure of the threshold take root as a means of distinguishing between the public image of moral and immoral women and between majoritarian and minority practices. My interlocutors in Pakistan expressed the line between good behavior or socially acceptable actions and transgressions using the term *hadd* [threshold, limit, frontier]. As well as being a figure of everyday speech, hadd is a familiar term in Islamic jurisprudence, referring to punishment for the transgression of divine boundaries. Describing hadd often requires taking a phenomenological approach to moral experience, in which the demarcation of limits is an intrinsic element of regulating natural instincts or passions. According to modernist Islamic scholar and liberal reformist Fazlur Rahman, the verb *hadd* in Arabic acts "to prevent" the intrusion of one thing onto another.[44] As a noun it heightens this preventative agency to express a limit that separates one thing from another by a moral obligation to be good as derived from the Quran and Sunnah (the traditions and sayings of the Prophet Muhammad). Rahman noted that the term underwent a change through its application in Islamic jurisprudence, moving from a limit or boundary marker to a term referring to the punishment of transgressing those limits.

Hadd or *hudood* in plural refer, in one sense, by their Arabic root, to the limits defined by Allah and provide a pervasive means of reinforcing social order through reference to tensile borders and boundaries.[45] Rahman believed that even though the actual limits of hadd are not clearly demarcated, punishable hudood are those that can be seen to do damage to others or to society, rather than neglecting performing one's daily prayers or drinking alcohol, which damage only the self.[46] While the context in which I heard the word was in reference to describing limits that are both moral and affective, such as those that divide recitation from song, the term relates to broader thresholds. I found that the greater my interlocutors' religious education the more likely they were to use the term, rather than interspersing their comments with the English word *line*. Almost all, however, were aware of the use of the term in Zia's Hudood Ordinances, which described five criminal laws split into separate punishments and evidence bases. Decisions that fell under hadd entailed fixed punishments like amputation, but these were never fulfilled. The most pronounced impact of the Hudood Ordinances was to exacerbate existing biases against women and minorities.[47] The Ordinances also introduced the idea that a limit previously the remit of intuition, that itself was to be guided by one's ethical disposition, could be disciplined and regulated by the state. It was not just behavior and conduct that could now be adjudicated by the state, but other forms of public leisure and entertainment like film that were subject to speculation over thresholds of permissibility.

The Second Placard: Ontologies of the Moving Image

The journey, from film actress to damnation, narrated in the first placard mentioned in the introduction to this chapter can be seen as part of an assemblage of residual sexual anxieties and patriarchal violence. The second placard's anxieties over "film pictures" are harder to pin down. As this section argues, worries over the ontology and materiality of the film image are often located on the surface of the film and are continually renewed by changing platforms for image access and availability. The permissibility of the film image—rather than the built and social space of the cinema—and its materiality was important enough to have been addressed by Muhammad Iqbal and Syed Abul A'la Maududi, both formative figures in the philosophy of Pakistan as a political and religious idea. Their arguments provide two divergent examples of the ways in which the permissibility of film—and by extension the moving images that have come to constitute television, internet, and social media content—in Pakistan has been expressed as an obstacle to politically infused piety.

Usually located in the social life of public affect and sexuality, the permissibility of film has also been questioned in relation to scriptural discourse. As Naveeda Khan notes, fatwas—Islamic rulings issued by an authoritative source—are useful for scholarly study as forms of performative text that reveal the social sphere of the everyday.[48] This is because, as Hussein Ali Agrama argues, the fatwa bears the tension between ethical agency and power wielded in its name.[49] The problem of the fatwa is a problem of inheritance and renewal, achieved by both the questioner and respondent, who together address the precarity not of situations but the affairs of the soul. Fatwas and answers to questions over film's permissibility often refer to the earthy materiality of celluloid and digital ontologies, the bodies of actors and laborers, and the permissibility of a kind of image with few easy parallels in the Quran or Sunnah.[50]

This is particularly evident in the extent to which the image is distributed and fabricated by cinematic technologies, or, in the case of the founder of the Jamaat-e-Islami, Syed Abul A'la Maududi, in the fixity of the moving image. For Maududi the mobility of the moving image played a key role in the ways film's materiality affects its reception across religious fields of experience. In the mid-1920s, Muslim disinterest in the cinema was of clear concern to the British colonial authorities, which in the wide-ranging

Indian Cinematograph Committee report of 1928 mourned that Muslims appeared particularly unmoved by film-going.[51] Yet their conclusions were reached even though the small number of ulama interviewed displayed neither an explicit aversion nor an overt enthusiasm for film entertainment. At much the same time, Maududi was eagerly consuming films in Delhi having yet developed his distinct brand of political–religious activity rooted in Deobandi thought.[52] As a young journalist Maududi argued that giving legitimacy to technology was the only means to effectively debate with the modern world, which could then be infused with a Muslim identity, thus pioneering the modernizing attempts of Islamic revivalism and its transformation of technology for its own ends.

In the second volume of *Rasail O Masail*, one of his many juristic compilations in which he responded to questions of religious comportment, Maududi answered an enquiry over whether cinema is permissible in Islam:

> Many times before I have shared this thought that cinema itself [*cinema khud*] is permitted. It is its non-permitted use that makes it forbidden. The image that is seen on the screen of the cinema is in fact not an image [*tasveer*], instead it is a reflection just like a reflection seen in a mirror. That is why it is not forbidden [*haram*], so long as the image inside the film is not printed on paper or any other thing, nor is the image applied [*atalaq*] to the film, nor used for any purpose relating to any of the operations [*kamo*] to be abstained from under any law that would proclaim the image forbidden. Because of these reasons, to me, cinema itself is permitted.[53]

Maududi's comments were accompanied by recommendations on the preferable genre and content of films—documentary, tactics of war, industrial, and educational—and the industrial labor that should undergird them—women must neither feature nor should men act their roles. Significantly, Maududi qualified his statement as entirely subjective: "to me." This was either to ensure that his comments were taken as contemporary readings and not as exegeses from scripture, or to emphasize his statements as an engagement with the experience of film which can and has been understood in different ways. It is interesting to see how these comments, written at much the same time as André Bazin's *The Ontology of the Photographic Image*, provide an analytical counterpoint to classical film theory and its conceptions of an objective, emancipatory film image released from its techno-material origins.[54] Maududi's reading of the ontology of the film image and its evasive "surfacism" relies on the notion that the inability of the social experience of cinema to self-archive, to impress its morality in material terms, resists assigning its visual data transcendental value.[55]

The question put to Maududi from an anonymous reader is also worth referring to in its entirety:

> I am a student and have attended Jamaat-e-Islami lectures and fol-
> lowed them in detail. With Allah's blessing I have gone through a
> radical religious change [inquilab] due to these lectures. For a very long
> time I have had an interest in cinematography and for that reason I
> have obtained a lot of information in that regard. After listening to
> debates for and against cinematography, my heart's wish is that if cin-
> ematography is permissible, I can use it for religious reasons and in
> the provision of ethical service to others [akhlaqi khidmat]. Could you
> kindly tell me whether this art can be used for beneficial reasons? If
> the answer is in favour of its usage, then could you please elaborate
> whether a woman is allowed to be shown on the curtain of the
> screen?[56]

It is important to note that Maududi began his reply by claiming that he had long authorized and permitted "cinema itself," what one might take to mean the techno-material phenomenon before its mediation or utiliza-tion. The word *itself* underlines the importance of the reciprocity of the subject and the perceived value-neutrality of the technology. Maududi gave a similar response to queries over the use of loudspeakers in prayer, saying their ontology was "pure" and that only the way that they had been used was immoral.[57] Use value, film's ability to be transformed into something in the world through application, suggests a familiar kind of porous screen upon which the self can be projected. By arguing that the image on the cinema screen is a reflection, similar to a reflection seen in a mirror—historically ruled permissible in Islam—and therefore immaterial, unfixed, temporary, and transient, Maududi suggested the reflection of light bifur-cates film and its image into separate things. What makes cinema forbidden for Maududi is the potential for the image inside the film to be manifested on paper or any other receptacle, as if the film were a capacious storage unit for embryonic forms that have the potential to solidify. A projection on a wall is thus considered something formed of light, whereas the static image, applied [atalaq] on paper, as opposed to the moving image, is classed as an image. It is the process that pulls one towards the other, complicating the ontology of the machine and the ethical aspirations of the viewer, which forms the social life of theology. Maududi's comments on the ontology of the film image thus attempted to define its material characteristics and effects so as to determine the permissibility of its use.[58]

Yet the interlocutors whose accounts inform this book rarely cited the Quran or the Sunnah when speculating on the mahaul of film or its permissibility, although some did refer to Maududi's guidance. Questions of permissibility stimulate what might be called everyday exegeses, that operate more on intuition or consultation of the internet hive mind than knowledge of juridical sources. A quick internet search reveals how the ontology of media interfaces and experiences are sites of frequent return for online ulama who are often asked questions that relate to the materiality of the still and moving image. On such sites pious authorities offer authoritative advice on Islamic law and codes of public and private comportment in everyday life. A few examples to which everyday exegeses variously respond include: those curious of the correct methods of respectfully disposing of Quranic and Islamic pedagogic DVDs; the morality of renting property to tenants who work in the film industry; rulings on employment in cinema-lobby customer service; the extent to which images projected on the screen of a cinema and the immaterial structure of digital photographs can be considered pictures in the theological sense [tasveer], and the extent to which they are prohibited. As in Maududi's time, the issue of film's permissibility remains not an abstract theological argument but a living sphere of debate over where moral thresholds lie.

Maududi's Islamic modernism was doubtless inspired by the nature, if not swayed by many of the arguments, of philosopher Muhammad Iqbal's focus on the materiality of religious experience. Iqbal's *The Reconstruction of Religious Thought in Islam*, a series of lectures given in Madras, Hyderabad, and Aligarh, and originally published in 1930, sought a greater understanding of the conception of religious experience and its place in early twentieth-century modernity.[59] Iqbal argued that unlike the Christian division between subject and object and the concomitant schism between the ideal and the real, Islam acknowledges the way the ideal and the real brush against one another. In identifying this relationship with the world of matter, things perceived in the world are subject to verification from one's sensory experience of them. As reliance is put on sensory faculties to decode the nature of matter, Iqbal asked whether religiosity as the ultimate character for reality can be maintained if the predominance of sense perception is adhered to. In many ways his was an attempt to divorce the natural sciences from materialism to emphasize spirituality as the basis of reality.

Yet Iqbal was more caustic in his criticism of the medium of film than Maududi, as expressed in a short poem titled "Cinema."[60] The direction of his critique was not over the politics of representation provoked by depiction, but what he saw as an idolatrous and parochial fetishism that the technology reproduced, composed of the very dust and ashes of modernity's disputed linearity.

CINEMA

Cinema—or new fetish-fashioning,
Idol-making and mongering still?
Art, men called that olden-voodoo—
Art, they call this mumbo-jumbo;
That—antiquity's poor religion:
This—modernity's pigeon-plucking;
That—earth's soil: this—soil of Hades;
Dust, their temple; ashes, ours.[61]

It is possible to see "Cinema" as a continuation of the theory of materiality articulated in *Reconstruction*. Its mutable, earthy matter points to the transformative potential of a dynamic and ever expanding universe, of which cinema is an expression of just one possible—and ultimately undesirable—modernity.

These textual sources provide an understanding of the ways in which repertoires of moving-image media, particularly in the history of Pakistan as a political and religious idea, might be better understood by acknowledging the multiple ontologies that coexist and circulate around disputed technological and image-based forms. Maududi's answer in *Rasail O Masail* contained more than a straightforward answer to whether film is permissible. It starkly referred to the ontology of film, pointing not as many others do, to the content, but to the surface of the moving image whereupon its moral body is located and can be renegotiated. Anxieties about misuse that ran throughout Maududi's advice on the moving image bring film back to the ambiguous and elemental ontology of first contact, as a transcendent and transformative medium. This the early filmmaker and film theorist Sergei Eisenstein identified in specifically drawn animation as "the *protean* element . . . which contains in 'liquid' form all possibilities of future species and forms," or what we might term the hypothetical origin of an image without an indexical relationship to divine or temporal authority.[62]

A New Wave

In Pakistan in the early 2020s, the mahaul of film can be seen as a kind of studied ambivalence, a way of not committing oneself to rejecting film or embracing it but leaving it as a force with the potential to act upon oneself in ways that might be both positive and negative. Central to the case brought against the Karachi Metropolitan Corporation over the use of an Islamic cultural center as a multiplex cinema was the belief that the moral atmospheres of faith and performance are incompatible. This correlates with building regulations from the colonial era that, still in use in Pakistan, dictate that cinemas must not be constructed within two hundred yards of any school, hospital, or mosque. While no mosque was constructed at the site, the judge presiding over the case agreed that the very fact that the building supported five domes and walls with Muslim prayers was enough to deem it intended for Islamic purposes. Even for the courts, film is a frequent site of return for those negotiating the varying regimes of permissibility that pervade everyday life. Whether it is a court case deliberating over the repurposing of an Islamic cultural center into a cinema or celebrity Islamic scholar Maulana Tariq Jameel taking film and stage actor Nargis on the Hajj pilgrimage to Mecca to strengthen her tauba— her renunciation of the performance industry—these ongoing negotiations instantiate a public eager to learn where thresholds of permissibility are located in relation to film.

By the end of the 2010s, the development of multiplex cinemas and the relocation of film exhibition to shopping malls looked to transform negative moral and class-based distinctions over film. In 2017, following Gulf countries like Qatar and the United Arab Emirates' sponsorship of film production and festivals, Saudi Arabia announced it would lift its thirty-five-year ban on cinemas, allowing chains to open, theaters to be built, and film production to begin. The opening of new, high-end multiplexes in cities across Pakistan coincided with a seminal change in the public image and morality of cinemas in Gulf Islamic polities that Pakistani investors sought to emulate. The resurgence of Pakistani cinema at this time found sources of funding due to an eagerness to fill these newly built multiplexes with domestically produced films, and to wean distributors off their need for Indian imports. This created a noticeable bifurcation between the entertainment associated with Lahore's historic "Lollywood" film industry and the return to aspirational, middle- and upper-class Urdu language entertainment being made in Karachi by a new generation of producers, directors, and actors who previously had little association with the old industry. While Lollywood films made in Lahore are easily recognized by their aesthetics, for those on the inside, the industry is delimited by labor organization and affiliation. To release a film, crew members must be signed up to their relevant union or association, whether it be for writers, producers, or directors. The lack of adherence to this measure for the new wave of films produced since the 2010s has further bifurcated these spheres of production into recognizably distinct industries. One professional body that cuts across the two is the Pakistan Cinema Management Association, whose chairman at the time of my research maintained a close relationship with the then chief minister of Punjab, Shehbaz Sharif. These professional associations were always quick to speak out against pornography and the exhibition of "vulgar" item numbers in films, pre-emptively striking out against accusations used to denigrate their industry.

This bifurcation between Lollywood cinema, with its recognizable aesthetic, its diluted colors from the overstretched developing baths at Evernew Studios' laboratory, and the "New-Wave" Pakistani cinema, with international-standard production qualities, was prefigured by that of Pakistani performance traditions. This associated female performers in Punjabi dramas with vulgarity while "educated" women forged celebrated careers in Urdu- and English-language drama and on the state-run Pakistan Television (PTV).[63] Such a bifurcation is part of an ongoing negotiation over the performance of film experience and its moral atmospheres. When the atmosphere of film leads to actors renouncing their career, singers committing to no longer singing, and industries becoming defined by normative inversion, it is here that moral thresholds become sensitized as palpable objects of social practice.

Recalling the placards erected at the entrance to Hall Road, the engaged inverse to cinephilia is often used to support arguments with much greater stakes, such as the TLP's calls for a stricter enforcement of blasphemy laws. As this chapter has argued, the latent potential of film—often used as a byword for the residual incursion of secular entertainment into public life— shows some of the ways in which the thresholds between morality and immorality are formed historically and reproduced in the present through forms of both political distance and emotional intimacy.

CHAPTER II

Public Demand

Interpreting Atmospheres

I dris insisted on accompanying me to the basement of the Dar-ul-Rehmat plaza, confident that any association with Durrani Electronics would assure me safety and polite treatment. Our destination was the last bastion of traders new and old who continued trading in film copies. Many used to run street-facing shops but could not afford the rising rents and moved to the basement of the newly constructed plaza. As I began my research looking at the marketplace circulation of Pakistani films, one of the methodological strategies I deployed was to ask DVDwallas for a film I knew was likely lost to history. As we discussed the possible reasons for this omission from the Hall Road repertoire, conversations turned to their usual strategies of retrieval, the infrastructures that brought about distribution, and the absence of state-led archival and preservation initiatives. One film I would often request was *Nai Kiran* [A New Dawn] (1960), a documentary produced on the orders of Pakistan's first military ruler, Ayub Khan, who seized power in 1958. It was produced in five versions—in Urdu, Bengali, Sindhi, Pashto, and Punjabi—to reflect the linguistic diversity of West and East Pakistan as the two wings were known before the Bangladesh War of Independence in 1971.[1] Despite being government propaganda, *Nai Kiran* was the first film made in Pakistan in the Sindhi and Pashto languages. The first East Pakistani film to be made in Bengali had only premiered two years before. *Nai Kiran* was a part of Ayub's attempts to legitimize military rule through the establishment of a system of mediatory local government he called "Basic Democracy," based on his assumption that Western-style democracy was ill-suited to the fledging Pakistani state.

Many of my interlocutors in the Dar-ul-Rehmat Plaza initially responded with fascination at this inexplicable omission to their repertoires but went on to explain to me that the film was likely lost because it had never been subject to *"public demand,"* using the English expression. A lack of demand would explain why no one kept the celluloid reels, nor transferred them to VHS for sale in the marketplace, and therefore why they were unable to find any analog copies to transfer to digital formats. Idris held a different opinion. To him, my enquiries were little more than a misplaced search for origins. Chiding me with his usual humor, he said, "If you look hard enough you might even find God." I think many of my interlocutors would have agreed; Islamic hierarchy is centripetal: it moves towards a divine and prophetic center. If Pakistani films on Hall Road are underwritten by the individual ethical and entrepreneurial decisions of their mediators, then the circulation of Pakistani media must also be contingent on the will of Allah.

For example, what my interlocutors on Hall Road called "demand" guides and buttresses the recording, retrieval, and reproduction of media content. Demand explains the non-existence of a rare film or speaks of the devotion, respect, and disciplinary character of the customer. Expressed through a clipped form of the English phrase "by public demand," it describes a felt atmosphere cleaved by a wish emanating from an undefined collective. The extent to which films are subject to public demand on Hall Road lends weight to the argument this book has made thus far, that enthusiasm for film can coexist with skepticism regarding its social utility, even within the moral world of a single individual. As the introduction and first chapter have shown, atmospheres provide a useful container for the oscillating moral moods borne when public conduct, ethical disposition, and religious permissibility come face-to-face with the social space of film. Demand is sensitive to atmospheres but requires a different interpretation. We know that as an economic principle, demand arises when there are a greater number of buyers in a marketplace. What is harder to ascertain is how demand is gaged and expressed. Through which networks does it reach an open mind or body? And more specifically, how does demand shape the reproduction and retrieval of films, as well as their censorship, regulation, and status as heritage objects? The act of assigning agency to an undefined collective seemed to me to willfully detract individual responsibility from those involved in the circulation of contested media. But it is not only traders who believe they are able to interpret what their public wants and needs. This chapter traces some of the ways that an attempt to read atmospheres and demands, despite their opacity, has come to shape how film is sold, collected, archived, and censored.

Demand

Research in South Asia at the intersection of anthropology and material and visual culture has been adept at showing how trading communities manufacture ways of reaching, and in a sense producing, distinct audiences, while doing so in ways that allow for mutually beneficial relationships between bazaar trade and popular piety.[2] In my use of the term *marketplace*, I refer to a bounded sphere of activity, but when my interlocutors referred to "the market" they also referred to a brand of mercantile conservativism that allows the engine of demand to decide the fate of things possessing unresolved ethical baggage. Perhaps I was preoccupied by the wave of populist politics that had come to dominate Britain and North America in the mid-2010s, and that, in a different form, would propel former cricketer Imran Khan and his PTI party to power in Pakistan in 2018, but the way my interlocutors described demand felt to me to be an assumption wholly in tune with the political zeitgeist.

As well as detracting individual ethical responsibility, the force of demand also propagated faith in the *awaam*, a term often voiced in Pakistan but rarely defined. Whenever I asked about the awaam, I was surprised to find my interlocutors on the defensive. This could perhaps be due to the word's dual usage, as either a pejorative, condescending equivalent of "mass" or as a possessive, communal "people" that evokes a sense of belonging. It is also used in close connection with the concept of a "public," the population in general, or as a motivational term to address a body of people at large. In many ways, the struggle to reconcile Islamic political structure with the mediatory face of democracy has made the relationship between the state and the awaam Pakistan's most enduring political problem.[3] Anthropologist Akbar Ahmed sees this relationship characterized by what he calls "the 'Pakistanization' of culture and the 'awamification' of society."[4] The former relates to a certain homogenizing tendency that attempts to crystallize repertoires of South Asian, linguistic, Islamic, and other expressions and fix them as emblematic of being Pakistani. "Awam-ification," on the other hand, marks a transformation of how "the people" are seen by power, rather than how they are allowed to exercise power. Ahmed explains that by the 1990s, the once vilified "people" were repositioned as the arbiters of public morality by power-brokers hungry for their votes. The extent of its use by political parties and forms of popular media references an eagerness to be on the right side of the awaam, just as one might like to be on the right side of history.[5]

It is here that we return to the Hall Road repertoire, a concept I raised in the introduction. This repertoire is a direct product of the absence of national film or sound archives, allowing the awaam to be considered the guardians, distributors, and censors of audio and visual material. The idea that circulating media can, under certain circumstances, be freely used by anyone instead of through payment or subscription has gained recognition in the online repository Wikipedia Commons and U.S. non-profit Creative Commons, both of which mix private intellectual property rights with the idea of the commons. The commons describes a natural resource, but, balanced as it is between altruism and self-interest, it is also an idea heavily laden with ethical concerns.

Garrett Hardin's influential essay on the biophysical commons as a pool of shared resources began with a call to look beyond science and technology to square the problem of the prospect of infinite growth with finite resources. Hardin's "tragedy of the commons" imagined a time free of the forces that aggregate human populations, when accessing the commons meant being locked into a system of competitive increase.[6] In his parable, the commons become depleted and the failure of human free will exposed. When it is easier to pollute the commons than dispose of pollutants in other ways, the tragedy of the commons is a problem of legislation and "temperance" that situates morality as a distributed element of the system to which it pertains.[7] Even then, for Hardin, individual conscience is doomed to fail. The answer lies in responsibility as a system that is socially produced at the same time as coercion, or what Hardin called "mutual coercion, mutually agreed upon by the majority of the people affected."[8] For my interlocutors on Hall Road the material accumulated was not always wealth, but often what Garrett Hardin argued was the system of responsibility co-produced at the same time as coercion. While this shows the moral background to circulation, its emphasis on self-interest does not account for the existence of the Hall Road repertoire. Elinor Ostrom showed that Garrett Hardin's "tragedy of the commons" neglected the place of collective management as a third way between private, exclusive use and state management.[9] Ostrom argued that shared resources can be governed by coexisting and often conflicting systems of regulation at the same time, such as by the market and the state, or in the case of the Hall Road repertoire, interdiction and reproduction.

The felt force of demand and practices of subsequent retrieval from the Hall Road repertoire therefore move in tandem. The collective management of the Hall Road repertoire is driven by the opacity of needs, demands, and atmospheres at the same time as aiming to make them transparent and readable at all turns. Demand is an idea in tune with the agency of others; a mutual coercion not yet mutually agreed upon. It creates a repertoire of both dissensus and common ground that operates through contestation and debate. In the following sections, I show how generative and censorial changes made to material and visual culture can be traced to the demands perceived to emanate from an undefined public.

Of Saints and Hidden Imams

Before circling back to the Hall Road repertoire at this end of this chapter, I want to briefly shift the ethnographic frame to consider instances in which other visual repertoires are subject to public demand. In many ways, the combined forces of responsibility, mutual coercion, and collective management are even more palpable in relation to religious media. Many of the roadside sellers of poster art that can be found on Hall Road's eastern edges are anxious about being accused of *shirk* [polytheism] and are therefore particularly sensitive to the force of public demand. By the late 2010s they mostly stocked Arabic calligraphic designs encased behind glass rather than the colorful, indigenous *aulia akram* [friends of God] posters that depict the shrines, personalities, and visual piety of Muslim saints.[10] Many of Hall Road's poster sellers remarked upon a recent censorial turn that had seen these posters decline from public view. At the shrines where they would usually be sold, adherents blamed their gradual disappearance on Islamist attempts to censor the mediatory power of saintly intercessors. Publishers, who affix their names and addresses on the bottom of the posters for repeat sale, tried to avoid becoming mired in accusations from far-right movements or vigilantes. Even if an image is overworked, burnished,

Figure 2.1 Poster traders selling calligraphic designs, devotional images, and decorative pictures. (Photo by author.)

and turned into something almost entirely new, its continual churning is reissued through conservative market mechanisms.

Once a week, poster sellers would rise early to visit Abu Islami Images and select the stock they would take by bicycle or on foot to sell by the roadside at the eastern end of Hall Road. They brought with them their estimations of what had sold well the previous week, knowledge of forthcoming religious celebrations, commemorations, or death anniversaries, and a set of assumptions about demand that they had accumulated through conversations and criticisms over the previous week. Abu Islami Images were one of the last publishers in a once burgeoning printing trade that centered around Lahore's Urdu Bazaar. They produced a varied array of devotional, syncretic, Christian, Shi'i, and Sufi saints posters that drew upon an extensive collection of templates. Returning after spending some time in his ancestral village, Jamil, the patient and sagacious foreman of Abu Islami Images, rushed to show me some new designs hot off the press. I was told that demand had called for the new Abraj Al-Bait Towers in Mecca to be included behind all images of the Kaaba, providing symmetry with the minaret beside the dome of Medina. The ruling House of Saud had transformed Mecca and Medina over the last century, bulldozing the homes, mausolea, and graves of the friends, family, and companions of the Prophet Muhammad. The new clock tower looming over the Kaaba is seen by many as the apex of this destruction and building surge. The mysterious force of demand had also consigned the production of visual materials relating to Pakistani and Indian film stars to a dusty storeroom upstairs at the offices of Abu Islami Images. For decades, they had been sensitive to the ambiguous and estimated tastes of regions and demographics, which had told them that demand for religious devotional images had risen at the expense of film posters.

Watching Jamil's team at work I saw how their repertoire was continually re-performed and how the moral atmosphere of market demand was channelled into a finished product. Demand, as an agential phenomenon felt in others but not wholly quantifiable, was expressed on Hall Road but always hard to gage in practice. At Abu Islami Images they spoke clearly of a "system," a chain of knowledge that connects the roadside sellers to the *murid* [followers] of the shrines, who express the needs which guide the creation of new posters. With a batch of copy-and-paste insertions that took him half a day, the in-house graphic designer Malik replaced the older Kaaba and Medina images that anchored all the five-hundred-plus posters in their repertoire with the new designs that featured the recently built Abraj Al-Bait Towers in Mecca. In other instances, the colors of turbans, cloaks, and even skin tones were changed to fit with the taste and aesthetics of different *mazhabs*, festivals, or just to create a brighter finished product. For this designer, color symbolism was the easiest alteration to make to adhere to public demand, whose chromatic trends are sometimes felt more palpably than others. In 2018, for example, a conference of clerics deigned that the consumer sales known in the United States as Black Friday should be known as Blessed Friday in Pakistan, so as not to associate the color of *jahannum*, Islamic hell, with the day of worship sacred for all Muslims. The following week, a morning's work turned all the black turbans and shawls green for future print runs.

The only exception were those posters designed for commemorations important to the Twelver Shi'a, most of which featured black as a sign of mourning. Shi'i posters have long complicated the reception of public demand among publishing firms. While Alid piety—devotion to the first Shi'i Imam, Ali, the cousin, son-in-law, and companion of the Prophet Muhammad—and love for the Ahl-e Bait is deeply engrained among Pakistanis of many faiths and alignments, Shi'i iconography is more open to depicting the figurative form of persons of importance in early Islamic history than is Sunni visual culture. Opening an old Photoshop work file on the company's computer, Malik pointed out to me the whited-out face of Imam Mahdi, the hidden Imam whose reappearance the Twelver Shiʿa await. He showed me this as an example of a poster that the company had sold in the past but due to the current conditions of felt consensus and dissensus, had been removed from circulation. Due to the contentious nature of so many divergent devotional images, demand must be negotiated carefully. Every creative decision regarding arrangement or design, Malik said, was "dependent on the demand of people in the market." For him, such decisions did not have the power to offend, as they were not one person's creative choice or act. Over many hours spent sitting behind Malik as he took scraps of older posters and, with post-production design software Photoshop, reconfigured the colors of turbans, the placement, hue, and direction of heavenly lights, and the configuration of domes, I found a performative practice at work in the continuation of this visual repertoire. Such images are honed through a process through which prevailing moral sentiments about them are absorbed and the images changed accordingly. If, as Malik frequently iterated, "*muwafaqat* [agreement or consensus] comes from demand," these demands for occasional infidelity to the source of an image negotiate a wider chain of transmission and authority in the commons of shared experience.

Such demands are sensitive to the mediatic flows of minority faiths, languages, and expressions. Managing the distribution and restriction of information is a primary characteristic of what Clifford Geertz called "bazaar economies," where traders jostle to apportion knowledge of prices and production scales to the advantage of themselves and to the detriment of others.[11] This distribution of knowledge is drawn from the "personal confrontation between intimate antagonists," of actors "at once coupled and opposed."[12] This resonates with Webb Keane's argument that economic transactions are events of mediation and therefore imbricated in ethical decisions, where "blaming and holding responsible, denying and justifying, are acts that *both* the agent, *and* his or her interlocutors, are doing . . . *for one another.*"[13] Situating the presence and morals of the other, as communicated and felt by mediums, drives the kind of speculation that questions whether such media are capacious enough to hold both the individual and the stranger, and from where the identification of atmospheres arises. In this system images themselves become events of inscription. Karen Strassler's study of the circulation and mediation of images in contemporary Indonesia examines a period of democratization that saw images factor heavily into a new sphere of mediation and circulation. Strassler calls this visual repertoire the bringing-forth of "public envisioning" in which "image-events . . . [are] a political process set in motion when a specific image or set of images erupts onto and intervenes in a social field."[14] In this theorization, the platforms, interfaces, and hardware that give shape to these repertoires also affect the rhythms of its reception. Unlike Strassler, however, I do not see "image-events" as related to a politics of collectivity, but a politics that defers agency to an imagined collective.

While I could never grasp with confidence the delineations of demand, there are four ways I came to understand it: first as an alibi; second as mutual policing of a commons of shared resources; thirdly as the mediation of an atmosphere of communal piety; and lastly as a warning system sensitive to thresholds of permissibility. Simultaneously, these ways of grasping the moral polyphony of the marketplace also serve as a way of understanding the moral atmospheres that frame this book. Mahaul can be comprised of a communal effort that shrinks the responsibility of the individual; it can be a coercive force that polices social reproduction; it can be akin to a plea for recognition among embattled minorities; and finally, it can also be concerned with demarcating the frontiers of permissibility.

The felt force of demand also closely resonates with Aasim Sajjad Akhtar's argument that the Zia era of the 1980s, remembered for its politics of Islamization in Pakistan, also inculcated structures of power in which "common sense" became located and mediated in the relationship between merchant traders and religious organizations. Akhtar argues that the ethical and political transformations of this time created a "common sense" politics rooted in the everyday.[15] The consequence of traders like those on Hall Road aligning their values with "common sense" is that Islamic piety often comes to legitimize the accumulation of capital. Demand as an alibi sees mediators place their faith in the awaam as the arbiters of moderation and morality. While demand could be considered as an atmosphere that halts change, an engine of intersocial reproduction, or a greater good for the majority, in its operation this needful atmosphere provided many with an alibi to protect against moral transgression. Demand infers a starting point of reluctance, or at least an air of ambivalence. In the same way that I heard religious trinkets described as "art" or "decoration" so as to remark upon their lack of efficacious or transgressive qualities, things relating to the public mass of demand also do not have the power to offend, as they are not one person's creative choice.

Taking It to the Market

Taking the moral consensus of the public as the measure of taste and judgement is also practiced in state institutions. For several weeks, day after day, I would sit waiting behind Mubaraka Hussain's palatial desk with its cracked glass counter, looking at nothing but the catalogues of the Punjab Archives. So proud was her team of the catalogues they produced over two decades, detailing the holdings of the archive, that visiting scholars often found themselves compelled to scrutinize them as closely as the evasive contents of the repository. Despite Mubaraka's efforts to change the reputation the archive held as a frustrating and impenetrable fortress, few managed to get further than her lively and effervescent company. Mughal-era papers in Persian, the court records of Indian nationalist Bhagat Singh, records pertaining to the immediate post-1857 era of British expansion in Punjab, and an unknown and unassessed trove of papers resided in numbered wooden lockers that lined the walls of the archive. Occasionally a locker would yield

Figure 2.2 The Punjab Archives, walled within the Punjab Secretariat and housed in Anarkali's Tomb, a sixteenth-century shrine to a mythical princess. Armed guards occupy the turrets. (Photo by author.)

a yellowed manuscript, other times teacups and sugar. While they remained tantalizing and within reach, the only documents I ever accessed were index upon index, catalogued by year—beginning in 1860 and ending in 1900— each of which took Mubaraka's team six months to compile. I was guaranteed not to find much researching the history of moving-image media in the Punjab Archives, especially in catalogues with a cutoff date of 1901. While the Lumière brothers first brought the cinemascope to the Watson Hotel in Bombay on July 7, 1896, Lahore had to wait until 1924 when the first film made in the city, *The Daughters of Today*, was directed by a North-Western Railways Officer, G. K. Mehta.

On every page of the hardbound catalogues, themselves now yellowed with age, Mubaraka had stamped her name, title, and department, an act that indexed her time spent making sense of the repository, her time spent making it knowable and showable.[16] A project to secure funds to catalogue the rest was "in the pipeline," Mubaraka explained, with the eyebrows of someone about to deliver a punchline, before exclaiming, "But the pipeline is blocked." As Matthew Hull writes in his ethnography of Pakistan's paper bureaucracy, "A Pakistani government file . . . is an unusual sort of artifact because signs of its history are continuously and deliberately inscribed upon the artifact itself, a peculiarity that gives it an event-like quality."[17] In Shaila Bhatti's ethnography of the Lahore Museum, many of those in charge of Pakistan's archives, libraries, museums, and heritage institutions adopt "the role of guardians who protect, maintain, classify and expand the archive, which in return . . . proffer a sense of authority and legitimacy linked to ownership."[18] In this way, the Hall Road repertoire that thrives outside of archival contexts operates in a comparable way to the constituents of extant Pakistani archives, whereby events—inscriptions, access, or indexing—maintain the circulation of objects, thereby sustaining the assertions of authority over them. On the other hand, the felt absence of the state brings to the surface of documents the idea that the political does not always have its own domain but various faces and interfaces.[19] For Mubaraka, the event of archival or bureaucratic experiences and its inscriptions directly reflect personal aspirations.

That day in the Punjab Archives was like many others I would spend thereafter. Inside, students and scholars waited awkwardly for something to happen, while dusty stray kittens lingered in the doorway. A university researcher looked questioningly at the typewritten, bound catalogues and asked, derisorily, "Are these the manuals?" To which Mubaraka responded, with her punchline eyebrow, "Not manual, *woman*ual; I made them!" This was not the first time she brought up the unusual presence of a woman in such a senior position in the bureaucracy, nor was it the first time she gendered the materiality of the archive, an act of performativity that implicitly cited the challenges faced by women in Pakistani workplaces. That day, the walls were lined with teenage girls, interns, and students, answering or handing in papers for their summary examination of their time in the archive. They had spent six weeks mentored by Mubaraka, who taught them about the processes of fumigation and lamination; about how to get their hands dirty. Like the others she put to the group, the question, "What is an archive?" had a right answer and numerous wrong ones. The correct response, which was expected to have been memorized through their time spent with her, was, "a record of non-current documents."

Walled within the Punjab Secretariat, the Punjab Archives is housed in an octagonal building built sometime at the turn of the seventeenth century (CE), many believe as a mausoleum to Anarkali, a Mughal princess said to have been buried alive by her jealous lover, Emperor Akbar. Under British rule the mausoleum was first used as an Anglican Church between 1851 and 1891 and converted into a clerical records office in 1923. In 1973, it was formally designated a Pakistani federal government archive. The biography of the Punjab Archives is a microcosm of Lahore itself: a Mughal tomb to a legendary princess, repurposed into a church, then reconfigured into a regional records office, with a reputation for being fiercely guarded and bureaucratic yet cut through by a pervasive informality. Mubaraka had worked in the archive since 1996. Facilitating the retrieval of research materials for scholars was her aim when joining the archive. But she was careful, as a young woman, not to appear to be challenging the status quo of her entirely male superiors. Her research output included scholarly publications in Urdu, this being her favorite part of the job, closely followed by the creation of indexes and metadata to ensure future access. She explained how "when I joined the archives, my slogan was 'give it to the public, send it to the market.' Can you believe that when I joined it was the first time the termite problem was treated? Some people before me were so scared of giving knowledge to people, worried that the awaam would get to know more than them. Can you believe this attitude? If I don't share information when I die the record will go underground too. It's better to give it away."

It is appropriate to acknowledge here that this sentiment would strongly contrast with the experiences of many researchers and scholars frustrated by Pakistan's repositories. Numerous rumors circulate around the Punjab Archives regarding the careless deaccessioning of objects and, in some cases, their clandestine sale to collectors. Despite Mubaraka's professed commitment to public engagement, the extent to which a public can be engaged is demarcated by those who can pass the Secretariat security, for which an appointment within its walls and a valid identification card is required.

A few kilometers away on Hall Road I would often hear the personal collections—from taped recordings of stage shows and master copies of rare films, to amateur cassettes of reciters and sermonizers long deceased—described as that community's or that trader's "record," using the English term, echoing Mubaraka's words. In a bureaucratic setting, the "record" describes the debris of authorized procedure that while defined as "non-current" still very much pertains to the present. However, procedures that make and unmake archival objects also serve to mediate the authority of individuals in a much smaller domain than the expansive reach of the state. In her desire to leave her mark on each and every aspect of the archive's processes, Mubaraka herself appeared to undermine her own definition of an archive as a repository for "non-current" documents. The ongoing events of use and inscription marked them not only as current, but critical agents of self-making, and indicative of personal morality and individuation. This draws attention to both the existence of a kind of non-government agency in the bureaucracy, and a kind of bureaucracy in public life, brought to the surfaces of objects when they become enmeshed in the way people define and locate moral atmospheres.

The Censorial Record

On a residential street in Muslim Town in Lahore I found an inconspicuous government office occupying the top portion of a family home. Among old desks that got dustier as they neared the floor, neat cardboard files, and the occasional moustachioed Punjabi film star could be found the Punjab Film Censor Board. The bureaucrat in charge welcomed visitors against an overpainted sky-blue wall, with the patter of a mild-mannered recruiting officer. Excitedly, he told me that they were expecting a delivery of a DCP (Digital Cinema Package) from India of a film for the board to review. Overhearing our conversation, an older producer of Punjabi films, with fire in his eyes, shouted the word *wasti*, or intermediary. The censor filled me in, "There is always an intermediary." Films are not imported from India directly, there must be a middleman. It was important for this producer to mention that, while cultural products of Indian origin are shown in Pakistan, there is no direct contact; while there is exchange, there is not intimacy.

After the Eighteenth Amendment to the Pakistan Constitution in 2010 the activities of the censor board were decentralized and split into provincial boards: Sindh, Punjab, and the Central Board in Islamabad, which at the time of my research also covered the Province of Khyber Pakhtunkhwa. The Punjab board was composed of thirteen regular members, seven officials, and three ex-members. I was told that every six months, after films were reviewed, they were burned in the presence of board members to guard against piracy. Such waste did not worry them. I was assured that the Central Board of Film Censors in Islamabad had a film library to ensure that, if a cinema was raided, a base copy existed to compare with what was submitted to the board and which scenes were ordered to be excised. But amid a decrease in the production of films destined for cinema screens and the reliance of some cinemas on older celluloid material, new problems had emerged with this central library of excisions. The mild-mannered inspector mourned the lack of a stable format on which to build a future-facing, censorial archive. "CDs melt, videos melt! What is the correct format? You tell me," he exclaimed.

The creation of this censorial record was originally driven by an urge to guard against *totay*.[20] Known in Bangladesh as "cut-pieces," these aberrant images became the basis for Lotte Hoek's study of a celluloid economy of concealment and revelation.[21] Cut-pieces were sections of a film that did not pass the censor board but were then illegally spliced into films during projection. Sometimes they would be completely extraneous sections of graphic violence or pornography added in by projectionists to generate rumor and satisfy demand. In Urdu *tota* means splice, with the plural *totay* meaning splices, frames, or strips of film. One could say that there has been totay as long as there have been film censor boards. Films exhibited with excised portions reinserted are mentioned in the Indian Cinematograph Committee of 1927–1928.[22] Totay in Pakistan were once a notorious feature of cinema-going in Lahore, which briefly competed with new media technologies by providing the contingency and surprise that television or home videocassettes and discs could not.[23] Such remembered transgressions lingered behind the murky reputation or bad mahaul of

inner-city cinemas, despite the reliance of totay on celluloid projection having led to their decline in the digital era. In Lahore, the Moonlight Cinema was once a byword for the exhibition of totay but closed when it could
not compete with the quantity of pornography available in copy on nearby
Hall Road.

In August 1974 a Punjabi film, *Khatarnak*, was certified by the Censor
Board and released. Soon after, allegations were registered at police sta-
tions. Claimants began to cry foul over "nude scenes" excised by the censor but re-inserted upon exhibition.[24] The police raided eleven cinemas in
Karachi where the film was being exhibited and took possession of the third
reel. The censor board found that in the item number "Touch Me Not,"
the impounded reel contained an excised portion featuring a low-angle shot
looking up a dancer's leg.[25] In the end, both the initial case and appeals
against the decision were quashed because it was felt that the 1963 Censorship of Films Act could not be applied to punish totay. But despite the
Khatarnak case having reached the highest courts in the land, the Motion
Picture Ordinance of 1979—which repealed both the 1963 and 1918 acts—
did not define that a film altered after certification becomes invalid or
uncertified by the act of being tampered with.[26] In a similar case brought
against the producers of the film *Maula Jatt* (1979) in 1981, the decertifica-
tion of the film was nullified, with the film continuing to remain certified even with fourteen scenes that were ordered to have been excised by
the Censor Board. In many ways the Zia-era Motion Picture Ordinance
was functioning as it may have been supposed to, drawing its efficacy from
being loosely defined and open to interpretation. Strictures ruling against
transgressions such as "offense to Islam" that replaced the clearer 1963
guidelines were so vaguely defined that it worked to make everyone an
interpreter and therefore a stakeholder in its policing. After a decade of the
Motion Picture Ordinance passing, films were being censored for scenes
including "Holding the wife's hand and making obscene movements . . .;
a woman confessing that she is carrying someone else's child . . .; vulgar
breast movements in the *mujra* dance . . .; shots of a mother picking up
pieces of bread lying before dogs . . ."[27]

Even in the earliest days of cinematography, moral panics around film
experience bore the curious coexistence of interdiction and reproduction.
Censorship allowed the constitution of a public sphere intimately entangled
with cinema exhibition and consumption.[28] In the Indian subcontinent,
this was tightly bound up with British-colonial ideas around public

morality. In the United Kingdom in 1917, the National Council of Public Morals established a "Cinema Commission" to look at the potentially adverse effects of film experience on British viewers.[29] Whether it was the dark seclusion of cinema halls allowing genders to intermingle or the depiction of violence and sexuality onscreen, the commission attempted to pinpoint the moral, affective, and educational dangers of a medium then merely two decades old. In several instances, the Commission's concern was avowedly visual, detailing the effect of flickering images on adolescent eyes. In other instances, the concern wavered between the aesthetic and the ethical. For example, schoolmasters and pediatricians were asked about the atmosphere of film and of cinema halls. From the ventilation of theaters to the positive environment fostered by film that might aid children with wayward parents, the ways in which atmosphere was deployed as a means of representing the possibilities of moral pollution are apparent throughout the report. Take for example, this account from a British policeman, one William V. Nicholas, chief constable of Guildford, and the free movement with which biophysical and moral atmospheres come together to produce an ecological notion of public morality. For this officer of the law, ideas around hygiene and airborne pollution provided a surface for ideas about the invisible, felt forces, newly unleashed by the cinema, to refract through.

> I am not an opponent of the cinema, but am strongly opposed to the absence of hygienic conditions in regard to the same. Generally speaking, the atmosphere is obnoxious and vitiated, the heat developed by the audience sickly, and the darkness most objectionable . . . Owing to the insufficient ventilation and heat there is undoubtedly a creation and free distribution of bacteria—a fact proved by the proprietors themselves in causing the deodorisation of halls by means of syringes at intervals during the performances . . . With reference to the darkness (difficult to overcome), it is the cause of many abuses, and one in particular where young men and young women attend together, not for the purpose of following the pictures, but, owing to the darkness, to become spoony, and to work up passions which may be described as "initiative immorality."[30]

It was these very real anxieties about "initiative immorality," and their impact on cultural products circulating under colonial rule, that led to the undertaking of a similar commission in the Indian subcontinent. The wide-ranging Indian Cinematograph Committee of 1927–1928 (hereafter ICC), attempted to understand audiences' reactions to film exhibition, and showed a growing interest in listening to what might be called public demand. The ICC's interests were located in both theatrical cinema settings and in the mobile film vans whose commercial or state-funded projects provided rural sites with open-air projection.[31] The ICC produced a four-volume report which included written and oral interviews with 353 "witnesses," namely film producers, exhibitors, distributors, actors, film censors, news-paper editors, and educationists working in India. The ICC project was conducted like an ethnographic or anthropological mission. Its members travelled 9,400 miles between mid-October 1927 and late February 1928, staging participant observation in forty-five cinemas and studying the activities of informal projectionists. The Committee received 320 written testimonies and interviewed 114 Europeans and 239 Indians, of whom 157 were Hindus, 38 Muslims, 25 Parsis, 16 Burmese, 2 Sikhs, and 1 Chris-tian.[32] How does film function? How does it affect cognition? In whose moral worlds does it become entangled? These are the questions that ani-mated the ICC and other attempts by colonial authorities and foreign powers to gage, express, and utilize the event of film exhibition. While the report noted that in North India there were "objections to the moving picture" on religious grounds, the entire basis of the investigation itself rested on the moral and ideological anxieties of the colonial regime that film had the power to destabilize.[33]

Despite the deep ontological and affective questions that animated the report, its final recommendations were pragmatic. These included finan-cial incentives to producers, the construction of new cinemas, a reduction in taxation on the import of raw film, and the establishment of an all-India censor board. What would become the Provincial Film Censor Code detailed examples of how a film could "demoralize" or "undermine the teachings of morality."[34] A revision of the code in 1949 added an element of opacity through the language of atmosphere. A film would be regarded as unsuitable if it "associates with institutions of co-education or mixed social life or mixed cultural activity, a general atmosphere of lax morals or indecent behaviour . . ."[35] This bad moral atmosphere conflated sexual, religious, and economic influences. Importantly, the film need not rep-resent or take these matters as its subject, but merely associate with them, be in proximity to them, or mediate their appearance in social life. Scattered through pre- and post-Partition legislation were value judgements like these that required interpretation and a degree of consensus to be made within the bounds of regulation. These included terms like *obscenity* or *indecency*. In Pakistani film and media law, referring to an object of adjudication in terms of its possible indecency is to invite interpretations that must look towards prevailing norms and decide whether the object is potentially transgressive of those norms. Indecency also refers to a realm of elicitation, to public sentiment, and to porous moral personhood.

Not all censorial decisions on the subcontinent were predicated on anxiety with film experience. A meeting of the Constituent Assembly of India in 1949 debated the Cinematograph (Amendment) Bill, which sought to amend the existing colonial-era censorship code that decreed that any film featuring scenes unsuitable for children was to be banned. They sought a classification for films targeted only for adults, to allow films of artistic merit to pass the board. This otherwise unremarkable debate provided a platform for a remarkable speech from parliamentarian and member of the independence movement Shri Mahavir Tyagi, who enthusiastically described the potential for films to shape the young nation. In his speech he argued not only for the legislation but for the nationalization of the industry: "If I had my way I would not allow this industry to go into the hands of any private individual. I would not allow people to make money at the cost of our morals—by making or unmaking them—because the cinema is nothing if it does not make or unmake our morals. No recreation remains as it is: every recreation goes directly into one's brain. It is the cinema which creates an atmosphere which changes our civilisation."[36]

Tyagi packed a lot into these lines: the notion that film shapes moral experience as well as deconstructs existing moral precepts; that recreation and leisure are not mere *time-pass* but constitutive of the life of the mind; and that the atmospheres that film harbors have the power to make or break nations and civilizations.

The period of my fieldwork was a busy time for Pakistan's censor boards. During 2017 and 2018, a period that marked a new era for Pakistani films, some felt that the censor board acted in ways antagonistic to this emerging national narrative. Unlike the Punjab Board in Lahore, the Central Board of Film Censors in Islamabad had the air of a long-established and long-functioning government regulatory body. Its grass well-trimmed; its peeling walls and high-ceilings cool and slightly damp. Inside an office room mostly used by its female staff for prayer, the censorial archive of

Pakistani films—in Urdu, Punjabi, and Pashto—was the largest state record of film content I came across during my fieldwork. Their "record," as bureaucrats describe it, was built only out of procedural necessity, to maintain the efficacy of their excisions, and to build up a reserve of potential evidence to use in litigation. In this case the record refers to the private debris that exists only as a guarantee that a film circulates as authorized by its base copy. If a film submitted for censorship reached the marketplace it would be the board members who would have to answer for it. Circulation here worked as a regulating force, as a threat of exposure. Having initially cleared it for exhibition, the Punjab Censor Board suspended screenings of the popular Pakistani film *Na Maloom Afraad 2* (2017) after the film had first been banned in the United Arab Emirates for satirizing the culture of exorbitant spending in the sheikhdoms. Next, despite outrage from Hindu right-wing groups across the Indian border, who believed an upcoming Indian film, *Padmavat* (2018), would feature a "love scene" between a Muslim ruler and a legendary Hindu queen, the film was cleared in Pakistan with fewer excisions than in India. Some users on Twitter joked that Pakistan should issue tourist visas to Indians who wanted to see the uncut version. Finally, another Indian film, *Padman* (2018)—about an entrepreneur from Tamil Nadu who introduced affordable sanitary pads to his community—received an outright ban after the Central Board of Film Censors in Islamabad refused to even preview the film. So powerful was the revulsion felt by the board that they were afraid to watch it lest it corrupt their own principles.[37]

It is an interesting conundrum. How does a film become so taboo that the people responsible for deciding on whether it is taboo or not refuse to watch it? These tacit economies of knowing and showing operate through what Michael Taussig describes as a *"public* secret," born of *"knowing what not to know"* or knowing what it is not possible to articulate. Returning to the marketplace circulation of film, we can see everyday acts of censorship evince a greater individual struggle with what is publicly permissible.[38] The informal spread of DVDs and VCDs, through small stallholders and DVDwallas, not only gave rise to repertoires of old media, but opened up space for micro-industries to finance new productions. One stallholder in Peshawar's own labyrinthine media bazaar, the Nishtarabad center, began to finance "CD films" or "minifilms," made for direct release through the networks forged by informal film distribution. He stated, "In the absence of a censor policy, '*insaan ka apna zameer censor board hota hai*' [man's own conscience is the censor board]."[39] While the Hall Road repertoire might be reactive to public demand, marketplace censorship also instantiates attempts to pre-empt and predict offense.

The Collector

When an object such as a film, an item number from a film, or a rare recording of a film song remains outside of the repertoire—such as *Nai Kiran* for example—the sole force of public demand is useless. The largest "record" of Pakistani film can be found outside of the remit of the state, in private collections sourced at great personal expense by individuals whose accumulated objects are closely entangled with their own biographies. Perhaps most recognizable of these is Guddu Khan, a devoted collector of Pakistani film memorabilia, who explained to me his methods of acquisition,

> Whenever cinemas are scheduled for demolition people inform me . . . One time I went to one of the cinemas scheduled for demolition and saw, past the padlock on the doors and through the windows, a number of posters on the walls. I requested the guards to allow me to take them but they replied that only once the building is demolished am I free to take what I want . . . Believe me, even *while* cinemas were being demolished, I would run and pick up pictures and posters in the rubble and dustbins. Next to the rubble would lie reels of films and the guards would remind me, "Hey, take those with you too," but I'd reply, "My house is not big enough to hold these reels." As you know, one full film in all its parts comes to seventeen or eighteen boxes. Where would I keep those boxes and what would I do with them? You have to dedicate time to take care of them with chemicals and maintenance, as they sometimes release a very pungent odor. I never had the resources to protect those reels in my house. Then I realized that all those films are on VHS and through that people will be able to access them, but my pictures and posters will be lost forever if I don't save them.

What he calls "Guddu's Film Archive" consists of objects primarily mass-produced during the 1960s and 1970s, the heyday of Lollywood film production. In a series of filmed interviews uploaded to YouTube, Guddu gifts film actors the publicity stills, posters, and clippings he collects from decaying cinemas and junk peddlers and hosts digital video or audio interviews. These interviews are interspersed with digitized clips from his videocassette collection, all of which are emblazoned with his ubiquitous watermark. Through these filmed interviews Guddu works to rescue from anonymity both formerly leading actors and jobbing extras, the poorly paid workers whose participation in Pakistan's baroque musical epics was restricted to non-speaking roles. Because many of the female actors and extras featured in Guddu's YouTube interviews have renounced the film industry and embraced tauba (see chapter 1), many consent only to conduct audio interviews in which their voices are finally heard over a montage of digitized film stills, film segments, or scanned artifacts from their earlier lives in film.

One might assert that Guddu's practice has little in common with the seriality of collecting, which usually relies on similar objects coming up at auction, being procured from junk shops, or, in the case of objects in the sphere of mass consumption, simply being bought and saved. From his

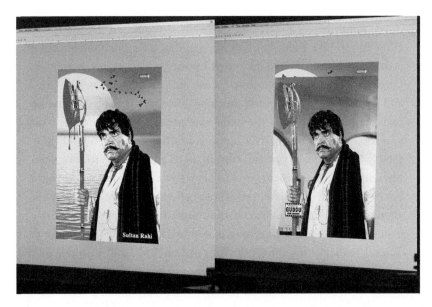

Figure 2.3 The designer at Abu Islami Images hides the source image of a poster of Punjabi film star Sultan Rahi by obscuring the watermark of film collector Guddu Khan. (Photo by author.)

networks in Karachi to Hall Road in Lahore, Guddu's accumulation and acquisition of objects requires an intimate relationship with the city itself, for the economic and political reality of Pakistani urbanity and its relationship to moving-image media dictates the accumulation of his objects. So too is a notion of personal history intricately interwoven into Guddu's description of his objects, noting as he does with relish any evidence of prestige conferred upon him for his efforts.

Unlike Guddu, other collectors are responsible for much of the material in circulation in marketplaces such as Hall Road. Eager to see if totay remained in a film during its long afterlife in the marketplace I bought a VCD of the film *Khatarnak* mentioned earlier. While I later found the controversial item number complete with censorial excisions, I could not help but notice a more pervasive incision, one less censorial than authorial. Throughout the film, from beginning to end, a permanent *pati*, or watermark, clung to much of the screen, its purpose being to tell the viewer that its master copy comes from a man named Mirza Waqar Baig and to provide his phone number. In Urdu, *pati* can refer to a hem, a line, or a straight mark, and in relation to film refers to a watermark or inscription asserting provenance or ownership. I found that most old, rare, and hard-to-find films on Hall Road bore Baig's pati. Also based in Karachi, Baig made videocassette to DVD conversions to order from his collection of 1,800 films dating from the 1950s to 1990s, most of which were on videocassettes produced by the once partly state-run Shalimar Recording Company. The circulation of these copies from his closely guarded collection to Hall Road began when his cousin, who manned a stall at the Rainbow Centre in Karachi, encouraged him to make copies of his collection for the "enjoyment of the awaam," as he put it. His reasons for affixing such a prominent watermark were similar to Guddu's. Both wanted to be appreciated for their acts of retrieval, a token of the same gratitude that they feel when people come to their homes to view their collections, but not in the impersonal, outward circulation of film copies, song compilations, and images in marketplaces and online. Pakistani collectors remain wary of the knowledge that objects, once collected, are always susceptible to appropriation. Therefore, their watermarked stamps imprint their name-logo as they travel from Hall Road to YouTube and its regional variants. In the lack of fan conventions, auctions, or museums, the internet has provided a network for Pakistani collectors and cineastes. These pervasive instances in which a desire for presence and ownership is expressed turn the surface of the screen into a visual site for interaction, negotiation, and contestation.

One afternoon I sat waiting for Fayyaz Ahmad Ashar in the Pak Tea House, at a rickety table with a sign reading "reserved for writers."[40] One of the last bastions of Lahore's literary cafe culture felt a fitting place to meet such an ardent collector of Pakistani film music. Fayyaz Ahmad Ashar called his collection the *"Awaz Khazana"* [Treasure of Voices], a collection he started in 1972 when he first listened to the sounds of Ceylon Radio and All India Radio. Like Guddu and Mirza Waqar Baig he lived off meagre resources, funnelling whatever money he had towards expanding his collection. Having spent much of his adult life working in Abu Dhabi, he began buying records among a community of collectors in the UAE, then expanded his connections to India, the United States, Canada, and the UK, from whom he continued to learn about objects coming up for sale. He valued this offline community; for him the internet was unreliable, full of disinformation spread by faulty and "unclean" copies, evinced by the sheer number of clips of songs and song sequences of heritage music on You-Tube. He told me, "In these videos, the actor's head or legs are missing or the songs are incomplete. In my eyes, these songs are worse than if they remained only in people's memories."

Recalling Mubaraka's work in the Punjab Archives, the books he has published are largely inventories of release dates, song titles, and singers. His and other such inventories are widely used; the Islamabad Censor Board use the online fan databases PakFilm and Motion Picture Archive of Pakistan (MPAOP), while television shows featuring segments on film music consult Fayyaz and his books for details. While others mourned the lack of financial support from the government, Fayyaz was mostly annoyed by a lack of reciprocity. He told me how "on a daily basis I receive phone calls from television channels asking me who sang the song for this film or that film . . . These same channels are only happy to take my book and promote it if I give it to them for free." A passionate love of vintage film music is considered a particularly urbane, Lahori object of appreciation. Such fandom is reminiscent of literary salons where poetic couplets are exchanged and recited. Indeed, the lyricists of a film song are often more clearly remembered than the actors. Flicking through old Pakistani film magazines one can see how widely the literary associations spread across social and economic divides. Letters from fans to the film and soft-porn magazine *Chitrali*, published in Lahore, were often phrased in the poetic form of a *sher* couplet of a *ghazal*.

Another dimension of public demand, one no less forceful and pervasive, is its relative opposite, the quiet violence of disposition. On Sundays, outside the Pak Tea House could be found one of Lahore's greatest pleasures, a book market that evinced the discursive breadth of the city and the lingering inspiration of the nearby Urdu Bazaar, once the publishing capital of North India. Biographies of English cricketers heaped beside Urdu chapbooks; one-of-a-kind plans for a tourist resort beside the Mangla Dam lay beside 1990s issues of *Chitrali*. One Sunday I came across a remarkable collection. On one table a scrap dealer was selling a singular collection of rare books on world cinema, from the 1930s to the present, including a large number of professionally bound film magazines, including: copies of the British Film Institute's *Sight and Sound* magazine dating to the 1940s; the short-lived *Cinemaya* journal; magazines on videocassette technology; and even a scrapbook of clipped comic strips about film culture from U.S. magazine *Mad*. They had been lovingly kept over a period of seventy years by a single owner. An *ex libris* stamp of Theodore Phailbus, a notable former resident of Abbott Road, indicated their provenance in the dust of the book market. I later learned that when he passed away, Phailbus's widow donated his collection of 1,800 videocassettes and celluloid reels of various films from 1930 onwards to Kinnaird College in Lahore. Either the product of disinterest or deaccession, his library, which by itself could have formed a research collection of Euro-American cinema possibly unparalleled in South Asia, seemed to have ended up on that table. Among his library was a poignant scrapbook, in which a young Phailbus had cut pictures from another volume and possibly even typewritten his own accompanying text on the left-hand page of each illustration. Evidently made as a child, the scrapbook was titled "Wonders of the Past," hand-dated Lahore, 1935.

Incisions and Excisions

Younger film fans without access to the collecting networks forged by Guddu and Fayyaz have found other ways to celebrate local Lollywood cinema, whose theatrical exhibition in Lahore I found almost entirely restricted to one street, Abbott Road. With the heavy onset of securitization having pushed many forms of public leisure behind the walls of gated areas, Abbott Road was buttressed by coils of barbed wire rolling over the high walls that divided cinemas from the street. Each of the remaining cinemas still screening celluloid operated as repertory theaters. The Metropole Cinema began "re-releasing," as manager Qasim put it, classic Lollywood films in 2016 when they screened *Banarsi Thuggi* (1973). A few weeks later the Capital Cinema followed suit, showing *Malangi* (1965), on the suggestion of the president of the Pakistan Film Distributors Association, whose uncle had directed the film. Soon after, another film was re-released, *Lahori Badmash* (1991), when the son of the film's producer wanted to pay homage to his father on his death anniversary. Unlike on Hall Road, where the recursivity of films are bound to the expertise of small-scale traders and to their receptivity to public demand, on Abbott Road kinship ties shape the experience of Pakistani film history. Yet while the formation of a repertory circuit on Abbott Road was ostensibly established to pay tribute to old stars, the decision taken by many cinemas coincided with the closure of the last domestic laboratory for the processing of celluloid film, and a shortage of new material to screen. Aside from the interiors of high-end cafes such as Hot Spot, which are decked out in Lollywood memorabilia from the collection of director Omar Ali Khan, the celluloid cinemas of Abbott Road were largely responsible for the continued visibility of Lollywood film in the alleyways and avenues of the city. The Metropole Cinema even retained the mid-twentieth-century method of advertising film screenings by rickshaw, with richly decorated vehicles driving around nearby streets offering reduced rates to patrons for that evening's screening.

I met Asghar, a part-time film programmer who screened old Punjabi movies in the analog cinemas of Abbott Road, while he was inspecting the seventeen cans of film delivered to the parking lot of the Odeon Cinema, along with some promotional material he was erecting with the help of some of the cinema's staff. From the remaining film poster designers in nearby Abbott Road, Asghar commissioned newly designed posters and flex banners to advertise aged and worn film prints. Some of these new posters featured actors with no involvement in the production, included just to draw crowds. The audience generally saw through such marketing techniques, with some even complaining that the cinema owners were trying to fool those vulnerable to the appeal of the new. A poster for one

Figure 2.4 An example of a censorial incision on the cover of a Pakistani film magazine, *Shama*. (From the author's collection.)

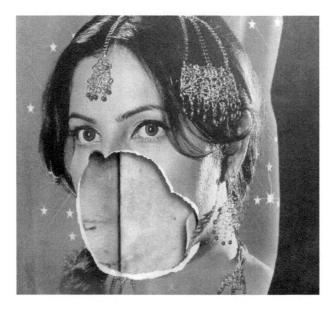

Figure 2.5 In a vigilante act of censorship, a film poster featuring a Pakistani film actress is torn around the mouth. (Photo by author.)

Punjabi film, *Badmaash Gujjar* (2001), had been censored since the film's initial certificate was granted. The designers of the new poster had not been made aware that the word *badmaash* [hooligan] was ordered to be excised from the title. Rather than re-designing the poster, they rectified the change by scrawling an X, crossing out the word and leaving it evident beneath the correction.

In the world of Pakistani film, it is common to see such blatant incisions as a strategy for responding to and acknowledging the requirement for censorial excisions. It is the moral equivalent of the mathematical pedagogy of showing one's workings. What I call incisions refer to strategies of visible concealment, such as the full-body stockings familiar in Pashto-language Pakistani films of the 1980s that responded to rules permitting the showing of bare (female) skin. In the public sphere, cosmetic advertisements could often be found with the face of the model scrubbed out. On the intercity buses I would take across Punjab, Hollywood films screened on overhead televisions had entire scenes depicting romance removed. On cable television, blurry squares hovered over the chests and upper arms of female actors, hosts, and sportswomen in shows imported from India, Turkey, and the United States. The same line, somewhere between censorship and expropriation, was drawn through watermarks for other channels on television dramas lifted from other networks. Whether it was casting aspersions on the modesty of women's dress or removing credits or intellectual property claims from other channels or producers, the surface tension of the image was a site for contested moral standpoints to interact. These incisions took the form of surrogated acts of violence on the bodies of women in the public sphere. On these surfaces easily scratched over, inscribed upon, or excised, the porous image located the aspirations and anxieties of an avowedly patriarchal form of public morality.

I refer to incisions both in the way Ann Laura Stoler describes knowledge made to incise and as the adaptive inverse of an editorial excision, what Jacques Derrida described as an act of defacement made to remain visible beneath the erasure.[41] The partial obscuring of ideas that are inadequate, yet still necessary, was used widely in deconstructionist philosophy to point to the polysemic dimensions of a text and its exterior. Derrida defined a method of writing *sous rature*—under erasure—showing both the excised word and its excising cross. Derrida explained, "The gesture of *sous rature* implies 'both this *and* that' as well as 'neither this nor that' undoing the opposition and the hierarchy between the legible and the erased."[42] Magazines and newspapers as far back as the 1980s—as well as in studies of Pakistani film and performance—similarly detailed these instances of self-appointed censorship. It is possible to find inscriptions with pen—from thick layers of color to neat lines creating a makeshift gauze—on posters, flex banners, magazines, and hoardings, most commonly covering the legs and breasts of film actors.[43] The violence of this act is heightened by the fact that most of these inscriptions were made on the copy of the photograph before it went to print. As Finbarr Barry Flood has argued, the surface of the image is one site where the distinction between "*instrumental* iconoclasm" and "*expressive* iconoclasm" plays out.[44] The former achieves a goal, the latter expresses the achievement of this goal through action. Unruly images become entropic images when allowed to continue in defaced form. By nature of how film objects travel in the present, an incised film object may form the base version for widely reproduced copies and come to form the standard extant version of that film. For example, during a mujra dance number in the film *Dubai Chalo* [Let's Go To Dubai!] (1979), unknown hands had drawn or scratched directly onto hundreds of celluloid frames, covering over the actors' breasts and skirting the fringes of her dress. As the film exists only in informal copies bought from sites such as Hall Road, the incised base copy comes to be more permanent than formal acts of censorship, which are often flouted with the inclusion of totay.

This provides a dark counterpoint to Laura Marks's sensuous engagement with the skin of film, in which "the image is connective tissue" and the aim of such sensuous engagement is "touching, not mastering."[45] By seeking retribution by one's own hands, the defaced poster is driven by the demands of its inverse, the intimate and the reactionary, through which visibility and concealment are negotiated. Touching becomes incising, and incising becomes mastering, not by means of an embodied gaze but by nature of a material engagement with the surface of the image. Such incisions rather than censorial excisions evince a masculine public culture open to its own forms of negotiation, experimentation, and debate, but one that shows its workings on the surfaces of media objects, and most violently when they happen to be representations of women's bodies.

Another kind of incision, less censorial and more generative, can be seen in retouched posters imbued with newfound efficacy through subtle tuning. Take, for example, the face of Ilm-ud-din, often known with the prefix *ghazi* [warrior], who was found guilty and executed in 1929 for murdering a Hindu publisher in Lahore. The publisher had printed a confrontational book titled *Rangila Rasul* that caused great offense to Lahore's Muslim community. The first time I saw his face—evidently a man from the early twentieth century by the look of the portrait photograph, long overpainted and retouched—was on a flex banner, advertising his death anniversary. Deeper into the neighborhood of the Walled City that now bears his name, several stores proudly exhibited decades-old oil paintings, explaining to me, "This is Ghazi Ilm-ud-Din, he did something for Islam." In a famous Lahori culinary stalwart in another part of the city, the young workers had no idea who this man was, understanding only from the surface iconography that he was a martyr, fighting for some cause that must continue to wield an agential presence.

Ilm-ud-Din's execution by the British colonial authorities and the depth of outrage felt by the Muslim community led to him being celebrated as a martyr of a quite different kind than revolutionary heroes such as Bhagat Singh, whose "afterlives" continue to be active agents for contemporary change.[46] Ilm-ud-Din's afterlife as a quasi-saint whose mausoleum in Lahore is one of the city's most visited minor shrines, and whose name is given to neighborhoods, schools, and hospitals, is similarly distributed across visual repertoires whose substance provides justification for contemporary debates over offense towards Islam. Each of the half-dozen stores that possessed a slightly different painting warmly encouraged me to take photographs of the picture and take them to a nearby photo-shop to be printed. This is common practice and, I was told, how his image remains so widely in circulation. This is why every time I found his image in the geographical confines of the Walled City it possessed a distinct sense of place, characterized by the slight differences to how the image had been touched up, straightened, vectorized, and realigned. By proudly boasting that theirs was the original from which others made a copy, such as to manufacture a new sign for the Ilm-ud-Din Memorial Hospital or for prayer gatherings in his name, guardians of his image located themselves in what they saw as a formative moment in pre-Partition Pakistani history.

Figure 2.6 A Hall Road trader previews a videodisc. (Photo by author.)

Figure 2.7 Cover of a three-pack selection of Pakistani Lollywood films, two of which feature biopics of the life of Ilm-ud-din. (From the author's collection.)

Having told him about my observations, I went with Idris back to the basement of the Dar-ul-Rehmat Plaza to pick up a copy of *Ghazi Ilm-ud-Din Shaheed* [Warrior Ilm-ud-Din, the Martyr] (1978), a Pakistani film directed by and starring the actor Haider. As we passed the entrance of the plaza, I noticed two reflective stickers had recently been affixed to a crumbling plaster entrance. The first, a gold circular design, displayed the ninety-nine names of Allah, with a tactile, gilded sheen; the second, a stark block of text, informative without any flourishes. The latter warned the reader that it was their duty to declare any members of the Ahmadi movement to be non-Muslims. The Ahmadiyya, who are prominent in Lahore and are arguably the most vulnerable minority group in Pakistan, were founded by a self-professed messiah named Mirza Ghulam Ahmad (1835–1908). For many Muslims, belief in this eschatological figure contravenes the doctrine of *khatm-e-nubuwwat* [the finality of Prophethood] that can be held by the Prophet Muhammad alone. Groups like the TLP and their adherents feel that the doctrinal faith of Ahmadis is blasphemous. By building upon these widespread feelings of religious offense, such groups argue that Islam is in danger of corruption by this most precarious of minorities. Such notices can be found in many other media and electronics markets around Lahore, including in the Hafeez Centre in Gulberg.

After making a few rounds to check whether any of the traders had the film to hand we came to an old man in a crisp white *shalwar kameez*. He appeared only to deal in recitations in praise of the Prophet Muhammad and some select devotional *qawwali* performances recorded at local shrines. His sensitivity to demand was specialized, reactive to what we might call counter-public demand. From beneath his desk, he pulled a bundle of three-pack compilations of old Pakistani films with suitably pious themes, darting his eyes to the left and right to hide these secret selections from his competitors. Without asking, he inserted the disc into a VCD-player atop the television embedded in the storage racks in the corner of his store and showed me the quality of the print. It is 1929; a young carpenter produces fine objects for which his grotesquely caricatured Hindu customers refuse to pay full price. Later, they choose to spend the money they saved on sex workers in the Walled City's red-light district. When the offending *Rangila Rasul* book is published, a furious crowd are shown streaming through Lahore's Delhi Gate, over which an advertisement anachronistically offers to procure visas and airplane tickets for those wanting to relocate to Dubai.

Fired up by the discourse of groups demonstrating on the street, Ilm-ud-din buys a knife from a salesman in the market. After he's imprisoned for the murder, the film depicts Muhammad Ali Jinnah, the lawyer and future founder of Pakistan, enlisted to defend the vigilante. The failure for Jinnah, who ultimately loses the case, to change the mind of the British-era judge becomes a reason for a gathering of supporters to begin to reflect upon the possibilities of their own government to decide upon such matters. As Ilm-ud-Din awaits execution, the videodisc glitched irrevocably and, with too much data compressed onto too small a space, the VCD-player spat out the disc. Disappointed by the failure of his hardware, and so eager for me to appreciate the story of Ilm-ud-Din, the trader gave me his own master copy, trusting me to return it once I had watched or copied it. In this case, it was neither age nor moral sentiments that put the *Ghazi Ilm-ud-Din Shaheed* disc under erasure, but rather the data limits that always stand between repertoires and their expansion.

The evident contrasts of my time in the Punjab Archives and on Hall Road helped bring some clarity to how ideas around public demand, as responsive to opaque needs and atmospheres, gain a sense of fixity in circulation. In light of the forms of censorship on paper objects, the insertion of presence on non-current documents, and particularly the anonymity demanded when talking about posters that publishers no longer publish due to the force of public demand, media surfaces can reveal the material evidence of a threshold being crossed. As a counterpoint to the impenetrability of the bureaucracy, its inverse, the trade in and transfer of copies permitted free reign, evinces a remarkable degree of transparency, an open non-government built on the force of public demand. Mubaraka's act of "sending it to the market" meant that agreement over permissibility and use comes to be attributable to consensus and from practice rather than to an individual, for whom the consequences might be social stigma, accusations of immorality, vulgarity, *shirk*, or blasphemy.

Owing to the coexistence of hostility and enthusiasm towards film, the state has maintained a certain distance from the materials and labor that undergird it. Yet film has been allowed far greater freedom of movement, circulating outside of authorized channels, than other forms of knowledge, perhaps so that its contested and complicated regimes of permissibility were not tangled up with any governing regime. Instead, roles usually adopted by the state—both the preservation and censorship of film—are taken up by self-appointed guardians of both material culture and morality. Demand shows that plural notions of the "good" become homogenized into simply what is available. When the absence of the existence of an external authority—a market-based censor board, a film archive, or a copyright legislator—is understood, the higher power invoked in legitimizing the repertoire becomes the public themselves. In these terms, demand becomes the entanglement of market mechanisms with faith in the good of public reasoning.

CHAPTER III

<hr>

Feeling the Threshold

In the alternation of day and night are signs for people of understanding.
—QURAN. SURAH ALI' IMRAN 3:190

The succession of day and night is the architect of events.
—ALLAMA MUHAMMAD IQBAL, *THE MOSQUE OF CORDOBA*

W henever I ducked down the stairs and into the basement of Hall Road's Zaitoon Plaza, I hoped to see Idris waiting outside Durrani Electronics, his legs slung in front of him like his overhanging moustache slung over his top lip, resting one broad shoulder against the glass doorway at the bottom of the stairs. He often looked pensive, as if he had yet to decide that day whether to be unhappy or not. Only twenty days older than me, he would often remind me, "That still makes me your *bhai-jaan*" [elder brother, lit. "brother-dear"]. He had just come back from fourteen years as an expat working in Dubai, having left Pakistan when he was seventeen. Back after spending his adult life abroad, Idris had returned full of hyperbole and self-possession, keen to reflect and opine on his ever changing society. He would tell me, loud enough so his work colleagues could hear, how he would spend his evenings sitting alone and writing reflections in a diary. This admission provoked smirks from those around him. Part confession, part demonstration of alterity, he told me, "I have come back to see this society greatly shaken." While for Idris this was a period of reflection, where he sat back and observed social life and its continuities, it was also a period of reorientation and immersion.

Unlike many Pakistani expatriates in the Gulf, who often return home every twelve to twenty-four months, Idris returned after fourteen uninterrupted years to find the country transformed. Former President Pervez Musharraf had liberalized the country's media and communications networks, leading to the founding of countless television channels, adding new ideas and forums for debate and disagreement. Following the military coup that brought Musharraf to power, Pakistan underwent a tumultuous period of instability, coupled with the beginnings of a period of democratization. The national elections of 2013 saw the country's first peaceful handover of power, repeated in the elections of 2018. With the country's population having grown by at least 40 million, and Lahore's doubling while he was away, Idris found a country both striving for new and improved infrastructural provision and rapidly becoming accustomed to changing media environments. For him, these new infrastructures were mere enablers for a widespread overconsumption of water, electricity, and gas supplies, itself the symptom of a pervasive moral decline. "Greed is in the seed," he told me. "Allah teaches us that this depends on you; if you are good, I will give you a good king. But if you are bad, the bad king will come. So, you see the smog? This is the result. This is our bad king." While Idris was true to his usual perceptive form, the smog was hard to miss; its particulate density seemed to materialize thresholds and chokepoints usually hidden.

It had become common to hear the extensive period of pallid smog, that Idris viewed as a kind of moral patina, described as Lahore's "fifth season." With a population of almost 13 million in 2020, Lahore is vulnerable to overload, be that resulting in a shortage of gas in the winters or electricity in the summers. Its delicate, fragile state is most visible in the smog season, whose fog muddies lungs, exacerbates traffic, and closes schools and hospitals. It is also a great leveller; it affects rich and poor as they sleep, drive, and work. Those laboring outdoors suffer far greater negative effects. One just has to look at the traffic controllers on the corners of busy intersections, who I only saw issued a paltry surgical mask a month into the worst of that winter's dense, low-lying smog, to feel the painful injustices that the weather materializes and amplifies. Respiratory illnesses, cognitive damage in children, cancers, and skin conditions—the effects of the smog are grave and numerous.

During Idris's time away, Pakistan's media environment had also heavily patinated the city. Mobile phone ownership and internet connectivity leapt to become so prevalent as to dominate many aspects of business and social activity. During this time, Hall Road, as the country's main electronics and wholesale market, played a central role in making electronic media feel elemental and omnipresent in urban Pakistan. The other palpable change Idris found was in density. He found Hall Road's once broad

Figure 3.1 Following an extensive city-wide power outage resulting from a malfunction in the energy supply from one of Pakistan's hydroelectric plants, solar panels began to be sold beside local "Lahori cooler" air conditioners. (Photo by author.)

street partly pedestrianized by the large number of near-identical motor-cycles parked at the entrance of each plaza and spilling out onto any available road space. Their engines were kept cool beneath the shade of trailing banners offering televisions, cable access, and training in smartphone repair. While film traders still resided in many of the plazas, selling cheap copies of Pakistani films on disc or loaded directly onto microSD cards, the street had become an example of the ways in which digital media has brought to attention the blurred edges between mediums. Most businesses, including Idris's family store, had moved from selling local Lollywood films and pirated Bollywood movies to other ambient media, such as internet data, air-conditioning, solar panels, and spare-parts such as USB connectors, screen-protectors, and chargers.[1] From the small row of stores dedicated to the blue foghorn-shaped loudspeakers seen on mosques to "Lahori cool-ers," local, water-fed air conditioners, and from internet data to memory cards with an ascending level of capaciousness, there was a recognizable logic in the communities of objects that Hall Road sustained.

In this and the following chapter, I trace the sensitivity to demand on Hall Road as being reactive to changing seasons and atmospheric disturbances, as well as religious commemorations, and the moral mood of the market. On more than one occasion during my time in Lahore, the transmission line of Pakistan's Tarbela Dam became untethered to the national grid, leading to a loss of power to the Chashma Power Plant and a total power cut for the provinces of Punjab and Khyber Pakhtunkhwa. Within days, workmen on Hall Road could be seen unloading a container delivery of large solar panels. In these instances, the bustle of entrepreneurial activity on Hall Road felt to me like the deft turns on a tuning peg, in which individuals brought the tone of the media landscape into harmony with the prevailing sensory environment. Reactive to the slightest changes, Hall Road's traders could source situation-specific hardware overnight. As the smog descended to lower visibility, Durrani Electronics sent their teaboy to the main street with a trolley full of facemasks, torches, and high-visibility vests that they had procured only that morning.

In this chapter I argue that to understand how demand is fulfilled on Hall Road, and the atmospheres that drive it, requires paying attention to the ways in which shared forms, such as infrastructure or airborne pollutants like smog, make thresholds present as objects of social practice. By a threshold, I mean the saturated sensation of being on the verge of change that is mediated by forces beyond your immediate control. For example, when entering some environments deemed at risk of attack, such as the Shiʻi Imambargah and shrine of Karbala Gamay Shah in Lahore, phone signals and internet data freeze. This is due to the site being fitted with signal blockers to forestall any potential of a coordinated attack. Similarly, during the climactic ninth and tenth days of the Islamic month of Muharram, when Shiʻi gatherings and processions take place, internet and telephone signals are routinely blocked. Only the expensive, Chinese-imported Zong Internet devices continue to provide internet data, producing not only the sensation of a communal threshold, but an economic threshold in which trade networks and purchase-power delimit the reach of the state even in its most urgent responsibilities. As Brian Larkin argues, infrastructures are not only subject to visual economies of progress and power, but formatively shape the ambient conditions of movement, volume, and scale.[2] In this chapter I want to follow this line of thought by exploring how infrastructures, and the atmospheres and intermittence they invoke, can provide a way of conceptualizing thresholds in moral terms. It is often through the felt conditions of these thresholds that people find templates for being peaceable or ways of living morally in the spaces that lie between themselves and others. In the thresholds made palpable and present by infrastructures and the airborne, uncertainty is the status quo. Such ambiguity neither "melts into air," to paraphrase Marshall Berman's work on the blurred lines between modernity and modernization, nor necessarily fixes into hard boundaries, but rather provides the materiality of indiscernibility that can make living with one another more tolerable.[3]

Yaseen Street

In the first chapter I recalled the anger felt by one of my interlocutors, Shamaila Begum, at the ways that performers were socially marginalized by Pakistan's economic elite and morally denigrated in debates over the permissibility of public performance. This perfect storm led to legislation that forestalled her daughter's much-anticipated dance performance in their local church in a Christian-majority colony of Bara Pind, an area divided by a dual-carriageway from a wealthy housing community in the south of Lahore. Employment in these partially gated communities was much in demand among Shamaila and her neighbors. Some of the economic elite prefer to employ Christians as domestic helpers and cleaners, beauty salon workers, and alcohol dealers, as it is felt that they are unlikely to pose a danger to the secular lifestyles of some of their employers. This association does not come without risks to the Christian community. It is well known to both workers and their employers that Pakistani Christians are disproportionately targeted by blasphemy allegations.[4] Domestic workers are also vulnerable to sexual abuse and coerced conversions to Islam.

After visiting Shamaila Begum's church, I spoke with the members of the congregation and promised to return for another service. Christmas approached, but there was little exchanging of gifts. Shamaila's youngest daughter told me that their church taught them that Santa Claus had died falling from his sleigh while delivering presents over Lahore. The star placed on the top of the Christmas tree represents his fall from the sky. I asked Shamaila what the church and its youth groups might find useful at this time. Knowing that I was spending my days on Hall Road, she asked me for enlargement lenses for smartphones and USB-chargeable torches, in order that pedagogic material could continue to be used in classes during power outages. She also remarked that as I regularly visited the poster printers Abu Islami Images (see chapter 2), I should procure sets of Christian posters for the church. However, she had no interest in acquiring any of these posters for herself. While she identified as Christian, the everyday contours of her faith involved greater adherence to Punjab's Muslim saints. On hot days, when she would procure glasses of water from whichever storefront was closest to her, she would squat to drink it rather than standing, and take it in three sips. She indicated to me that this is what the Prophet Muhammad taught his followers to do. During the mourning period of Muharram, when Pakistani Shi'a mourn the sacrifices of Imam Hussain and his followers at the Battle of Karbala in 680 CE, she would refuse to listen to music and chastise anyone else for violating the atmosphere of solemnity. Yet she was always keen to remind others that after the Karbala tragedy, when the female survivors were humiliated and paraded unveiled through Damascus, it was a local Christian community that threw shawls to them with which to cover their heads and maintain their dignity. As with many traders on Hall Road, despite fluid affinities in practice and identification, Shamaila experienced her multiple selves and the ideas that shaped them as whole. For Shamaila, the bleeding edges between religious communities were not indicated by outward practices but a sense of inner orientation. Perhaps this is to do with the precarious position of Pakistan's Christians, for whom it is more pragmatic to express thresholds as similarities rather than differences that widen the gulf of separation. Emphasizing commonalities also contains its own dangers. It was an important point of contention in the family that Shamaila Begum's eldest daughter had not only converted to Islam, but to Salafism, a form of Sunni jurisprudence that promotes a literalist approach to piety that is often associated with radical conservatism. While her eldest daughter made no attempts to convert other members of the family from Christianity, she was adamant that Shamaila should stop visiting Muslim shrines and praying for saintly intercession, acts which Salafism strictly forbids.

As I went shopping for the items on Hall Road, Idris pointed out the spire of the Cathedral Church of the Resurrection. Built on the Mall in 1887, the construction of the church led to the demarcation of service roads, including Hall Road on its eastern side. Today, the church houses what many Pakistani Christians call "the first cross," a type of cross associated with the apostle Saint Thomas (who died around 72 CE), excavated from near Taxila and said to belong to the ancient community of the Saint Thomas Christians of India. After the death of Jesus, Thomas helped spread Christianity through Kerala and on to Sri Lanka. As I looked at the spire, I remembered the diversity and richness of Shamaila's beliefs and thought about how the thresholds between faiths become atomized in practices held to be particularly resonant, rather than in coherence with a normative system of beliefs. This line of thought correlated closely with my own attempts to navigate the thresholds that demarcated Hall Road's economic environment. Without any discernible organizing structure, the street and its radial spread was split into sub sections based on the elemental qualities of electrical items. Loudspeakers for mosques were sold beside traders who installed car stereos; internet data was sold beside dealers in smartphones; and back-up generators were sold beside chargeable LED lighting. The newest items, those usually procured cheaply from users of the Chinese wholesale and e-commerce site Alibaba, as experiments in gaging public demand, were usually carted round by street hawkers connected to one of the larger and more prosperous permanent stores. On Hall Road, technological obsolescence was managed well. Shops went into business selling the technology that rendered their previous stock obsolete, the unused hardware quickly sold wholesale to the "parts market" formed by the outlying alleyways to the north. Even though he had just returned, Idris had come to know the segmentation of the market well. Indeed, for those who work on Hall Road, the plazas are a second home. There are at least a dozen mosques on the street, with many plazas housing a mosque on the roof, with loudspeakers connected to each floor for amplification of the azan. Traders get through the day with teaboys on speed dial, fountains for performing ablutions, and struggle with a notable absence of toilet facilities.

Idris told me the items I was looking for could be found in a street formed in the shadow of the two oldest shopping plazas, named Rafi and Zaitoon, shaded by flex banners and darkened by gangways, overhanging wires, and power cables. As with the spontaneous streets formed by Hall Road's plazas and its encroachments to the north and south, this passage is not officially named. But to the traders who rent or occupy any available space with footfall, it is known as Yaseen Street, after the Quranic surah (Quran 13:3) of the same name that similarly examines the "signs" referenced in surah Ali' Imran at the beginning of this chapter.

Figure 3.2 Yaseen Street. (Photo by author.)

Figure 3.3 The Sunday DVD market at the entrance of Yaseen Street. (Photo by author.)

The creation of passages between built space had been a part of Lahore's urban growth from the beginning of the twentieth century. The influential town planner Patrick Geddes, who visited Lahore in 1912, noted, "The confused maze of telegraph and telephone posts and wires, their overhead tramway cables and power-cables; . . . the clumsiest girder forms taken from beneath overhead railways . . . this grim and wastefully complicated web overhead."[5] Over a century later, the web that troubled Geddes had taken over from the town planner. Over Yaseen Street loose wires lay deactivated and dormant. Access ramps, built as afterthoughts between plazas, hung precariously in the air. Connecting the archipelago of plazas were power pylons with their clusters of wiring, like date fronds heavy with fruit. As with its constituent produce, within the market's growth lay a built-in obsolescence. The establishment of the plaza model in other parts of Lahore decentralized the importance of Hall Road. But it was always more of a concept than a street, an interlocking set of alleyways gravitating around the short-lived reign of the newest media commodity.

At the mouth of Yaseen Street from Hall Road, the traders who could stand the bustle of people and motorcycle traffic set up stalls, hawking whatever had recently been unloaded wholesale from containers fresh from their Chinese importers. It was here that I found "3D" enlargement screens designed to be used for mobile phones to magnify the images for group viewing. With the texture of a human fingerprint, its screen was housed in a frame that gave it the impression of a contained television unit. The shade provided by the side panels helped the clarity of the image by omitting surrounding light pollution. The salesman told me how to use it to become semi-independent from the central power grid. I would be able to watch an entire film during periods of loadshedding while powering the phone through my USB power-bank, the salesman told me, pointing to the back of Rafi Plaza where they could be bought. Regardless of government restrictions on internet service, the film itself could be streamed through a USB-powered mobile internet device, as the salesman made an about-turn and pointed to a franchise of the Chinese internet provider Zong. If that was not enough, when settling down to watch a film I would not even have to use the Roshan App to check scheduled power outages. The Roshan [power, light, energy] App is a smartphone application (courtesy of the government of Pakistan) that allows users to monitor the scheduled loadshedding in their district. Loadshedding is a strategy used by energy suppliers to ensure the central electrical power supply does not overload by

Figure 3.4 Participants at a music festival in Lahore enjoy an element of Sharmeen Obaid-Chinoy's *Look but with Love* project—a virtual reality (VR) documentary. (Photo by author.)

withholding energy flow to certain sectors for certain demarcated times. This prevents failure when the central system is nearing capacity. It is different from a blackout or power outage because it is a preventative measure before the uncontrolled loss of power in an electricity network. Semi-independent from the central power supply, smartphones became an ideal medium for navigating intermittence. The same could not be said of Lahore's cinemas. While newly built multiplexes possessed their own automated backup generators, in Lahore's remaining celluloid cinemas projectionists had to keep a keen eye on the fading of the image, the waning of the sound, and the speed of the wall-mounted fans in the cinema stalls, before rushing to regulate the flow of energy between the central system and its manual generators. While this happened, patrons patiently took out their mobile phones and played film music to pass the time while the frames found their rhythm and the sound rose in pitch to become synchronous again.

For Idris, whose individualism set him apart from his colleagues, the digital solitude brokered by smartphones affected the ability for certain forms of contemporary media to mediate a moral atmosphere. He pointed this out to me as we passed a trader with a recent delivery of virtual reality (VR) headsets, augmented to work with the smartphones that most customers on the street possessed. "We achieve nothing, shutting ourselves off from each other in these environments [*mahauliyat*]," he exclaimed, loud enough for the trader to hear. I posed a counterexample to him. At a recent music festival in Lahore, I had seen the filmmaker Sharmeen Obaid-Chinoy's interactive documentary *Look but with Love*, part of which was screened on VR headsets, allowing the wearer to become immersed in the places featured in the films. The premise of the documentary was to cultivate empathy in the viewer through the simulation of ambient co-presence. The situations the viewer was shown were often banal, but ones likely to be outside of their milieux, such as the bustle of life beside railway tracks or a hospital filled with female doctors. The title, derived from a slogan featured widely in Pakistani truck art, engages with subcontinental ideas around the harmful effects of embodied vision known as *nazar*.[6] The most potent force that drives this surveilled form of vision is jealousy, such that a seemingly admiring glance or complimentary word can harbor malevolent powers. Idris stuck to his initial judgement. "Avoiding nazar does not mean turning ourselves into ghosts." He seemed to be asking, how can one develop empathy, rather than jealousy or judgement, through a simulated environment? For Idris, media environments are made between people and mediated by the air and the ethics that lie between them, not *about* them. This recalls another subcontinental visual concept, that of the Hindu notion of *darshan*, in which the act of both seeing and being seen by a deity radiates outward to shape the importance of relationality and reciprocity in a wider public sphere. There are also echoes here of Inayat Khan's philosophy of atmosphere as alterity. "No matter what a person may try to hide," he wrote, "his atmosphere will speak of it. No one is ever able to create a false atmosphere . . . an atmosphere that is different from his own condition."[7] Atmospheres possess the qualities of both opacity and transparency, which obscure at the same time as disclosing.

Whether on Hall Road or in the celluloid cinemas of Abbott Road, whose ticket stubs advertise air-conditioned halls, my interlocutors were always keen that I, a visitor, and one from outside South Asia no less, always sat closest to a cooling fan. This kind of hospitality was particularly pronounced in May and June, when I was warned of the *luu*, the hot summer wind that dries vegetation, imparts heatstroke, and builds to a suffocating crescendo until the arrival of the monsoon rains. On summer days spent walking towards Durrani Electronics, I saw birds, mainly large black kites, tumbling down the branches of trees or succumbing to heatstroke on the road. On the counters of street-facing stores, some traders would keep small birds, similarly afflicted as the black kites but chosen for their diminutive size and beauty, submerged up to their chests in bowls of water to help them cool and rehydrate.

The cooling economy is one that has long intersected with that of Hall Road. On the southern edges of Yaseen Street, Hall Road as electronic market passes an imperceptible threshold to reach the outer edges of Beadon Road, a street lying almost perpendicular to it, and famous as a conglomeration of ceiling fan and pedestal fan retailers, repairpersons, and wholesalers, in a trade dating back to the early twentieth century. I found the threshold between these streets as compelling as I did the blurred lines between Shamaila's self-identification as a Christian and her daughter's objection to her seeking intercession from Muslim saints. On one alleyway the expansive tangle of streets that make up the markets of both Beadon

Figure 3.5 A Hall Road trader helps a small bird rehydrate and cool down in a bowl of water on a hot day. (Photo by author.)

Road and Hall Road mingled into one another. The Hall Road–Beadon Road limit was filled with computer parts, computer mouses that hung like meat in a butcher's shop, desktop hard drive cases, and finally a number of stores selling the internal cooling fans for standing computer hard drives. It was at this threshold that a new street began, not only one recognized by municipal authorities but one known to the public through its association with a particular commodity zone.

On the same alley, traders who repaired and cleaned the blades of wall-mounted fans provided their labor to the aging cinemas of Abbott Road. The first air-conditioned cinema in the subcontinent, the Regal in Bombay, opened in 1933, while the first Pakistani air-conditioned cinema, the Gulistan, was built in Dacca, then East Pakistan, in 1952.[8] Less than a decade later, a report conducted by the Government of Pakistan between 1960 and 1961 on the condition of the national film industry, found the ambient conditions of cinemas a primary concern among respondent interviewees. Responses from cinemagoers indicated that many wanted cinemas categorized under different economic brackets, so that taxation could be levied in an evenly distributed way that ensured attendance for both high- and low-income groups. One suggestion included categorizing cinemas by their air-conditioning. Class A would be air-conditioned, Class B would be "other than air-conditioned," and Class C would be decrepit cinemas that should be "compulsorily" renovated.[9] A few pages later, the report went on to describe the "three distinct classes" of people "as far as taste is concerned" who might correspond to this hierarchy of cinemas.[10] Class A were the "high-brow" who wholly avoided Pakistani films in favor of foreign imports and would not relent until an "aura of respectability is conferred" on the local industry.[11] Class B was made up of the everyman, "educated or illiterate," who attended the cinema out of habit, and whose dedication to the local industry despite its failings should be awarded with productions of which they could be proud.[12] Finally, Class C was the "*masses*" who were easy to satisfy despite the failure for Pakistani film to understand "mass psychology" or "Mass Taste."[13] The report itself appeared to possess a language, if not of mass taste, but of mass morality, that was framed in relation to the atmospheric and the airborne. The problems of the industry were to be addressed by various means, including liaison with the press, to "remove much of the atmosphere of disrepute and unreliability that has managed to envelope in the public mind."[14] It is hard not to see this connection between hygiene and comfort, on the one hand, and morality and modernity on the other, as mediated by air-conditioning. As Muhammad Qadeer remembers of 1960s Lahore, "Watching an English movie in the air-conditioned Plaza cinema on a searing June afternoon was the badge of modernity."[15] Some four decades later, in Mohsin Hamid's novel *Moth/Smoke*, air-conditioning remained the most enduring class division in Lahore, separating the economic elite from those who served them at the same time as draining the electricity grid common to all.[16]

Much evaporates upon encountering cool air. The thick, vivid smell of the city, dense, polluted, and fresh, mingling with the sulfurous smell of sewage and fresh meat dissipates when greeted by the cool air of a modern multiplex, and the inequalities manifested by the air, themselves usually ambient and unseen, suddenly take on an atmospheric form. Echoing the class hierarchy proposed in the 1960–1961 report, Asghar, the part-time programmer introduced in the previous chapter, described to me the ranking of cinemas, and extended it to his audience. "You can say that there is an A-class section of the society, a B-class, and C-class. My customers fall between B and C." The airborne also mediates the decay of sound. Several music collectors told me that many archived recordings held by Radio Pakistan, dating back decades, were irrevocably damaged in the 1980s, when the air-conditioning in the vaults was turned down too low, causing spools to succumb to the heat and fuse together. The interaction between the aesthetic and the ethical is not simply mediated by the air. The air becomes an interface, allowing cinema attendance and social class to be hierarchized. Class anxieties about the cinema are also often expressed in moral terms, in that "lower" ranks of people are seen to enjoy film differently and be more easily perverted by the content. At the same time, these same audiences possess a heightened ability to shape or pollute the atmosphere if cohabiting with A-class audiences and spaces. It is when infrastructural elements extend to the rights of persons and their characters that the movement of the aesthetic and the ethical manifests in moral thresholds.

Pressure Points

In the introduction, I suggested that when my interlocutors speculated on the atmospheres that surround film, they were interested in the ethics of persons and things transcendent to them and beyond the range of their everyday lives. Then, in chapter 1, I argued that the Zia-era Hudood

Ordinances helped to turn the idea of a moral threshold [*hadd* or *hudood* in plural] into something that anyone can identify and police. While such a threshold previously referred to a divine boundary, its relocation in social and legal space equipped it with the possibility of a social or legal punishment. In their book on the Hudood Ordinances, Asma Jahangir and Hina Jilani asked what else the new laws introduced to the country, besides exacerbating patriarchy and acting as a symbol of Islamization. One answer might be that the "Hudood laboratory," as they called it, helped supplant a heuristic in everyday speech that tracks the speculative move from divine to legal sanction.[17] Atmospheres, airborne and as common as shared breath, and thresholds, the felt or assumed feeling of imminent change, do not smoothly map onto the differences between the internal and the external. Rather, their interaction shows how they lend the other a moral form.

My use of the term threshold differs from how it has been used throughout the history of anthropology, where it has been an important and long-running theme. In his 1909 *The Rites of Passage* Arnold Van Gennep wrote, "To cross the threshold is to unite oneself with a new world."[18] This radical notion inspired Victor Witter Turner's explication of Van Gennep's work on the centrality of the threshold in early anthropological thought as well as his own ideas around the subjunctive qualities of ritual.[19] While marshalled to do analytical work in the discipline's early history, few saw the need to explicate their deployment of the term. Other than in the title of his 1909 book, *The Threshold of Religion*, R. R. Marett only used the term twice, and in both instances in close relation to the cultivation of a particular "*mood and attitude consisting in a drawing near in awe.*"[20] In its association with awe, Marett revealed the two explicit assumptions that undergird the paradoxical use of the term threshold that his work would inspire. Firstly, that there exists a clear-enough boundary between the sacred and the mundane that it can be described in spatial terms. Secondly, that the magnitude of mood and awe is so affectively vast that it cannot be spatially located.

This is a reminder that anthropologists often conflate two semantic uses of the term.[21] In one guise the threshold can be a boundary marker of ritual crossing derived from the word for a point of entrance. In another, the threshold expresses the magnitude or level that, once exceeded, manifests a reaction, a change, or the coming into effect of a phenomenon. It goes without saying that these two senses of the term lose much in their conflation into one concept that expresses both a frontier and the magnitude of intensity and energy that looms at its boundary. At the same time, thresholds in anthropology have long hinted at the vastness and immensity of cultural praxis that serve to register intensity, rather than the actual location of change. It is magnitude that makes things new and that drives social change, not necessarily the act of crossing. Coming to grips with the scale and spectrum of these magnitudes provides a method for studying thresholds on their own terms, rather than in relation to the apparent binaries they motion towards or away from.

The way I use the term *threshold*, as a space of affective intensity, has a rich scholarly trajectory. This includes Susan Leigh Star's suggestion that "boundary objects" that dwell within shared social space "allow different groups to work together without consensus."[22] Equally valuable is Mary Louise Pratt's call to understand the arts of the "contact zone," or the "social spaces where cultures meet, clash, and grapple with each other, often in contexts of highly asymmetrical relations of power."[23] More recently, Ilana Gershon has called for ethnography to account for "porous boundaries," or the multiple social commitments that overlap and intersect.[24] But as Marett appeared to suggest, awe does not have to be bound to something as socially productive or instrumental as ritual. Thresholds, as magnitudes rather than processes, can refer to the level of intensity felt before the manifestation of change. One example of how thresholds might take on moral contours is through the feeling of pressure.[25]

Despite the relative prosperity of the traders who populate the main streets of Hall Road, as with many small businesses in Punjab their enterprise is characterized by feelings of pressure, expressed through the English word *tension*. Idris told me that while many may admit feeling submerged in day-to-day pressure, its disclosure is often obscured by sensitivity to social class. Feeling depressed is not a malady appropriate for his social station, he reminded me. Once, after being told off for coming in late, he was called for a private chat with Faisal. He explained to his uncle that his *tabeeyat*—his inner being or consciousness—felt disturbed. Faisal told Idris that he was neither aristocrat nor landowner; he was a laborer and laborers do not have an inner being. He could break a bone or catch a virus, but existential malaise was not an excuse that would be accepted in the future. There was something about the term Faisal did not like, something that evoked for him entitlement and idleness, or navel-gazing and self-obsession. Why then, did atmosphere matter so much for Faisal, but not the condition of one's mind or body?

Tabeeyat is a matter of self and of interiority, while mahaul finds its stakes in the promises and dangers of alterity. If everything was a matter of inner being, then there would be no mahaul to perceive. But just because moral assumptions about film saturate public culture, it does not mean that all are touched in the same way. Shamaila Begum, for example, was a big fan of Punjabi-language cinema, with a repertoire of tunes that she sang to her family. Or so her eldest son told me. Her humility stopped her from singing in front of my family. She also turned down our offer to take her to a nearby multiplex, after telling us that she had never visited a cinema in her fifty-or-so years of life. Whenever I suggested regaling us with a tune or joining us at the cinema, she responded that as she did not listen to music during the ninth and tenth of the Islamic month of Muharram, nor should she watch films. I was perplexed. As my suggestions never coincided with the days when Pakistani Shi'a mourn the tragedy at Karbala in 680 CE, I blamed the misunderstanding on my Punjabi language skills. I later realized that not singing or visiting the cinema was for her an opportunity to draw attention to qualities in herself that she considered far more noteworthy. Each time singing or films were discussed, she told me of the commitments she found most virtuous in herself. During the ninth and tenth of Muharram she fulfilled a *mannat* [a vow to a saint or deity in relation to a wish, either realized or unrealized] in gratitude for being provided with a son, in which she walked barefoot through the unpaved streets of her colony asking for money to feed the poor. If the atmosphere of film and music provides a somatic index for moral ambiguity, it also provides one ingredient in a holistic approach to ethical life, in which turning away from the emptiness of public leisure is to turn towards the outward practice of individual virtues.

An Infrastructural Sphere

Thresholds such as that between Hall Road and Beadon Road were also the by-products of a public sphere predicated on infrastructural ambience. As mentioned in the introduction to this book, Hall Road's trader community were often caricatured as being politically devoted adherents of conservative religious groups. In the September 2017 by-election in the Pakistani parliamentary constituency of NA-120 in which Hall Road falls,

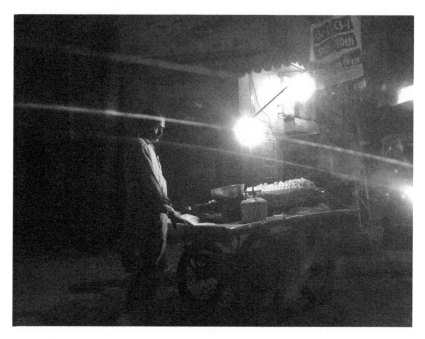

Figure 3.6 A street trader selling sugarcane works late into the night with the aid of a cheap chargeable lightbulb bought from nearby Hall Road. (Photo by author.)

many owed the sudden rise of Tehreek-e-Labbaik Pakistan (TLP), the Barelvi Islamist group who earned 5.7 percent of the vote, to the area's population of merchant traders, like Faisal, and their employees, like Idris. Like all political parties, the TLP had a registered election symbol. In their case it was a yellow crane signifying their commitment to construction, building, and infrastructural development. The Milli Muslim League (MML), a far-right Islamist party that included banned cleric Hafiz Saeed, chose as their symbol an illuminated, energy-saving lightbulb, to support their promise to halt loadshedding and improve energy provisioning.

During my fieldwork Pakistan was being transformed by a collection of infrastructure projects known as the China–Pakistan Economic Corridor (CPEC). News reports and politicians measured success in the form of "returning to surplus" of both food and energy after years of intermittent power supply. The state's economic and political entanglement with Chinese infrastructural development had already seen cities rapidly transform at the expense of the expulsion and dispossession of residents in informal settlements.[26] Yet hydropower and energy infrastructure are passionate subjects, allied as they are with the prosperity of nations.[27] What Islamist parties like the TLP's and MML's appeals to public opinion suggested was the existence of an infrastructural sphere open to illiberal forces that was quite different from the archetypal notion of a deliberative, liberal public sphere centering on congregation in coffee houses and discussion in a free press.[28] Instead, infrastructural intermittence creates what Christopher Pinney calls a "performative public sphere," where users mediate the nation state through ears, eyes, and bodies tuned to a complex sensory terrain.[29] Rahul Mukherjee has argued that because infrastructures are seen by many Indians as markers of progress, development, and digitization, their "radiance" is mired in complex and ambivalent feelings.[30] Mukherjee finds that the imperceptibility of radiation felt to emanate from cell-phone towers and nuclear reactors, in contrast to the visibility of air pollution, amplifies fears over negative health effects. He argues that while the mediation of these anxieties by journalists and broadcasters expresses the stakes at play in gaging the "threshold levels of radiation" that mark the limit between safety and danger, in striving to do so they largely fail to challenge the power of energy companies.[31] Permitting a certain degree of pollution requires what Max Liboiron calls a kind of "threshold-thinking . . . [that] allows for a certain amount of population death."[32] The airborne is also where anxieties find an interface. Mukherjee examines how internet connectivity in the air is felt through the case of people who declare themselves to be "electrosensitive," with medical symptoms brought on by an atmosphere saturated with wireless internet networks.[33] Performative public spheres need not be aspirational to be recognized as such. Anxieties, pressure, and fears of saturation or overload make thresholds palpable public affects.

The support of many sole traders for the Pakistan Muslim League-Nawaz (PML-N) party in Punjab was owed in large part to their partial reduction in loadshedding in their five years of rule between 2013 and 2018. I remembered, in the months before the 2013 elections that swept the PML-N to power at the expense of the Pakistan People's Party (PPP), whole days and nights spent by candlelight, without internet, air-conditioning, or ceiling fans, and the sudden synchronic blackout of whole sections of the city while a sector beyond an invisible border remained illuminated. Perhaps this was why Yaseen Street seemed to personify for me the thresholds which the city usually allows to remain hidden. Loadshedding, as infrastructural intermittence, creates spatial relations. During loadshedding power outages, it is hard to miss the vegetable sellers who can operate at night simply by affixing a single cheap LED light to illuminate their stalls. Continuous power without intermittence or breakdown had rarely been accessible to all in Pakistan. Loadshedding is itself a threshold experience of magnitude rather than spatial crossing, creating an infrastructural sphere materialized on Yaseen Street by the offsetting of energy, and from overload rather than breakdown. While infrastructures are material entities that facilitate the interaction, distribution, and cohabitation of object-forms, their physical networks give shape to the conditions of ambience. While infrastructural breakdown gives rise to an awareness of how governing systems attempt to mobilize the invisibility of failure and the inevitability of collapse, the kind of infrastructural intermittence I have described here operates through performative reciprocity. The imminence of breakdown is felt through the certainty of its eventual restoration; it is a certain uncertainty that draws attention to how precarity is internalized and absorbed by marketplaces like Hall Road into thresholds that become perceptible, in some degree, to all.

The Road

Having acquired the 3D screens from Hall Road, and on my way back from Abu Islami Images, I found the smog so much worse in Shamaila Begum's colony. Perhaps this was because of the colony's proximity to the brightly lit dual carriageway that divided her economically deprived Christian-majority colony from one of the many elite, securitized housing communities to have sprung up over the last two decades in the south of Lahore. Shamaila Begum met me as I was laden with materials from Hall Road at the nearest Metrobus stop, to supervise my then familiar dash across the motorway. Just a week before, an attack had taken place targeting a Christian church in the western city of Quetta as they prepared for Christmas. It had been the third terrorist attack on Christian communities within the previous four months, during which time at least fifteen people had been killed. Despite the increased police presence at the roadblocks that surrounded her colony, that day Shamaila was even more self-possessed and animated than usual, wearing a new white pashmina that she fingered with a studied humility that bordered on disdain. Even though thousands of people in Shamaila's community worked as household staff, such as cleaners, drivers, and cooks, on the wealthy side of the road there was no footbridge or pedestrian crossing over the six-lane dual carriageway. One must either travel by motorbike a kilometer to the nearest passage to the other side or climb over the embankment—which doubles as an open sewer—and dash fifty meters across the busy road. In Pakistan, infrastructural projects, such as roads, are often subject to the anxiety and unease of a "coming modernity," yet in housing communities constructed in once rural areas that contain extant villages, roads also serve to demarcate the boundaries between modernities open to some and not to others.[34]

In clear weather, the brightness of the lights on the dual carriageway cast everything not as powerfully lit into deep shadow. That evening a power cut had, for once, laid both sides of the road into darkness. At night, the luminosity of individual billboard screens yet to be filled with advertising content distributed pale white lights from each lamppost and created an even more palpable border between the two colonies. As the 2018 elections loomed, the incumbent PML-N party had hung a series of plastic posters over the digital signs, featuring five images of the party leader and then-Prime Minister Nawaz Sharif wearing different hats indicative of the different provinces of Pakistan. Sindhi Nawaz followed Pashtun Nawaz followed Balochi Nawaz, and so on. If you looked from the bus stop outside Jannat Cottages, the road seemed to run alongside inky black scrubland. The word used interchangeably for light and power supply in Pakistan, *roshan*, well articulates the political economy of luminosity in Lahore. Light is power, power, light. At the end of the dual carriageway a monolithic gated shopping mall lit up the darkness, coloring a square mile of unlit houses. Shamaila remembered before it and Jannat Cottage were built, the enclosure was used as a garbage disposal plant, where plastic bottles and packages would burn throughout the night, throwing out a continuous plume of poisonous smoke into her colony. The dual carriageway also served as a threshold that marked different sectors of the power grid. This meant that Shamaila's home, where she lived with her five teenaged children in a dwelling that consisted of a single room with a double bed and a courtyard with a chicken pen, had different scheduled periods of loadshedding to her employers over the road. While Shamaila would often boast to me that she received far fewer hours of scheduled power outages than Jannat Cottages, that December her colony had suffered an extended period of gas loadshedding. As they did every smog season, her family were beginning to have to make wood fires in the courtyard. On the other side of the road, electrical loadshedding had increased. With fewer air-conditioning units being switched on due to the drop in temperature, energy providers felt able to apportion more frequent outages without drawing the ire of those who had come to rely on cool air. These thresholds are important, not merely as anthropological thick description, but because they reinforce an environment securitized in ways that far exceed the labor of those who enforce it. While Jannat Cottages was supposed to be the safest place to live in the city, it had only privately policed road cordons upon entering the area, cordons which only saw the odd motorbike or van stopped and checked. Instead, dividing Jannat Cottages from the Christian colony was an ambient wall that ensured social division in the same ways that a different kind of threshold, the particulate matter of moral experience, works to aggregate the fluidity of religious practices into categorical distinctions.

The Pulse of the Atmosphere

In English, the word ambience has been used to describe a mental or moral environment since the late eighteenth century and, along with the term atmosphere, appears to have been adopted to describe the kind of tonal and textural effects that emerged in Romantic poetry and art. These changes in vocabulary allowed social commentators, like the cleric and popular writer Hugh Reginald Haweis, to describe the virtues of music as determinate on the "moral atmosphere of feeling."[35] Haweis's popular book *Music and Morals* went through several reprints in the late nineteenth century, charting a journey from Christian music to the ways in which it might be possible to recognize the constitution of "emotional atmospheres" through sound.[36] Evidently thinking on the same lines as his contemporary John Ruskin on the connection between art and morals, in which the question of "public taste" is one with connotations of social order, Haweis's use of the term atmosphere varied in ways that reflect its use in this book.[37] He went from describing an intersubjective climate of emotion and morality to describing the conditions of polluted Victorian England, echoing the relationship between measurement and mood found in the term threshold. For Haweis, the idea of public taste as the judgmental nature of aesthetics, is closely related to social order, class, and hierarchy. When we read again his description of "the moral atmosphere of feeling," with this mixed use of the term in mind, we can imagine Haweis experiencing music as active to a moral life as pollutants are to the patina of a church building, layered in black residue. In the Victorian era, the omnipresence of pollution allowed musicians and art critics to argue that an aesthetic disposition was needed to regulate social order. Public discourse in Pakistan uses a similar heuristic of purity and pollution to argue for a different social regulator. Taking one of the origins of the name *Pakistan* as the "land of the pure," Farahnaz Ispahani has shown how the term has been embraced by Islamist activists whose "drive to 'purify' Pakistan has become a quest to impose religious conformity, which in turn requires the social and economic exclusion and marginalization of people believing in religions or practices other than those of the 'purifiers.'"[38] This notion of purification relies on assumed ideas about cleanliness and pollution, and their social causes, and shows how atmospheres and thresholds play off one another.

For Haweis, it was only the arts that could purify a polluted space, providing a counter-atmosphere that, like a musical refrain, continuously reasserts its moral sentiment.[39] Haweis's work on music cohered with a late-nineteenth century effort to take back the study of ecological concerns from those who wished to divide empirical philosophy from the natural sciences. In 1803, industrial chemist Luke Howard published the first major meteorological treatise on clouds since Aristotle's *Meterology* (circa 350 BCE) and its rediscovery and reapplication in golden-age Islamic philosophy. Howard's *On the Modification of Clouds . . .* aimed to depart from the associations of clouds with literature, mood, and symbology. He deemed philosophers and aesthetes only capable of studying the "*pulse* of the atmosphere."[40] He argued that while sailors and farmers became accustomed to the cycles and signs of weather formation, their means of expressing and mediating their own intuitions rendered their knowledge largely esoteric. To address this, Howard introduced a shared lexicon of cloud formations, such as *cumulus*, *stratus*, and *cirrus*, and its intermediate modifications. Writing at much the same time as Haweis, and in ways quite contrary to Howard, the art critic and historian John Ruskin dedicated himself to contemplating the pulse of atmospheric morphologies and advocating that students and scholars of art undertake daily observation of dawn cloud movements. In an 1884 essay titled "The Storm-Cloud of the Nineteenth Century" Ruskin experimented with the symbology of prophetic fallacy that Howard had critiqued. Ruskin described a kind of cloud formation specific to his industrial late nineteenth century, one observable by art critics rather than meteorologists.[41] In the essay, he described the "plague-cloud" and its then residual associations with bringing illness and death to the land. For Ruskin, meteorological instruments were incapable of measuring the oscillation and movement of the "plague-wind," hampered by the qualities that he felt were able to be inculcated through aesthetic training, and on another level, the ethical faculties possessed through observation and reason.[42]

If infrastructures are ambient or shape how people perceive the atmospheres that surround them, it is their detritus—pollution, smog, and intermittence—that allows one to speculate on the thresholds that first make atmospheres perceptible. These include the ways in which Idris perceived moral choices to determine atmospheric conditions, the ways in which Haweis wrote of the "moral atmosphere" capable of being formed by music or pollution, or Ruskin's description of clouds as a punishment for moral inequity. Like Idris's characterization of smog as the "bad king" that reigns because of the moral failings of his subjects, infrastructure materializes these thresholds and brings them into a sphere for debate and contestation.

The Smog Clouds of the Twenty-First Century

It was early evening, and the smog was thickening. The panicked rush across the road was exacerbated by the cars that habitually appeared to accelerate to speeds nearing one hundred kilometers per hour on the two-kilometer-long stretch of straight road. From the other side, I could only barely make out the compounds of the squat mansions of Jannat Cottages through the smog and the traffic. All I could see were the flames spilling out of burning drums as security guards outside the mansion walls warmed their shins underneath sun-bleached parasols. This soft border became more palpable amid the particulate matter of the dense smog, which seemed to acknowledge the contours of everything on which it fell.

I glanced back at the curb that ran down the middle of the road, trying to get a closer look at the brightly lit advertising screens that were causing most of the light pollution. I spotted the outline of an animation on the row of screens affixed to lampposts. Having been left unused since their construction—and only omitting powerful tones that passed the color spectrum from red to blue—a television cable-company, WorldCall, had taken up advertising space on the flashing signs. In the advertisement, the company promised, *"Aisay Clear. Jaisay Real"* [Clear Like This, Like Real(ity)], itself barely visible through the smog. Making claims about the clarity of their cable broadcasts by comparing the resolution of the moving-image adverts on the street to the clarity of the cable signal, and then to the ineffable quality of reality, the company tried to make a connection between the atmospheres brokered by visual patina and its aftereffects.

Despite the extent to which the powerful pale lighting exposed the particulate matter in the air, Shamaila believed the smog was nothing other than winter fog, waving away the warnings on the radio and in the newspapers with a dismissive shrug. To her, it was almost a kind of mirage. In Pinney's political history of mirages, their evasive form has long provided ways of thinking through religion and power. Mirages are airborne, not only in their technics, but in their imagined efficacy, and experienced in various places as "exhalations."[43] In South Asia, mirages have been marshalled to impart important moral lessons, such as that "desire magnifies the illusory."[44] Unlike mirages, mahaul is not an illusion; it is there, in front of you, shaping you and others. But like mirages, mahaul has a politics. It exerts pressure that can lead to legislation, censorship, or pedagogy.[45] Atmosphere is a motivation and an alibi, and therefore pertains to some experienced presence in the world rather than an individual's description of it.

On the other side of the road, we walked along looking for a way up and clambered onto some strategically placed bricks to a higher escarpment. From there we came to the billowing mouth of the colony's open drain, climbed over it and onto one of the rubbish tips where the row of houses that abuts the bordering street throws their garbage. I felt that, having climbed the escarpment and its open sewer, I had ascended to the kind of altitude where one might find houses perched amid the clouds. From there we clambered down, skidding between a pathway in the trash made by well-trodden steps. As we arrived at her colony amid a pungent layer of smog that made the air almost unbreathable, the incandescent glow of street-lights layered at odd intervals cast the cuboid houses of Jannat Cottages into silhouette. It was becoming hard to see. Due to it being wedding season, the roads had been full of traffic all day. The chaos of the smog had begun to take a toll on people's lives, with flights rerouted, school times changed, chest infections, and road accidents. Mixed with the detritus of construction, the poisonous PM2.5 takes on a more tangible form. It is there in the tissue when you sneeze, and the stringy late-autumn leaves are dusted with a layer of the stuff.

Smog crystalizes social inequalities. Smog also limits the potential for an atmosphere to lead the way to social change, for it gives the impression of shared investiture in a common danger. Thresholds as the materiality of indiscernibility provide the promise of ambiguity, while meteorological ecologies foreclose the ability to feel the "pulse" of the atmosphere in all its radically subjective glory. Taking an environmental approach to media, it is biophysical forms such as the air, and material, visual, and digital interfaces such as images, figures, and sounds, that mediate and give form to conceptual ideas, atmosphere, and thresholds.

I tried to take in the view in front of me. The whitewashed walls of the colony were adorned with plastic posters, their surfaces—doomed never to be anything other than crumpled—reflecting the dazzling glare of the light pollution. They all featured Maryam—the virgin Mary—for whom that evening's event was held. The entrance to the church was signalled by a large sheet hung between the entrance to an alleyway, in front of which a security guard stood on watch, casually frisking anyone, and buzzing a bomb detector over them. Inside the open-air church courtyard, bright halogen spotlights, whitewashed low-rise walls, and a crowd of at least five hundred families were celebrating Christmas, facing a group of priests taking turns to deliver sermons through a distorted microphone.

At one point, it is hard to say exactly when, the threshold of visibility dropped to less than one meter and nothing other than the taut surface of the amplified sound remained.

CHAPTER IV

Atmospheres of Moral Exception

Atmospheres that both divide and bind become issues of national interest during the first ten days of the Islamic month of Muharram. During this time the minority Twelver Shi'i branch of Islam refrains from consuming film or music while observing a period of ritual mourning to mark the death of Imam Hussain, the grandson of the Prophet Muhammad, and his family and supporters at the Battle of Karbala in 680 CE. Muslims from different *mazhabs* and reform movements, and many of Pakistan's religious minorities, also avoid celebrations and secular media such as film and music. From the eighth day until after the climatic tenth day, known as Ashura, television broadcasts turn solemn and austere and media markets close to preserve the annual period of mourning. One must observe Ashura as one mourns a death, enjoying neither festivities nor anything that distracts the mind from sadness and remembrance. Pakistan's numerous private news channels transform. Their bright color schemes shift to monochrome and their coiffured hosts don mourning clothes, while on other channels the sound of music or the broadcast of films are notably absent to preserve the mood of this period of mourning. Preceding and following these annual commemorations, film and media traders on Hall Road attempt to strike an appropriate balance between benefiting economically from religious media and publicizing minority beliefs. For media traders and consumers, the practices of abstaining from celebratory sounds, images, or entertainment media during the first ten days of Muharram requires an improvised approach to where moral thresholds lie. This period of commemorative mourning was important for my interlocutors on Hall Road. I found that at no other time in the year is the source of "public demand" so apparent yet so mired in overlapping stakes as it is during Muharram.

I was memorably warned, almost rebuked, by Idris and my interlocutors at Durrani Electronics for wearing black clothing, associated with the communal mourning of the Shi'a, during the first ten days of Muharram. I was unsure if their guidance was intended for my safety or due to their disapproval over the prevailing atmosphere of Muharram. Over recent years, targeted attacks on Shi'i processions had killed thousands. From the 1990s to the early 2010s anti-Shi'a violence had affected every corner of the country, with militant Sunni groups claiming that core tenets of Shi'i faith were constitutive of religious offense. While instances of anti-Shi'a violence in the provinces of Punjab or Sindh has risen and fallen several times, attacks on Shi'a Hazara communities in and around Quetta in Balochistan have been more sustained.

Perhaps it was frustration with the annual loss of revenue that annoyed Idris and Faisal, due to the days surrounding Ashura, when media markets such as Hall Road habitually close to preserve the period of mourning. On the first seven days of Muharram, however, the audiovisual atmosphere of the city transforms more gradually, and Hall Road's film traders reflect this change in their stock. Three-pack sets of vintage Lollywood films, foreign pornography, and pirated Bollywood films fade into the distance on the racks behind the counters, and devotional releases relating to Muharram and Ashura are brought into view. This temporary addition to traders' repertoires includes professionally filmed *majlis* [plural: *majalis*], sold in packaged VCDs featuring as many as a dozen orators of laments and elegies. A majlis is a mourning gathering central to communal worship for Shi'i Muslims that has traditionally been held to commemorate ritual occasions in which the virtues and sacrifices of the family of the Prophet Muhammad, the Ahl-e Bait, who suffered after the conflict over succession, are remembered. Various social and economic changes in Pakistan, where the Shi'a account for around a fifth of the population, have seen such gatherings held so frequently as to have become daily occurrences in big cities. Produced and released by what are still referred to as "cassette," "video," or "CD houses," which I found operating near Shi'i places of worship or shrines associated with Shi'i communities, majlis videodiscs travel on the circulatory networks maintained by the trade in informally distributed media in Pakistan.

The atmospheric contours that characterize the first ten days of Muharram rely on the absence of film, as well as tonal changes on television and radio networks. As this book has argued, when people give a name to disquiet, they also give name to the collective as well as the individual who perceives it, as to name an atmosphere is to describe possible cohabitants as well as strangers. People also identify atmospheres in absences and exceptions. In this chapter I leave Hall Road and follow the flows of Shi'i religious media that fill the gap in traders' repertoires during Muharram, when film finds itself temporarily eschewed during a period of commemorative mourning.

The Absence and Presence of Film During Muharram

The involvement of the state in closing cinemas for Muharram can be traced to Iran as early as the 1920s.[1] Before Partition, Muharram-specific radio programming flourished on the Indian subcontinent, featuring lectures on Shi'i ethics, theology, and recited laments. In the mid-1950s, anthropologist John J. Honigmann noted the informal practice of closing cinemas during Muharram in Pakistan.[2] Even in the comparatively louche days of the 1960s, Radio Pakistan did not broadcast music during the first ten days of Muharram, culminating in the *Majlis-i-Sham-i-Ghariban* broadcast given by the famous orator Rasheed Turabi since 1951. By the end of the 1960s, Pakistan's one television channel, the state-run PTV, had started screening Turabi's oration, and did so every year until his death in 1973, after which other leading orators took over.

This annual period of abeyance became firmly integrated in state attempts to wield religious sentiment in late 1978, when Pakistan's General Zia-ul-Haq was midway through his tenure as chief martial law administrator. He would become president of Pakistan in September 1978 after declaring martial law and seizing power in a coup in July 1977, a position he held until his unexplained death in a plane crash in 1988. On December 1, 1978, Zia addressed the nation on television and radio on the subject of Nizam-i-Islam, a term often rendered in English as the programme of political "Islamization" long associated with his period of rule. This remarkable speech outlined the juridical and social reforms he intended to implement, all delivered in his singularly threatening manner. He joked that daily prayers would only not be made a legal obligation because of his inability to police it. "For the time being we want to rely on persuasion rather than compulsion," he declared.[3] However, he did begin his speech with a request that quickly segued into an order.

> I appeal to all my countrymen that generally throughout the year and in this first month particularly they should demonstrate like true Muslims, forbearance, mutual understanding and oneness so that with full confidence and solidarity we are able to march forward towards our destination. As a mark of respect to *Muharram-ul-Haram* [Blessed Muharram] all cinema houses would remain closed at least on the 9 and 10 of Muharram.[4]

Nizam-i-Islam was to begin with this act, a practice that had likely previously been voluntary or undertaken as a precaution during times of communal tension. While Zia's attempts at Islamization institutionalized an approach to public piety underwritten by majoritarian Sunni Islam, his use of the moods of Muharram showed him unafraid to draw upon wider religious repertoires, even of those practiced by groups his regime and supporters often persecuted. Whatever his motivation, "persuasion rather than compulsion" did not apply to the public space of cinema-going.

Forms of legislation followed Zia's Muharram declaration and consolidated the growing sentiment that Islam and film should not coexist in the public sphere. The 1981 Ehtram-e-Ramazan Ordinance, for instance, ordered all cinemas and theaters to remain closed three hours after sunset during the holy month when Muslims immerse themselves in prayer and reflection. Building on the 1981 Ordinance, during my fieldwork the then-incumbent PML-N government of Pakistan made violating the periods of abstinence during Ramadan a punishable offense. As part of the Ehtram-e-Ramazan Amendment Bill 2017 [Respect for Ramadan], supported by the Religious Affairs and Interfaith Harmony Division of the government, it was decreed that cinemas should not open during fasting hours. The preceding bill that had been in force from 2014 to 2016 prohibited the screening of movies during iftar, the sunset meal when the fast is broken and *taraweeh*, the period of prayer and contemplation that follows. The 2017 Bill, however, stated that cinemas must not show films during the fasting times as well as iftar and taraweeh, leaving a narrow gap from around midnight until sunset for them to legally open. The highest tier of fines to be imposed during Ramadan—between 25,000 PKR and 500,000 PKR depending on the violation—were levelled at cinemas and TV channels that trespassed upon what has been described as a mass-mediated "sacred time."[5] While governments may legislate on these periods of moral exception, the intercommunal practices that shape Muharram and Ramadan are not given. Familiarity is required to understand which media practices are and are not permitted. Often, this familiarity is gleaned through the circulation and mediation of film and media, and proximity to the ethics that undergird these exchanges.

While not explicitly concerned with film, it is also during Muharram that Section 144 of the Pakistan Penal Code is often enacted, leading to a temporary ban on the display of arms, pillion-riding, and, in some provincial cases, broadcasting music on television or radio. Having been a historic flashpoint for sectarian violence between Shi'i and Sunni groups, Muharram is marked by the looming presence of the state. In these instances, atmospheres, moods, and public demands suddenly take on legislated form. If the closure of cinemas, as preeminent sites of public leisure and secularity, was once the primary sign of Muharram as a moral exception, during the period of my fieldwork it was also the suspension of mobile phone and broadband networks across entire cities during the 9th and 10th of the month. The government, army, and police argued that this measure was designed to forestall coordinated attacks.

It has become a cornerstone of a century of political thought that sovereignty is defined by the ability to decide upon states of exception that see legal and constitutional rights frozen to guard against perceived threats to social order.[6] Less well defined are how states of exception are sensed and felt before they are delimited. Muharram provides a unique view into a state of "moral exception," a term I borrow from Samuli Schielke.[7] I use the notion in a different sense to Schielke, who uses it to evince the importance of ambivalence and contradiction when considering the ethical lives of people who happen to be Muslim. Schielke asks his readers to turn their attention to Muslims who understand themselves to be imperfect, and sometimes immoral. In his work on Egyptian youth during Ramadan, food, feasting, material consumption, and restraint followed by excess are not simply steady paths to piety. Ramadan can instead be a period of "moral exception" when people of different Islamic orientations try to be good because of the likelihood of reward. Rather than the result of the cultivation of a particular ethical subjecthood, the period surrounding Ramadan reflects the wider coexistence of differing approaches to wealth and consumption, modesty and sexuality, and the contradictions these introduce into people's lives. Where I find the idea useful is in the way periods of "moral exception," such as Ramadan or Muharram, also become mediums for establishing the hierarchy of other values besides their faith that people hold dear.

True to his oppositional nature, on the eighth day of Muharram I found Idris looking for ways to flout this period of moral exception. He had decided to communicate his dissent through a customized dial tone. During Muharram, Pakistan's telecommunication providers send promotional text messages offering extracts of laments to disclose love and condolement to those who suffered in the Battle of Karbala. The wide focal range of Muharram commemorations invites the participation of those who would usually have little to do with Shi'i ritual or practice. This is not a new phenomenon. The material and visual culture of Shi'i faith contributes much to the aesthetics of Islam in Pakistan. As mentioned in chapter 2, this is because Alid piety, meaning devotion to Imam Ali, the cousin, son-in-law, and grandson of the Prophet Muhammad, and first Shi'i Imam, is shared across jurisprudential schools of thought and faiths. While the Shi'a are frequently othered in majoritarian discourse, the Ahl-e Bait are also loved and mourned by many Sunni Muslims. Perhaps aware of these shared affinities, Idris was eager to find a way to act differently. Rather than subscribing to one of the dial tone laments (in Pakistan, phone users can choose the dial tone their callers will hear before they're connected), Idris chose to have a *na'at*, a poetic recitation celebrating the virtues of the Prophet Muhammad. He told me that he did this as a way of communicating to his network that he was not a Shi'a, not engaged in mourning, and instead broadcasting his all-embracing love for the Prophet. While sitting with him, he told me to give him a call. As I raised the phone to my ear, I heard a familiar tune. He had chosen the na'at "Meri Baat Ban Gayi Hai," based on the tune of "Chalte Chalte" from the Bollywood film *Pakeezah* (1972). This was the same na'at broadcast by the visually impaired man with a loudspeaker in the prologue to this book, whose labor Idris saw as "purifying" the atmosphere of the street. By choosing this as his dial tone during a time when Barelvi na'at recitations or film songs were rarely aired, what Idris felt he was doing was demarcating a moral threshold that also expressed his position on several issues. These included his standpoint on the role of secular music in devotional recitation, his attitude towards Muharram as a period of moral exception, and his dissenting, but not defamatory, views regarding Shi'i practices of public mourning.

These moral thresholds, that manifested from feeling the surface tension of public sentiment, differ from Laura Ring's powerful ethnography of women's spaces in a Karachi apartment building, where the "nonresolution of tension" is central to making peace in the everyday.[8] Instead, competitive displays of individuality, like Idris's dial tone, become a way of challenging the ethics and equilibria that exist between faiths and communities of practice. Where moral thresholds are a question of unresolved tension is in relation to the broader question of consensus over the public place of Islam or what Muhammad Qasim Zaman calls the "hardening of boundaries" between minority and majoritarian faiths.[9] Idris's dial tone was a provocative attempt to locate himself at this limit of unresolved tension. Thresholds like these are forged by pressing oneself up to the surface tension of public sentiment and feeling the boundaries of toleration; on one side lies an often-fraught equilibrium and on the other side communal strife.

Concealment and Revelation

On the morning of the ninth of Muharram all of Hall Road's modular units were shuttered, their lattice grills hiding darkened staircases. Over at Lahore's last working film studio, the picture was much the same. Muharram is also a period of moral exception in the film industry, due to it being comprised of many Shi'i actors and directors, many of whom refrain from recording musical sequences from the first of the month until the commemorations that mark the fortieth day after Ashura, known in Pakistan as Chehlum [Arba'een in Arabic]. On television, entertainment channels refrain from broadcasting films and music and rolling news channels change their color schemes and scrolling news tickers to shades of red and black. In the gaps between programming, many channels play video recitations of laments with dramatic green-screen animations situating the orator on the desolate battlefield of Karbala. In the absence of musical instrumentation other techniques are used to expand the acoustic space, including echo and reverb effects on vocals. These conditions coalesce to give Muharram in Lahore a very particular emotional atmosphere produced both by the state—which is required to provide expansive security arrangements for public processions—and sustained by religious others whose beliefs and practices often do not align. In this case, Muharram as a period of moral exception provides an atmosphere conducive to the circulation of *azadari*. Meaning "the doing of mourning," azadari is a central tenet of Shi'i Islam and refers both to practices of mourning and to the creation of an atmosphere conducive to this collective mourning for Imam Hussain. Writing on Shi'i traditions of lamentation, Mahmoud Ayoub suggests there exists a doctrine of redemption in Shi'i Islam. Writing shortly before the Iranian revolution, after which Shi'i mourning became entangled in its revolutionary project, Ayoub describes "fulfilment through suffering," an action-centered, rather than emotion-centered form of grief.[10]

Despite his interest in the atmospheres and emotions of azadari, Ayoub's attribution of redemptive suffering to Shi'i mourning aligns too easily with the social-contractual ways that death is bound up with the promises of redemption in Euro-American philosophy, theology, and political thought. Whether it was the force of empathy, providing condolement, appealing to adjudication, or calling for justice, the situations that my Shi'i interlocutors attempted to bring about through azadari became a kind of mediated mourning that was also directed towards non-Shi'a in the here and now. This mediated mourning expands in all directions, variously bridging gulfs and blocking paths, and challenges the usual distinction between grief as an internally felt emotion and mourning as its outward manifestation. It does not pursue an end but in its subjunctive state aims to widen the zone of activity through which new forms and possibilities might take shape in the wake of death. It does this by reconfiguring what is present and what is absent from public perception.

For example, the first ten days of Muharram, when celebratory performance forms such as music or film are considered an ill fit with the period of communal mourning, are the only time when a type of usually concealed image is seen in the public sphere. I had only seen figurative representations of the Shi'i Imams Ali and Hussain once in Lahore before Muharram, in the locked storehouse of a Shi'i *hussainiya*, or prayer hall, where inherited wooden models of the mausoleum of Imam Hussain used in ritual processions are kept.[11] I had been taken there by Nameer, a friend whose family owned a hereditary license to take out public processions during Muharram. He had been taking a young colleague in the marketing firm he had established on a tour of his neighborhood, and, having run

Figure 4.1 A cover of a DVD showing the kind of material brought into view and sold on Hall Road during the commemoration of Muharram. (From the author's collection.)

into me in the Walled City, agreed to take both of us to his family *haveli* [a traditional townhouse or mansion]. When the month of Muharram came around, Nameer's haveli was filled with mourners, and the storehouse was used as a stage from which orators delivered laments and elegies. During the first ten days of Muharram every year, he and his father bring out a gallery of framed pictures collected over a century or more and passed down the generations like their hereditary license. Nameer's family heirlooms, pictures of Hussain brought back from Karbala and Najaf in Iraq and from journeys to Iran, were partly concealed during the daytime and uncovered during processions and communal worship. That day when he opened the door of the storeroom, his young colleague, a Sunni Muslim with little exposure to the practices of those outside his community, was surprised by the sight of human faces in a room where holy objects and texts were kept. He was particularly perplexed by the claim that one framed image was supposed to depict Imam Ali, the cousin and son-in-law of the Prophet Muhammad. He iterated that there are no pictures of Imam Ali, nor is it permissible for the family or companions of the Prophet to be depicted. Understanding the rising tension, Nameer closed the door of the storehouse and assured his colleague that the image is *khayaali*—imagined—and that before Ayatollah Khomeni's rule in Iran there were even coins struck with an image of Imam Ali.

The tentative reconfiguration of what is present and what is absent also affected Hall Road and the Shi'i media that traders appropriated for sale. While Idris was keen to demarcate and disclose his own ambient boundaries, many traders in the basement DVD markets were taking down their customer-facing discs showing films, music compilations, and pornography. For the first ten days of Muharram, they stocked professionally filmed Shi'i remembrance gatherings featuring laments and elegies produced and released by media producers who often operate near Shi'i places of worship or shrines associated with Shi'i communities. This incremental transformation saw a temporary repertoire of Muharram-appropriate materials occupy the threshold between media usually in circulation and that which was suitable to the annual period of moral exception. One trader, Qasim, who manned a store called Kasur CD House, was eager to suggest I write about this Shi'i media, particularly, "how they punish themselves for killing Imam Hussain." His advice drew upon the defamatory misrepresentation held by many non-Shi'a in Pakistan that demonstrative acts of grief and bodily mortification are acts of public penance. On the contrary, Islamic history is clear that Hussain and his followers were killed by the armies of the Umayyad caliph Yazid. Closely tethered to this seismic event, azadari and its media are seen by Shi'i adherents as a bridge between the emotional atmosphere of communal grief and the virtues and personages of the Imams and the Ahl-e Bait.

Hasan Mir, a producer of recordings of sermons, recitations, and processions significant to his local Shi'i neighborhood, saw his procession videos appropriated by traders on Hall Road, who purchased discs from his store and used them as master copies to create their own Muharram-specific repertoire of content. Yet he did not complain of copyright infringement or lost revenue. His desire to start his store in the 1980s, while working as an expatriate laborer in the Gulf, was to spread azadari within and beyond his community. His guiding sentiments were well expressed by the motto "#AzadariNoCopyright" that his son Haider hashtagged on Facebook whenever reposting videos of famous Shi'i orators. One particular shareable image of the motto in circulation across Shi'i social media pages was accompanied by a short couplet: "One flame lights another and the chain continues. Whether we live or die, azadari remains." When uploading rare recordings of long-deceased Shi'i orators to YouTube, Hasan Mir appealed in the comments box for viewers to save and re-upload the recordings. He did this because of the frequency with which his data storage devices had broken down or with which he had seen platforms and file types become unreadable. Predicting its unfettered onward circulation, each of Hasan Mir's releases of local Shi'i processions began and ended with an identification of their origin. A short segment showed him performing ritual self-flagellation with a tangle of curved blades. After a period of intense bloodletting, there was a brief shot of two pre-teen boys doing so with much shorter blades, including his eldest son Haider.

When I met Haider, he was in his mid-twenties, taking his undergraduate degree in engineering from a Lahore university. When Muharram came around, he would resign from his night-job at a call center, unable to keep up his commitments to his community at the same time. Haider explained that just like ritual mourning, the circulation of recorded material publicizes and magnifies condolences to the Ahl-e Bait and those mourned during Muharram. Hall Road traders, he explained, make such media commensurable with Alid piety in the public sphere by abstracting it from its context.

They take our recordings and put their logo underneath. They've removed the ritual flagellation at the beginning and end and even turned our watermark black to hide it. Our logo is still slightly visible there, but we don't say anything to anyone. The more the public sees it the better it is. It is azadari and there is no need to take any action . . . After all, for them, Muharram lasts from the first to the tenth of the month. For us it lasts from the first of Muharram to the thirtieth of Al-Haj [the entire lunar calendar].

While Haider found the lost revenue no cause for complaint, his father made a moral distinction between intimacy with the recording and its mediated experience. Hasan Mir would warn me that such recordings of busy processions and religious gatherings are characterized by the kind of "noise [*shorr*]" that can only be enjoyed by those present at the moment of recording. He explained that the enjoyment is only for those who have the "mahaul" fresh in their mind, still ringing in their ears and reverberating in their hearts. It was this added ingredient of mahaul that drew them towards the recordings he described as "*live*."[12]

Hasan Mir's identification of a good moral atmosphere recalls the ways in which Nida Kirmani's interlocutors conceptualized mahaul and identified it as a variable boundary that possesses the impression of fixity.[13] In

Kirmani's fieldsite, a mahaul is shaped by the call to prayer, by clothing, cuisine, and institutions and infrastructures for prayer and worship. This good mahaul sticks with you, reminds you of your roots and values when distant from the place you associate with its emanation.[14] In the instances in which Kirmani's interlocutors did not identify a community in whose conviviality they could find membership, they did recognize a mahaul that acted as a temporary container for persons, things, and ideas, that could feel just as binding.[15] The ways in which Hasan Mir described atmosphere mediated by its elicitation of liveness also underline the importance, raised in the previous chapter, of understanding the magnitudes that make thresholds recognizable as levels of intensity.[16] For Hasan Mir "noise" possesses an atmosphere that evinces the mundanity of co-presence with divine figures, fellow worshippers, or ethical exemplars. This recalls the work of Inayat Khan, who wrote, "There is another world besides the world that our physical eyes can see and whose sound our physical ears can hear, and it is not even very far away . . . This is the world of the atmosphere . . . It is something we feel; it is something that will touch our body. And though the body may not perceive it, yet it is influenced by it."[17] This quality of aeriality that mediates between the opacity of minds and the transparency of physical bodies, takes shape through ideas like liveness.

By speaking of mahaul in the positive, Hasan Mir also made direct reference to its inverse. Aware of the similarity in appearance between his religious media store and the film and music traders on Hall Road, he was eager to emphasize, "It is all *deeni* [faith-based] CD and cassette work. I don't do film." So influential was his enterprise, as the only production company that recorded the processions and mourning gatherings around the Walled City of Lahore, that Hasan Mir had long been the one who decided where that very threshold between film and faith lies in the context of religious media. "You won't find songs or singing here," he would often iterate. "We've never done that, since the beginning." It is among producers and traders in religious media, who must factor in the negative associations many have with the film and music stores with whom they may bear more than a passing resemblance, where the sale of audio and visual content is most acutely sensitive to moral atmosphere.[18]

Leaning on the relationship between film and music to define good practices by negative comparison is commonly heard in the critiques of some popular devotional na'at recitations praising the Prophet Muhammad, and in the anxieties around other devotional genres that incorporate film songs, such as *bandiri* in Northern Nigeria and Hindu forms of recitation.[19] For traders in religious media, a part of this ethical labor is to define what secular media is in Pakistan, so as to define what their media is not. The threshold between film, singing, and entertainment on the one side and pious moving-image media on the other is socially and materially constituted as a space of normative inversion.[20] In the circulation of religious media, mahaul as atmosphere acts as both a prophylactic and a magnet towards which the good in ambiguous media environments might flow. Pathways to impermissibility—with the faithful halting before crossing the threshold—must be well-trodden to gain an intimate understanding of the precipice to identify the guises through which it might be unintentionally crossed.

Atmospheres also animate scholarship on Shi'ism in South Asia. Atmosphere has been seen as the reason that majlis sermons can be both polysemic and draw a common repertoire of responses from its congregants.[21] Atmosphere has also been seen as indicative of tipping points towards communal violence that provided a reason for colonial intervention.[22] Throughout recent scholarship on Shi'i practice also lies evidence of the existence of a co-produced boundary between permissible and impermissible practice, such as the "fine line" between veneration and deification of devotional objects.[23] Toby Howarth, in his study of Shi'i oration in the Indian city of Hyderabad, discusses the heightened awareness held by orators of the criticisms levelled at the practices they represent. Orators are required to possess an awareness of where the threshold lies in the eyes of the others, and in the interpretation of prevailing Shi'i consensus. Howarth gives the metaphor of two riverbanks that demarcate the boundaries of how such pious expression may flow, guiding orators on exactly who is fit to speak and what they are permitted to say.[24] The performative event is an essential part of the production of moral thresholds. Syed Akbar Hyder documents examples of orators in the Indian subcontinent displaying caution to ensure that their audiences—or potential detractors—did not feel their orators had crossed the threshold into theatrical performance.[25] In another instance, while laments are often performed in the present tense to conjure a sense of immediacy and intimacy with the Ahl-e Bait, there is also a compulsion towards restraint, to guard against listeners becoming overwhelmed. Hyder calls this "the informal pact" that exists between orators and their audiences.[26] These felt limits and boundaries, even in their circulation beyond the bounds of Shi'i communities, recreate the boundaries that undergird periods of moral exception, giving a fleeting sense of certainty at times when there is no affordance for debate or contestation.

Moral thresholds within Shi'i media also exist in anticipation of their reception by unknown, particularly non-kin, others, the most pronounced reception being the general interdiction towards recording female participants in commemorative events. A message that appeared on the page of the orator Zakir Ghulam Abbas, and circulated widely on Shi'a Facebook sites, summed up these concerns, "Attention all believers, women, and patrons of the majlis. Make strict arrangements for your female committees to ban making videos [during the majlis]. This includes participants making their own videos on mobiles. If someone makes a video, delete it, because the enemies of azadari are editing these videos for their satanic purposes. Send this message to every *azadar* [ritual mourner]."

Despite these anxieties over misuse, for Shi'i media traders the value of devotional media is enacted in their circulation. Perhaps because of his

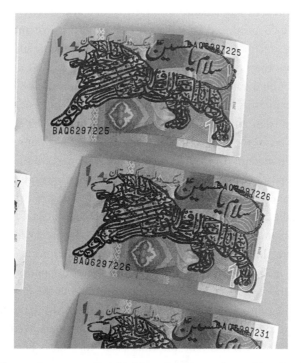

Figure 4.2 Ten-rupee notes stamped with a salutation to Imam Hussain, designed to circulate during Muharram. (From the author's collection.)

insistence on circulation rather than profit, Hasan Mir could no longer economically rely on electronic media. For some years he had come to specialize in devotional materials and paraphernalia, including prayer shawls, armbands, and shackles worn to recall the bondage endured by those at Karbala. Aside from encouraging the spread of his procession recordings, he also exchanged ten-rupee notes for notes he had stamped with a salutation to Imam Hussain, so that they could circulate within his neighborhood and beyond during the first ten days of Muharram. The materiality of Hasan Mir's stamped notes illuminates how the media environment during Muharram is formed. A particular moral atmosphere is created by adapting things already in circulation in the belief that such changes will expand to the environmental space of their exchange. In its direct form, this gesture also demands a contract of commensuration from the recipient who, by choosing to accept this defaced currency, runs the risk of its possible economic devaluation and removal from further onward circulation.

Circulating Guardianship

On the ninth day of Muharram devotees from villages surrounding Lahore journeyed to the shrine of Bibi Pak Daman in the center of the city. As they passed through the security bottleneck, they came to a commodity zone packed thick with stalls selling devotional items from beneath the awnings and behind the jangling *zanjeer* [lit. chains, referring to blades for ritual flagellation] of small modular stores. The market is a prominent center of public leisure for local Shi'i. Behind its security cordons and roadblocks, it felt almost akin to a gated community. One day, walking down the narrow market street that led to the shrine, I heard a women's majlis taking place behind a thick black curtain, held by members of the Twelver Shi'i community who are the primary, but not only, adherents of the shrine which is also shared with Sunni worshippers and Sufi devotees whose allegiance to jurisprudential schools can often be ambiguous or undefined. Pakistani Shi'a believe the shrine is the resting place of several pious women including Ruqqayah bint Ali, the niece of Imam Hussain, who was said to have made her way to Lahore from Iraq after the Battle of Karbala. Outside, while the women's majlis took place, a contingent of black-clad men signalled their arrival to the shrine with recited greetings to the women buried in the shrine, before removing their shimmering black polyester tops to reveal backs deeply etched with diagonal scars from earlier acts of flagellation. Together the men recited a popular lament, with the wavering yet consistent tune of the lamentation repeating itself to powerful off-beat slaps on bare skin, like a deep, raw, and elastic bass note thundering on the lowest register.

Despite the security guards' strict prohibition of cameras, anyone assembled who was not participating lifted their smartphones in the air, recording the bodily gestures of communal mourning. Inside, men pressed their phones against the black curtain capturing the women's majlis on their smartphones' built-in sound recorders. So resonant and affective was the demonstration of grief that one could not help but want to retain what visitors referred to as a *nishani* [memento] of the immediacy of the event. Fulfilling this demand, a number of Shi'i cassette and video houses beside the shrine had long offered new and old recordings of majalis, procession footage, compilations of laments, recitations, and documentaries. Due to the demographics of the area and its visitors, most of the recordings were

Figure 4.3 A Shi'i cassette and video house in the market beside the shrine of Bibi Pak Daman in Lahore. (Photo by author.)

in the Punjabi or Saraiki languages. The oldest store in the area, Jaffriyah Video House, was run by Tahir Jafri, who had collected, reproduced, and retrieved majlis recordings since the mid-1980s. Behind his counter was a collage of rare Shi'i poster art, all sourced from journeys to Iran, and unavailable in the commodity zone beside him. In the same spirit, the visibility of the videocassettes—master copies of recordings made by himself and his brother—boasted of the antiquity they had at their disposal. Over the last thirty years as many as a dozen cassette and video houses came and went, leaving Jafri's the oldest in the market.

In the late 1970s, home recording technology and the availability of removable magnetic tape cassettes allowed people to document events that were important to them. What was previously the remit of the elite, the act of commissioning records of events, became widely available and affordable, the residual effect of which is visible today in the widespread use of smartphones to capture and circulate images, video, and sounds. Like the digital present, analog home recording media reconciled individuals to the social solidarities inculcated by the circulation of the audio- or videocassette. During the era that audio- and videocassette hardware was widely adopted in Pakistan, broadcast television programming was dominated by the theocratic and ideological hallmarks of General Zia-ul-Haq's state, where Pakistani Shi'a, increasingly the target of polemic and physical attacks, found tools for creating their own media trajectories.

I was surprised to learn that Jafri was also in possession of perhaps the most notable omission from the Hall Road repertoire, Jamil Dehlavi's *The Blood of Hussain* (1980), a film that remains unofficially banned in Pakistan and whose reputation circulates more tangibly than physical copies. Usually, searching out this legendary film turns up only second-hand information, yet its presence continued to resonate—like an overheard rumor—through the history of the cinema in Pakistan. Filmed in and around Punjab and the Walled City of Lahore in 1977, *The Blood of Hussain* is an allegorical tale of revolutionary struggle against injustice and oppression and unfolds against the backdrop of Muharram commemorations. Faced with a military coup, a local landowner refuses to recognize the new regime and, like the historical personage of Imam Hussain, flees with his family and followers towards an uncertain future. Dehlavi's observations proved to be startlingly prophetic. One month after the shooting of the film was completed, the Pakistani military, led by General Zia-ul-Haq, took power in a coup d'état and imposed martial law. Even during

Figure 4.4 The one-hundred-rupee note entrusted to Tahir Jafri. When it was legal tender in the 1950s, the note would have been worth a significant amount. To some of my interlocutors the safekeeping of Pakistani films or religious media was comparable to collecting or keeping paper Pakistani currency once they fell out of circulation. (Photo by author.)

production Dehlavi was accused of subversive activity, but when martial law was declared, the filmmaker's passport was seized. With great difficulty, he managed to send the unedited material out of the country, before himself relocating to the United Kingdom to complete postproduction. Paradoxically, it is during Muharram, when films and music temporarily dissipate from the Hall Road repertoire, that Jafri prepares as many copies as he can from his own videocassette of Dehlavi's *The Blood of Hussain*. At that time, his was perhaps one of the only master copies of the film in Pakistan, acquired from a relative who recorded it from a late-night television broadcast in the United Kingdom in the 1990s. His copies came complete with his own censorial excisions of scenes of nudity that he found incommensurable with the moral atmosphere his store aimed to cultivate.

For Jafri, his collection was both a personal archive and a reserve on standby for future deployment. He defined the act of collecting, preserving, and shifting recordings onto new carriers as "guardianship on behalf of the community" [*imanat hai quam ki*]. The anthropology of Shi'ism has paid great attention to this kind of activism and advocacy, allowing piety and politics to play off on one another.[27] For Jafri, circulation was closely entangled with the agency of its mediation, and the disputed power relations involved with custodianship and inheritance. "In Pakistan," he told me, "every new government tries to destroy the previous government's data." And to illustrate his point he took out a one-hundred-rupee note from the 1950s. A local boy was given it by his employers, and he in turn gave it to Jafri. "Now we are talking about old things," he said, "not about media. You can see that this is a dark side of our society. These old things are our culture and they do come back." That Jafri was seen as the man in the market most worthy to be entrusted with "old things" underlines how media for recording and distribution amplified the prestige usually associated with mediating religious sensations. There remained great value to being the mediator of prized, rare, or high-brow religious content among trader-guardians like Jafri, without whose efforts at safekeeping they would not have survived. With their reputations in the market closely aligned with the analog formats that made their name, these stores distinguished themselves from other traders of audio- and videodiscs by their collections of master copies of recordings of processions, gatherings, and laments. The strategies they employed in the marketplace and within their communities aimed at retaining their position as trusted guardians of valued objects relating both to the past and the proselytization and publicity of communal belief.

Jafri's daily routine consisted of fulfilling customers' requests for majlis sermons new and old, *marsiya* elegiac poems, or *noha* laments while monitoring the little green bar on his desktop computer that showed the progress of customers' USB and microSD cards being filled with curated content. These requests might span time periods, languages, and national and international points of origin. In his trade, the difficulty of retrieval is paired with the physical and organizational effort of recording and duplication. Jafri remembered that "during the cassette era there was a lot of demand . . . demand still exists but an atmosphere of disrespect has come . . . Previously people would come from far away, as far as Karachi, to buy the recordings. They would come from so far to procure it and there was a lot of hard work in that procurement. In turn, they would put a similar amount of hard work in keeping it safe."

While the substance of demand had remained the same, Jafri saw an increase in platforms for the accessibility of devotional media correspond with a decrease in moral, devotional, and disciplinary virtues. Jafri associated this decline with changes in listening and viewing habits. Jafri remembered when half a dozen people would sit together and listen to majlis cassettes and videos. For him, these modes of consumption had been disrupted by the personalization of the smartphone, which allows one to listen while on the way to work or while doing other tasks. As a much cherished reminder of the cassette era, his store aimed to recreate these deliberative conditions. The bench in Jafri's store was a diverse meeting place of different classes, castes, and professions. The leather-cushioned seat acted as a waiting area for customers while their requests for the reproduction and compilation of content was fulfilled, either by loading up a USB or memory card with digital content, or by making copies from a master disc or cassette. The act of loading files provided a small break from the back and forth of the market. Jafri's decision to retain the long bench in a

Figure 4.5 The interior of Jaffriyah Video House. The waiting bench, used by customers since the cassette era while requested content was copied from master copies, was also a place of discussion and debate over newer styles of devotional recitation. (Photo by author.)

Figure 4.6 Tahir Jafri searches through cassette master copies to fulfil a customer's request for a majlis given by a particular orator in the 1980s. (Photo by author.)

store so greatly starved of storage space aimed to produce an inviting and homely atmosphere for the discussion and consumption of Shi'i media. While copying many hours of audio and video files to memory cards took much less time than the minute-for-minute copying of analog media, my time spent waiting with others for devotional content to be digitized from cassette master-copies or loaded onto microSD cards suggested that the durational exercise of waiting was still associated with being provided with an object of great spiritual value.

Jafri referred to these objects as the "assets" of the Shi'i *qaum* [nation, community] and, for him, the best way to ensure the continued existence of these assets was to distribute them across as many formats as possible. Jafri remembered the first footage of Shi'ism in the public sphere were the televised sermons of Rasheed Turabi. If it were not for majlis collectors like him, who managed to share and distribute recordings, the footage would have languished in the fiercely guarded and largely inaccessible PTV archives. He blamed this mindset on the problems of inheritance and custodianship in the political sphere. "During Zia-ul-Haq's time they destroyed all the data made in [the preceding Prime Minister] Zulfiqar Ali Bhutto's time. Every new government tries to destroy the previous government's data. When politics gets personal, important things get lost," he told me. From the dozen cassette and video houses around the shrine of Bibi Pak Daman, most had closed a few years after Pakistan saw widespread connectivity to the internet. Jafri explained that without the weight of a reserve of original material behind them and without the importance of the connection between those doing the recording and its reproduction, other traders' roles as mediators were nullified when they were only able to trade copies of content easily procured on the internet. Jafri was not afraid of circulation undermining any rights he had over the monetary value of his recordings. Instead, he was sensitive to the intimate connection between the recording itself and the labor of guardianship. What he described as "guardianship on behalf of the community" was predicated on the logic of demand, as nuanced by its location among the Shi'a qaum, rather than the public awaam, as arbiters of public morality.

Amplification and Immediacy

As we spoke, evening fell, and the exposed light bulbs of the Bibi Pak Daman market lit up the night with a piercing brightness. Two women and their children came in and sat down, massaging the soles of their feet. They had come barefoot to the shrine from a village north of Lahore. Exhausted, they asked Jafri for a glass of water, which he had already reached over to pour. To the younger woman, whose small baby bivouacked beneath her thick shawl, clung a young boy: thin, shy, serious, and no older than six. The women sat down next to me on the waiting bench and sipped the cup of water that Jafri had given them while the boy addressed him in a quiet and focused manner. It seemed he had been preparing for some time for what he would say. He asked for videodiscs of Shi'i orators because he wanted to become one himself. He did not want audio content because he wanted to see the orator and learn by imitating his rhetorical style and gestures.

When they left, Jafri packed the paper-covered discs they had flicked through back into bundles and sighed, "Nowadays the copying style is very popular." He had come to the realization that circulation preserves but also inhibits change and originality. Previously, orators would recruit and train adherents through direct oral mentorship. He explained, "Nowadays people just buy discs from here and start reciting. No one tells them that they have proven that they can recite. With the change in technology the orator's job has become easier. When there were no amplifiers, they would have had to exert more energy." Usually calm, strong, and forceful in the clarity of his ideas, Jafri found himself uncertain of how to historicize the influence of marketplace recording companies, having never been asked to trace their development. Caught between a preference for less elite forms of recitation, with their roots in vernacular Punjabi, on the one hand, and the authorized transmission of knowledge that comes from teacher–student relationships, on the other, Jafri appeared surprised to find himself in a network of circulation and amplitude that mediates the tradition of *ustad* [teacher] and *shagird* [student] for those who may not be visible to each other face-to-face. He was struck by the paradox. For him, while copying distributes knowledge widely, electronic mediation submerges the immediacy of presence that gives majlis orations an affective force. Perhaps this is why some Shiʿi cassette and video houses preferred to deal in live rather than studio recordings. Studio recordings, of laments and panegyric elegies, are insulated from the good moral qualities of a Shiʿi mahaul that Jafri sought in recordings. In his live recordings, he and his customers felt the presence and participation of other co-present believers and the benefits of being among them.

As a trader and guardian of primarily analog recordings of orators, Jafri was an exception in the marketplace. Other traders of his era managed to keep their businesses alive by continuing as videographers of Shiʿi events but for broadcast on livestreaming platforms in which the qualities of liveness remained a central ingredient in simulating co-presence. As a new arm of Shiʿi media production, these videographers and the social networks they manage have come to be known as "Azadari Networks." Like their forebears, their recordings are built on feedback, striving to mediate the felt co-presence of fellow worshippers or important exemplars like the Imams and the Ahl-e Bait, and communicate through multiple technological interfaces, such as Facebook Live, WhatsApp, and YouTube. Gesturing towards the shrine of Bibi Pak Daman, Jafri told me, "Last night there was a majlis being watched all over the world. For the last two years more and more networks on the internet are playing all of it live. Previously it would only be those present inside the majlis. Now the audience includes the live people. But you don't get that sense of awe and *rohaniyat* [spirituality] . . . There are even specific sects within our community who say that the live should not happen."

Despite marking his distance from the conservativism of some of his peers, Jafri had his own reservations about "the live" as temporal co-presence. This is because it is not simultaneity of presence, being together at the same time and watching the same thing, that matters to faith, but the extent to which a recording captures the atmosphere of the majlis, procession, or recitation. For Jafri, the liveness of online broadcast loses its "spirituality" when the intention and reception of liveness is predetermined by international social media networks.

While for Jafri live broadcasts flattened the magnitude of awe that gave a majlis oration its affective force, for Hasan Mir the technical conditions of recording possessed their own affective means of persuasion, place-making, and moral atmosphere. As the first ten days of Muharram reached their climax, all attention in Lahore turned to the Mochi Gate area of the Walled City, and to Hasan Mir's Shiʿa-majority area known to its residents as the Mohalla Shian. A *mohalla* describes a neighborhood of an urban quarter which usually carries with it the implication of a caste identity. While the boundaries of districts are delimited by local government for the purposes of elections or taxation, a mohalla is porous to the changes in social or corporate groups identified by profession or religious affiliation. As the Day of Ashura approached, one unnamed street—the widest in the area—was resplendent in flowing black flags. There, Hasan Mir's store smelled more overwhelmingly of rose petals than ever, a product of the home-bottled spray he had made from pure extract and water, decanted into a large Coca-Cola bottle affixed with a spray nozzle. He told me it was made locally, explaining that even perfumes that say on the package that they are from the United Arab Emirates are all made in the bazaar next to his. "This is just rose; it's not so precious [*Gulab hai, gulab nehaab to nahin hai*]," he said. Opening a branded bottle from under the counter, he lifted it to my nose. "Now smell the original. The public can't tell the difference."

Hasan Mir claimed to have been the first to have hit upon the idea of recording majlis and processions at the nearby Nisar Haveli and on the streets surrounding his store. What began as a strategy for remembering the Ahl-e Bait through recording technologies soon turned into a thriving marketplace for religious media. He decided to become a videographer in the early 1980s, when he worked with a contingent of the Pakistan Army in Saudi Arabia. There, Ashura processions and public mourning were strictly regulated, having been banned in much of the country since the early twentieth century. Returning home for a year between 1984 and 1985 he recorded Ashura processions for the first time on videocassette on the street in which he lived. Hasan Mir brought back hardware from the

Gulf unavailable in such quality and quantity in Pakistan outside the state-owned television and radio network. During his time abroad, he rarely ate and quit smoking so that he could buy audio- and videocassettes at a time when their legal import had been left ambiguous by the Zia regime in Pakistan. When I met him, he kept a few behind the counter as mementoes of the time, still sealed in a crisp blue Sony-brand plastic wrapping.

What Hasan Mir continued to find so special about his personal archive of recordings was the addition of mahaul, the sense of locality, a feeling of proximity, but also a sense of moral atmosphere. Picking up a DVD copy of the 1984 procession he told me about the traces of the contemporary Shi'i public it captured, the memories of those men and women now departed, and his own presence on the streets, improvising techniques of sound and video recording for such a large and dispersed event. Editing in-camera, rather than in a postproduction unit, he was able to begin making copies as soon as the event was over. The public, by which he meant those who attended the event and wished to own a keepsake of it, saw in the roughness and contingency of his technique something that resonated with the atmosphere that defines that mohalla as Shi'a. They also perceived something else in the recording, something hard to put into words but something that transcended the events it captured. "*Live* has a *mahaul* of its own [*Live ka apna hi mahaul hota hai*]," he told me.[28]

Unlike Tahir Jafri, Hasan Mir remained adamant that there was a radical subjectivity to the moral atmosphere of communal mourning and its "noise" that was impossible to mediate.[29] The theoretical problem of the presence of *live* in this sense, is also one which strives to understand whether such media are capacious enough to hold both the individual and the stranger.[30] This sense of being attuned to the moral presence of difference plays an important role in the identification of moral atmospheres, creating both ambiguity that can sustain everyday interaction and certitude for periods of moral exception, such as for Muharram, in which lines between permissible and impermissible must be more clearly drawn.

Sustained and held together by the kind of thresholds that Idris's dial tone was keen to provoke, Muharram is an uncanny state of exception. I have borrowed the term "moral exception" from Samuli Schielke, writing on how Ramadan in Egypt provides an intermission to the ambivalence with which many outwardly practice their faith throughout the year. Unlike Ramadan, Muharram is mediated by a precarious minority community, by Shi'i material culture, devotional laments, on- and offline media networks, and broadcasters, which come together through affective holding patterns. One of these is the Shiʻi concept of azadari, that makes mourning and condolement convincing and persuasive to those not in its grip. The mediated mourning of azadari also helps to define states of exception differently, perhaps beyond the political, as that which cultivates solidarity rather than cements sovereignty.

As suggested by Hasan Mir's preference for liveness, in contrast to the ways in which moving-image media is described as harboring a bad mahaul, Shiʻi media traders speak of atmosphere as a positive attribute to media. For many, the rough grain, shaky sound, grainy images, and proximate bodies in recordings of ritual processions can evoke the positive affects of a religious collective. As indicated in the introduction to this book, the first time I became aware of the positive moral attributes of recording the atmosphere of Shiʻi events marked the turning point in my Lahore research. The more time I spent with Shiʻi media traders the more I realized, when previously I was unable to understand my attraction to the palimpsestic surfaces and visual noise of mass-copied film on Hall Road, that my own ethnographic interest in the qualities of live recordings was part of an overarching concern with how affect can be mediated through a reorganization of the usual hierarchy of what is present and what is absent.

CHAPTER V

The Absorptive City

Hall Road's Urban Form

S tanding at a newspaper stand beside the Lahore Zoo, I remembered
the stories I had been told of the days when Hall Road was a byword
for the reproduction, retrieval, and sale of Pakistani films. Apparently,
the animals thrived on the tinny vocals and deep bass of Punjabi-language
filmi music that managed to reach them from traders' sound systems over one
kilometer away. To a question from one reader to the film magazine *Shama*
in the early 1990s, asking for advice on how to get into the industry, the
editors answered, "Move to Lahore." This was a time when film was in
the air.

In the weekly film newspaper *Rang-o-Roop* I was reading that day, a
group of leading film artists and television stars were calling for the public
hanging of a suspect in the recent rape and murder of a child in the nearby
city of Kasur. As I read on, I began to hear the heavy drawl of low-fidelity
amplifiers and the rough grain of urgent voices coming from Hall Road.
I put the paper down and walked towards Regal Chowk. When I arrived, I
saw the preamble of a large public meeting at the entrance to Hall Road,
rather than finding any amplified film music. A canopy had been erected
over a single line of tables facing outwards towards Zaitoon Plaza, one of
the largest and oldest shopping centers on the street. Hung on top of the
canopy, a banner featured a series of macabre pictures purporting to represent the violence then raging against Rohingya Muslims in Myanmar's
Rakhine State, while a caption implored the Pakistani government to act.

Figure 5.1 A man reads Pakistani film magazine *Rang-o-Roop* outside a newspaper stand on Lahore's Mall Road. (Photo by author.)

Another banner in black and red, evidently representing the murder in Kasur, featured an image of a girl with an adult male's hands clasped tightly over her mouth, its borders fringed in dripping blood. As someone dropped a purple fifty-rupee note into a clear plastic donation box steadily filling up with cash, a man seated in the center of a dozen others nodded solemnly. The small throng of white-clothed men gave the tent the feel of a pop-up abattoir, fenced in as they were by all the gore and horror around them.

An edition of the *Tajir Log Lahore* [Lahore Tradespeople] newspaper was being handed out to coincide with the demonstration. Its cover, emblazoned with the edition's sponsor, "Khidmat Group, Hall Road," showed graphic, grainy photographs intended to evoke outrage over the violence in Myanmar and the murder in Kasur. Atrocity images were once a familiar sight on the slew of rolling-news channels which had long competed for the most graphic and sensational footage of the decades-long insurgencies that had blighted Pakistan with sporadic and ferocious violence. Even on quieter days, a tangle of banners hung between the buildings of Hall Road. The most prominent banners, usually situated at the entrance to the street from Regal Chowk and the Mall, were festooned with the face of Kamran Mehsud and the name of his organization, the Khidmat Group, a combined traders' union, charity, welfare organization, and development firm. The gore and the outrage of that day's banners were erected to coincide with upcoming elections for the street's trade union representative, pitting the established Anjuman-e Tajiran [Union of Traders] against the newer Khidmat Group.

In the previous chapter, atmospheres in Shi'i media practice became both intimately local in their liveness and objects of national concern in their centrality to periods of moral exception. This chapter asks how the experience of urban form holds together these kinds of public affects and provides a heuristic for people to conceive of the political character of atmosphere. In the instances explored so far in this book, the disquiet or solidarity expressed by identifying atmospheres shifts alongside auditory, visual, and material repertoires. These repertoires can be mined as sources of public affect that attempt to locate consensus in already existing flows. Take, for example, the issue of the *Lahore Tajir Log* that coincided with the rally held to gather support for the Muslim victims of violence in Myanmar. On the cover of the special edition of the magazine—printed to coincide with the demonstration—grainy and pixelated photographs illustrated and attempted to draw an emotive response. A closer look revealed that one photo depicted dozens of burned bodies from an attack in Nigeria by Boko Haram and another a Tibetan man self-immolating at an anti-China demonstration, while another showed a heavily pixelated pile of animal carcasses intended to evoke butchered human corpses.

On Hall Road, such appeals to public opinion and outrage play out against the backdrop of a wider battle for recognition, authority, and patronage. This chapter examines how these claims are often tied to the street's urban form and how they, in turn, come to shape the circulation and reproduction of Pakistani entertainment media. This follows the logic of the book so far and its argument that the atmospheres shaped and mediated by media environments like Hall Road are central to the stakes at play in the contestation over the public place of Islam in Pakistan.

Khidmat and the "New Pakistan"

Those responsible for the panoply of banners that united the street in outrage, the Khidmat Group and their leader Kamran Mehsud, were less a union and more a loose professional guild known for getting things done. Meaning "service," the word *khidmat* also has connotations of religious philanthropy and has long been used by members of the merchant middle-class to refer to an idea of corporate social responsibility undergirded by Islamic faith.[1] For political parties vying for votes, the Khidmat Group were also mediators of clientelism. To their detractors, they were known as the "plaza mafia," whose actions were seen as abetting the destruction of Lahore's architectural heritage, or as the largest of several *"qabza* groups," using a term meaning occupation, possession, or encroachment. A plaza is a cheaply constructed vertical bazaar formed of modular units for small-scale traders, often electronics or clothing retailers, who run workshops, ateliers, or storefronts, as well as draw upon other providers in the same building for craftwork, repair, or wholesale trade. Demand for plazas grew with the segmentation of electronic media and the trade in its constituent parts and hardware.

Approaches to social welfare or public service have taken two distinct trajectories since the birth of Pakistan in 1947. The first motif is what the country's first prime minister, Liaquat Ali Khan, referred to as "Islamic socialism," that he posited as a third way between capitalism and communism. Having long established itself as an American ally and capitalist bulwark against Cold War-era Soviet expansion, Pakistan's Islamic socialism could never fully align itself to the ideological principles of many other Muslim-majority countries across Asia, Africa, and the Middle East in the 1960s and 1970s. Approaches to Islamic socialism that flourished in the early twentieth century saw thinkers like Ubaidullah Sindhi and Khalifa Abdul Hakim locate within Islam the seeds of a progressive economic model in which affluent individuals serve the needs of the vulnerable in society.[2] This correlated with an overwhelming acceptance of free, private enterprise among the ulama in Pakistan, which was also predicated on their rejection of the Marxist-materialist basis of socialism. Despite the attempts of philosopher Ghulam Ahmed Pervez to provide a revolutionary interpretation of the Quran that would replace the Western concepts of "religion" with an emphasis on *deen* [faith] as a means of cultivating change and moral agency, the rejection of socialism among leading Islamic clerics stifled its emergence in any tangible form.[3] It was the ill-fated Pakistani prime minister Zulfiqar Ali Bhutto who last wielded the banner of Islamic socialism as a means of reconciling his populist deployment of Islam (for example, by prohibiting alcohol and declaring the Ahmadiyya non-Muslims) with policies such as the nationalization of all major engineering and electrical industries. Having failed to disentangle socialism from Marxism and situate its origins in the doings and teachings of the Prophet Muhammad, Bhutto was removed in a coup led by one of his generals, Zia-ul-Haq.[4] Instead of using the language of Islamic socialism, Zia's decade of military rule took up the mantle of *nizam-i-mustafa*, or the "system of the Prophet Muhammad," as a means of integrating Islamic jurisprudence into most spheres of legal, economic, and political life.

In many ways, the Zia era crystallized the second motif, the Islamically infused public service of khidmat, into a widely held public demand. Proposals for an "Islamic welfare state" in Pakistan have long been predicated on the belief that the economic and political organization of any Muslim-majority state should strive to guarantee social welfare. To fulfil this, various forms of charitable giving exist as obligations under Islamic jurisprudence or as exhortations that can be taken up voluntarily by believers. In the latter category is *zakat* which sees all Muslims donate a certain share of their wealth each year. In 1980 the Pakistani state began to take control of *zakat* by managing the withdrawal of funds directly from citizens' bank accounts. Voluntary donations include *saqdah*, an act closely allied with the cultivation of virtues such as sincerity and humility and which can range from smiling at a stranger to mediating between conflicting parties to resolve a dispute.

Public service undergirded by a sense of obligation to others, all as a means of maintaining one's obligations to Allah, continues to drive recent political transformations in Pakistan. In 2018 a wave of Pakistani voters brought Imran Khan, a populist politician long at the periphery of mainstream politics, and his PTI party (Pakistan Tehreek-e-Insaf) to power on the promise of a *"naya* [new] Pakistan." While this was supposed to mean many things to different people, in his victory speech he clarified his promise to transform Pakistan into an "Islamic welfare state." With the promise that Pakistan would bring forth the ethical ideals of seventh-century Mecca into a "new" Pakistan based on welfare, Imran Khan and PTI party workers pinpointed the populist thrust of khidmat. The idea deftly expressed the deep-rooted association in Pakistan of civil society and common decency with pious frameworks of how to live well by others. It also referenced the perceived failures of the last two civilian governments and the tangible feeling of the absence of governmental infrastructure and security provision. For example, the kind of shared investiture in a sensory environment documented in chapter 3, forged by the discontinuity of energy provision, proved ripe for guarantees of formalization, not by governing schema but through an ethical project integrated with the promise of Islamically infused public services. As such, Imran Khan's attempt to nationalize khidmat, in ways that only entrepreneurial and community welfare organizations tied to religious movements did before, proved appealing to many.[5]

To examine the political character of atmosphere that animates Hall Road's constitution and character, I ask how my interlocutors' understanding of the built environment provided them with the tools to navigate the circulation of media and the systems of ethics that undergird it. In so doing I explicitly conflate the circulation of objects and their re-inscription with the atmosphere of the built environment. By conceptualizing attitudes to urban atmosphere this chapter serves to define and explore, through the activities of varied representative interlocutors on Hall Road, the associations of the street with the assimilation of change. I do this for various reasons; one of which is to challenge the dominant language of economic informality and remark upon its analytical unsuitability for the study of film, media, and public morality in Pakistan. In its place I suggest that two central ideas about urban form might provide a way of understanding the backdrop to Hall Road as a media-elemental environment. Firstly, the Indic binary concepts of the *kacha* and the *pakka*, and *qabza*, a term used for land appropriation, provide a language of urban phenomenology, authority, and ownership. Secondly, the latter half of the chapter comes to consider how ideas around urban appropriation and encroachment become entangled with nativist conceptions of authenticity. Here, believable untruths and conspiracy theories show how atmospheres get wedded to politics at the same time as undermining the transparency so desired by voters and promised by politicians.

Focusing in this way on the technical and social grounds of media circulation builds on two decades of sustained interest in the informal infrastructures of Indian film and its dispersed archives, as documented by the research groups SARAI, the BioScope journal, and affiliated scholars such as Lawrence Liang and Ravi Sundaram. This diverse body of work shows postcolonial urbanism to be characterized by breakdown, recycling, and extra-legal space. Any attempt to challenge the utility of informality in the study of Pakistan's media environment, particularly ideas around mass mediation such as piracy, must first acknowledge the critical trajectory that has brought such issues into clarity. Liang's influential body of work explores how piratical practices assert claims over urban space, through goods, objects, and commodities in circulation. The ways that individuals make a claim over, say, land tenure must consider the varying dimensions, stakeholders, and forms of access which govern how such land comes to be used, rather than owned.[6] These observations came at a time in which the perceived illegality of slum housing and utility theft was joined by a phenomenon similarly infrastructural in scope: the piracy of media. While building on Liang's findings, the language of urban form I propose differs in an important respect from his call to better understand the lateral spaces through which piracy unfolds, Ravi Sundaram's call to explore the relationship between the copy and the city, and Kamran Asdar Ali's interest in the connection between urban experience and the moving image in Pakistan.[7] Preparing the ground for the subsequent chapter, I want to direct attention towards how forms of individualism serve to order objects in circulation. I propose that it is individual acts of mediation that take place within informal systems or infrastructures that are constitutive of the oscillating relationship between economic value and ethical values, rather than the systems themselves.

A Short History of Idris in the Plazas of Hall Road

Idris spoke proudly of his descent from a long and prestigious line of professionals who had worked with animals. His grandfather, the son of a bureaucrat in colonial Peshawar, came to Lahore and was made senior zookeeper at Lahore Zoo, where he worked for fifty years. Subsequently, his father and uncles became taxidermists. At home Idris maintained a family collection of two thousand photographs relating to his paternal lineage of hunters, colonial zookeepers, and taxidermists. "This is my *virsa* [heritage]," he told me. "When I am not feeling happy, I look at the pictures to remember that I came from this tradition." His outlandish tales of the animals in the zoo, each beloved of his grandfather, all seemed to impart a moral lesson at the expense of the injury of one of his younger family members, less kindred with its caged inhabitants than Idris.

Figure 5.2 Banners trailing over Hall Road. (Photo by author.)

Idris's fourteen years in Dubai were spent working as a dispatcher for a chain of car-rental firms. On the side he sold pirated telephone minutes and internet data. He named these data tokens the "Universal Card" and illustrated them with designs featuring monuments of Pakistani cities on some, and Hindu symbols on others, to appeal to the cosmopolitan labor force residing in the United Arab Emirates. He told me stories of his friends from Dubai: the Chechen bare-knuckle boxer; his Kosovan friends from Pristina who venerated Abbas ibn Ali, the brother of Imam Hussain; and the English Muslim who deserted while serving with the British Army in Iraq and whose panic attacks were only calmed by reciting the *kalma*, the Islamic declaration of faith. He told me, "I could only have seen this humanity outside of Pakistan." Idris's upbringing amid his grandfather's employment at Lahore Zoo and his life in the Gulf were his sources of personal pride. His stories about his cross-species cosmopolitanism brought these together into self-conscious attempts to challenge the social conservatism of his peers and kin group.

Idris remembered when, as a young boy growing up at his uncle's shop on Hall Road, almost the entire street dealt in videocassettes and, just before his departure to Dubai, VCDs and DVDs. On the top floors of the most popular plazas could be found large duplication factories for making film copies. Many extant videocassette master copies transferred onto digital formats on Hall Road retained a trace of their reproduction. While duplicating films, sometimes on hundreds of videocassette recorders wired together, an interruption in the electrical supply would occur and the recordings would stop. Rarely would those employed to monitor their transferal rewind every nascent copy and start again. Instead, they would simply restart the process where they left off, permanently archiving that short outage in its onward journey into other futures and onto other formats. These "long, picaresque journeys" that film prints take coalesce to create what Sundaram describes as a "pirate modernity, a contagion of the ordinary."[8] I found these same outages and their contagious ordinary on YouTube, on VCD copies, and even on cable television channels broadcasting films with a common provenance, and whose intermittences were often hard to discern amid the persistent layers of glitches caused by censorial excisions and incisions, burned celluloid from long circuits in cinemas, or in their encoding onto digital carriers.

Plazas are also more closely connected with another kind of ruination. Across the city, rapidly constructed commercial properties are blamed for the disappearance of pre-Partition buildings, with plazas having become a byword for heritage destruction. From the Walled City's Tarannum Cinema to the urban caravanserais in New Anarkali, it is common to hear of the destruction of a derelict building so that its owner can build a plaza in its place. High-rise-building began in Pakistani cities in the 1960s with the foundation of the Lahore Development Corporation. The Rafi Group, a private real estate and land development corporation established in 1978, created the "plaza" style of architecture that has redefined Lahore's urbanity over the last four decades. The first plazas, named Rafi and Zaitoon, were built in the early 1980s to accommodate the sudden popularity of home entertainment technology. In a remarkable study of Lahore's urban form written around the same time, Muhammad A. Qadeer argued that the city "absorbs development."[9] Hall Road gives urban form to Qadeer's notion of absorption. To facilitate the delivery of discs, tapes, and copies between Rafi and Zaitoon Plazas, precarious gangways were added after their construction, linking each floor at

Figure 5.3 Zaitoon Plaza. Yaseen Street is to the left. (Photo by author.)

Figure 5.4 Rafi Plaza. Yaseen Street is to the right. (Photo by author.)

various points, creating arcade-like burrows and warrens beneath which became Yaseen Street.

Qadeer observed absorption manifest in the vacuum left by urban development in postcolonial cities still held back by foreign influence. Absorption can be seen as the unintended consequence of the kind of cyclicality of the development paradigm, or a symbol of the assimilationist, nation-building project of postcolonial Pakistan. Qadeer's notion of absorption bears similarities to Arjun Appadurai's later argument that the circulation of media and commodities does not homogenize difference but instead sees cultural texts indigenized through hybrid processes of reception.[10] The porosity of reception is one of the "internal dynamics" that Qadeer argued is key to understanding urban form, through which scholars must remain sensitive to the "disturbances and accommodations" of an environment in flux.[11] Bringing Qadeer's notion into the analytics of this book, absorption is perceptible only on its threshold. Absorption is an idea resistant to the idea of the city as palimpsest popularized by Walter Benjamin in his study of the arcades in urban Paris, whose contribution to the city's urban form can be compared to Hall Road's plazas.[12] Instead, in Lahore, absorption necessitates the permanent submersion of what came before. Idris found that the absorptive qualities of Hall Road—its ability to assimilate change rather than be transformed by it—also marked its interpersonal environment. As he settled into life as a trader on Hall Road, his desire for the inverse of public space, a private, personal, exclusive space so often elusive for men and women of his age, was swiftly curtailed by the conservativism of the world he found himself within. While much of Hall Road's fortunes were made in the Gulf, the continual arrival of young returnees marked it with a generational disjuncture. Idris's push for individualism, common to young male returnees from periods of employment in the Gulf, was quickly forced to re-acculturate to a cooperative and hierarchized merchant community formed through kinship, faith, outrage, and empathy.

The Kacha and the Pakka

While the trades that Hall Road comprises might be understood together as an informal economy, and the labors of its constituent traders as informality, my interlocutors in Lahore were not aware of such a distinction.

For most, the definition of the informal, as that which possesses market value but is not recorded by its inverse, the formal realm of government, taxation, or legislation, would not stand up to scrutiny in a country where corruption is evident in every government sector. This distinction also does not account for the ways in which legality and illegality often coexist in an economic sphere driven by external demands and competing stakes. When I asked Idris and other friends on Hall Road how they would describe this distinction between forms of trade, they gave me an example that, like the Euro-American concept of informality that first arrived in academic discourse in relation to urban planning, is used to describe land and built structures. The example they gave, the distinction between the *kacha* and the *pakka*, roughly defined as temporary and fixed, was one which relates to the product of informality rather than the labor of the traders themselves. The masculine and feminine cases of *kacha/kachi* and *pakka/pakki* also refer to the distinctions between "raw/unripe" and "cooked/ripe," namely in Claude Lévi-Strauss's influential proposal to think through the structural binaries at play in societies, but also the temporary, crude, imperfect, and permanent. In his study of caste hierarchy Louis Dumont argued that the Indic concepts of kacha and pakka, both "tinged with hierarchy," open out into a more expansive set of value distinctions than the states of simply being raw or cooked.[13] This is because kacha food, so "vulnerable to impurity" is associated with "lower castes," and pakka food is often seen as more transmissible to "higher caste" groups.[14] The kacha is the domain of "precariousness and imperfection" while the pakka is characterized by "solidity, perfection."[15] In the urban domain, it is the precarious kacha that is more often heard, standing as an exception to the preferred norm, in reference to slum housing or areas of slum housing known as *kachi abadi*. Kacha can also refer to temporary bridges over torn-up streets awaiting resurfacing, or a makeshift road demarcated by a collective decision to drive over a section of undeveloped land. Although to be kacha is to be rough and ramshackle, to be kacha can also be communal and unplanned. It is not surprising then, that many of my Hall Road interlocutors felt this a more appropriate heuristic with which to understand the economic character of the marketplace. Although the formal authorizing agent embodied in regulation and taxation is absent, power is not absent from kacha and pakka phenomenology, but rather it comes to the surface in the possibility of change. To address the state of being, kacha requires a process of transformation and approval to turn it into pakka.

Scholarship on informality first stemmed from research into parallel economic practices centered upon trade, housing, and urban planning, and crystallized around the turn of the twenty-first century in studies of informal labor, the constitutive character of informality to urban form, media piracy, and pirated film distribution.[16] Pakistan has long been associated with media piracy, despite this reputation being complicated by the extent of the procedural informality of the formal sphere of governance and trade. In 1994, the World Trade Organization (WTO) authored the Agreement on Trade-Related Aspects of Intellectual Property Rights (TRIPS), effectively ensuring that copyright compliance became a prerequisite for continued participation in global trade. The early years of the twenty-first century saw the Office of the U.S. Trade Representative (USTR) threatening the nations of the world with inclusion on their annual Special 301 report's "Watch List" and "Priority Watch List." From being branded as an economic outcast to trade sanctions, the punishments can be severe. The Philippines was only removed from the list in 2014 when they capitalized on every haul of seized pirated goods with public destruction ceremonies where discs were steamrolled, hard drives smashed with hammers, and materials burned. In 2016, after Pakistan's establishment of Intellectual Property Tribunals in Lahore, Islamabad, and Karachi, USTR promoted Pakistan from the Priority Watch List to the Watch List.

Unlike the international language of piracy and its focus on rules and compliance, studying the circulation of media in Pakistan requires an understanding of specific social, urban, and phenomenological conditions that are separate from traditional understandings of informality. Focusing only on the rights of owners in the case of piracy, or relationships with dominant structures in the case of informality, withdraws the agency of their individual mediators and maligns the complexity of these acts within webs of social relations.[17] The specific conditions of film distribution in Pakistan require focus on what Jeffery Himpele calls the "counter-itineraries" taken through the cracks in urban infrastructure.[18] The extent to which these counter-itineraries might benefit marginalized persons is up for debate. On the one hand, as Sundaram argues, the kind of media urbanism that characterizes Hall Road as marked by the possibility of radical, anti-capitalist subversion can act as a "giant difference engine" that brings subaltern populations into "permanent technological visibility."[19] On the other, Hall Road is inseparably linked to the colonial logic of "zoning," that sees industrial, commercial, administrative, and residential areas subdivided to become more public and present objects of secular governance.[20] In the early 1980s, when studies of urban informality were in a nascent phase, Qadeer saw a third way, between radical subalterneity and colonial path-dependency. Qadeer, like Sundaram, was sympathetic to what he called the "bazaar sector," after Clifford Geertz, seeing it as a creative economy forged under conditions antipathetic to its existence, if paradoxically conducive to its growth.[21] By looking to these conditions, Qadeer felt that Lahore's urban form could be adapted to city planning, and that the bazaar sector could come to be recognized and reflected in land use, transport policies, and housing, to interrupt the path dependency of the city's colonial inheritance. He was quick to notice that the relationship between the firm—his own term for formal—and bazaar economies is related to the hierarchical flow of wealth, power, and income, and therefore does not produce a mutually dependent binary but a "hierarchy of circuits."[22]

Despite the prevalence of the language of the formal and the informal outside Pakistan, few on Hall Road were familiar with the distinction, so fluid and malleable were their potential networks for trade, housing, urban infrastructure, and the consumption of media. Due to the felt absence of the state in the enforcement of intellectual property legislation or taxation, concrete categories assigned to material culture and commodities beyond ethical designations appeared inconsequential and unnecessary to many of my interlocutors. Instead, the more conceptually malleable distinction between the urban kacha and pakka, or the temporary and the fixed, proved a more appropriate language to describe the atmospheric character of things, the built environment, and the threshold of "absorption."

At the liminal point between these two states, at the threshold point of absorption, lies another term for describing urban form. Qabza [occupation, possession, or encroachment] refers to infrastructure and the built environment. It is an act of disturbance that works on the threshold of kacha and pakka phenomenology. If qabza is taken up by a collective or a powerful corporate group, it must be one that is incapable of asserting the kind of authority that would allow them to manage the transformation from kacha and pakka. This process of formalization requires an established upper echelon capable of authorizing the move from temporary to fixed. As I have already noted, besides being known as the "plaza mafia," Hall Road's populist trade union the Khidmat Group were known as one of many "qabza groups" or the "qabza mafia." There was a palpable fear of these shadowy groups that newspapers and my interlocutors talked about as if they were a single unit or corporation. It is significant that they were recognized as authoritative enough to usurp urban power but not able to manage the transformation from kacha to pakka. Qabza groups were said to illegally take possession of land through government bribes or coercion and on a larger scale often occupy swathes of land by constructing an illegal mosque and building outward to create *kachi abadi* [slum dwellings].[23]

In colonial Punjab the term *encroachment* was used as the antonym to public space.[24] Naveeda Khan's Lahore ethnography has demonstrated the wide semantic field of qabza. Studying the illegal construction of neighborhood mosques, Khan found that qabza as a form of seizure could be either an expression of anxiety—that a mosque as a place of prayer or stand-in for Pakistan itself is being appropriated—or an aspirational form—that it is being reclaimed. Those supportive of qabza used it in a benign sense of taking up ownership of something left behind by non-Muslim refugees during and following Partition. While qabza is used to describe the illegal occupation of land and occasionally the necessary settlement of land following displacement, the term can be used to describe the friction between social actors. For Khan, qabza elucidates the "state of striving and the obstacles to it in within everyday life in Pakistan."[25] The polyvalence of qabza is reflected in the reputation of the Khidmat Group, who work to depict themselves as shepherds of the kind of "striving" that Khan defines in her ethnography as an instantiation of a future-facing Pakistan open to experimentation and debate. The polyvalence of qabza also operates on the threshold of absorption, in an atmosphere of potential and imminence judged in moral terms.

On Hall Road, differences in what does or does not constitute qabza can often be traced to one's allegiance to one of the streets' two trade unions. The estimate of Hall Road's working population of thirty to one hundred thousand that I was given by the street's older, "official" trade union, the Anjuman-e-Tajiran Hall Road, was based only on registered store-holders; many operated in temporary premises, had yet to register, or chose not to show their presence to the traders' union and allied themselves with the Khidmat Group. The head of the Anjuman-e-Tajiran, Nadeem Chohan, whose decision it was to hold a bonfire of "pornographic" discs back in 2008 (see chapter 6), had been working on Hall Road since 1969. He began repairing radios and sound systems, before establishing a successful firm installing and improving audio systems in cars. Nadeem considered the

Khidmat Group and their charity to be merely a front to siphon money into building plazas on evacuee property. In theory, buildings or land left over by former residents who migrated to India after Partition are supposed to be managed and rented out by the Evacuee Property Trust Board. He believed that the then-incumbent Pakistan Muslim League-Nawaz government (PML-N) led by Nawaz Sharif feared the power of the national traders' unions with whom Hall Road's Anjuman-e-Tajiran were allied and encouraged organizations like the Khidmat Group to compete under the guise of a union while functioning as private developers. He told me that in exchange for their support, evacuee property in areas of prime real estate would often fall into the hands of the Khidmat Group.

I would later tell Adil, the youngest and usually most sedate member of Durrani Electronics, about the union's claims about the "mafia" Khidmat Group. When I did, his eyes flashed red and he began, in uncharacteristic fashion, telling me of his passion for their mission. For him they were mosque-builders; they assisted in dowries to allow underprivileged women to get married; they were men who, like him, worked themselves up from nothing and focused their energies on welfare and development, two premium political desires.

Hearing his impassioned speech, Idris sneered and twisted his moustache. Whenever this happened, one of two things followed: an argument, or Idris was sent on an errand. In that instance, he was sent to deposit money in the bank. On the way, he took me on a brief tour of Hall Road's pre-Partition heritage. Between the heave of Beadon Road and the chaos of Hall Road lay a haven of quiet and domesticity: Lakshmi Mansions, upscale, early twentieth century apartments built around a central garden. Idris and I walked around, looking for the blue plaque installed by the family of the controversial short-story writer Saadat Hasan Manto (1912–1955) to mark the apartment he lived in after migrating to Pakistan after Partition. Instead, we found half the apartments recently demolished, a shiny-looking plaza in its place. The number of Manto's apartment—31—was the last one on that side still standing. The apartment's blue plaque, marking the author's habitation, had been removed and replaced by one bearing the name of the "Khidmat Group," into whose possession the property had somehow recently fallen. Such assertions of qabza operate at the threshold of absorption. As it was not the Pakistani government who installed the plaque, due to their reluctance to celebrate a poet once tried by its courts for obscenity, the building was considered an appropriate site upon which to play out

an urban power grab. While the Khidmat Group could have easily demolished this wing of the Lakshmi Mansions, as many other sections of it had
been to make way for mobile phone plazas, the Manto family's attempt to
imbue the site with heritage status in the form of a blue plaque was met
with a counter-assertion of ownership similar in many ways to the incisive acts explored in chapter 2 of putting image-events "under erasure."

Yet the state was not entirely absent from these contestations. Governmental responses to kacha developments and qabza in the form of urban
appropriation took the form of anti-encroachment drives. In November 2018, Karachi's Empress Market, home to the Rainbow Centre, saw
the destruction of a vast marketplace similar in form to some of Hall
Road's connecting and outlying alleyways such as Yaseen Street. With
some businesses having been in residence since the 1970s, and with most
paying rent, the extent to which such markets are held on the threshold of
legality makes them prime opportunities for qabza groups to exert a kind
of shadowy non-governmentality. The provision of welfare, charitable
work, and civil protest help to build the ambience of pakka over the precarity of being kacha. It is this liminal point of being fair game that makes
these thresholds of ownership so porous to Pakistani marketplace media.
While Qadeer saw in Lahore's "bazaar economy" the foundation of an
indigenous approach to urban development, he overlooked how the tendency of the city towards "absorption" provides an opportunistic space to
catch hold of objects, places, and things, as they are left to linger by a weak
state reluctant to turn the kacha into pakka.

Nativism and the Refugee Mahaul

As we reached the dead end of Yaseen Street, Idris stopped outside a whitewashed, nineteenth-century building of four stories that starkly contrasted
with its surroundings. I squinted at a faded, hand-painted sign: Cheema
Sons, bookbinders and booksellers since the mid-nineteenth century. In
Lahore, pre-Partition buildings identified themselves by their patina: a
combination of rich ochre, a pastel *décollage* of chipped paint, and the gnarl
of rotting wood. Through the passages between plazas, one could glimpse
several ruinous buildings that seemed to be toppling backward, time having slowly eviscerated them of their mortar. They folded into the surrounding area so seamlessly that their antiquity was hard to gage at first. As Idris

wandered back to Durrani Electronics, I knocked on the door of Cheema Sons. Inside, the Cheema family's urbane and articulate eldest son Usman recalled an old friend, Chaudry Buzdar, who was the first to run a small radio shop on the street, just beside the entrance that leads to the rear of their property. Even that shop, Usman said, was built on the property left vacant by an illegally demolished Hindu temple, which itself sat beside a disappeared Sikh gurdwara. For Usman, the chaos of encroachment did not begin with the radio, videocassette, or electronics shops; instead it origi- nated in the extent to which Hall Road was left practically vacant and given out as evacuee property to Muslim refugees from India or occupied by internal migrants in the new state of Pakistan.[26] Qabza, as the illegal encroachment of new buildings, served to remove any traces of the Hindu temples that could once be found on Hall Road and its outlying edges. Many temples in the Civil Lines areas in Lahore were also damaged or destroyed by crowds in 1992 demonstrating over the demolition of the Babri Masjid in Ayodhya in India. Indeed, in other parts of the city the *sikhara* spire of a former Hindu temple might suddenly come into view. Finding the rest of the building often presented a challenge, so totally had the rest of its form been integrated into surrounding buildings and put to other uses.[27]

A few doors down from Cheema Sons was the Shrine of Hazrat Ismail Lahori, a breezeblock mosque built around a tree and housing the grave of an eleventh-century saint purported to be Lahore's first Muslim seer, pre- dating that of the city's patron saint Data Ganj Bakhsh. White-tiled and compact like an industrial refrigerator, its small grave was delicate, lonely, and almost entirely ignored. Having once housed Hazrat Ismail Lahori's hermitage, the land continued to be used as a graveyard during Mughal times, evinced by the presence of another small mausoleum on the street, that of Shah Abdul Menan, where babies and children were taken to restor- ative waters to be cured of contagious skin conditions. Many old families still resident on Hall Road recite the oral history of their ancestors; when the foundations of their homes were laid, they would find skeletons, all facing Mecca.

Following the Indian Rebellion of 1857, Lahore saw a sudden influx of British colonial building projects that forged physical and commercial space for the expansion of an urban middle-class.[28] When the British needed a sizable church for their congregation, they built the Lahore Cathedral Church of the Resurrection on Hazrat Ismail Lahori's graveyard that had been left untouched during the years of Sikh rule. One of the suppliers of the bricks for the church was a local contractor, Muhammad Sultan Thekedar, who erected a small residence for his engineers. The building survived until the middle of the twentieth century and briefly housed one of Amritsar's deputy commissioners, C. M. Hall, after whom the street was most probably named. The first half of Hall Road, accommodating the commercial spillover from the Mall via the Regal Chowk junction, was historically a busy place where people gathered to protest. This was due to the concentration of lawyers' offices there, including that of the late Asma Jehangir. The famous demonstration of the Women's Action Forum on February 12, 1983, against Zia-ul-Haq's anti-women Hudood Ordinances was held at the entrance to Hall Road, marking a significant moment in the history of feminism in Pakistan. The other half, its lands belonging to the church and adjacent government buildings, was once flanked by tall, shady trees, and was wide enough for public buses to course down it, as they travelled from the Mall to McLeod Road. Before Partition, Hall Road was full of Anglo-Indian families employed in nursing and education, and a sizable Chinese community, with restaurants, dancing halls, and bars, including the Clifton Bar, where Saadat Hasan Manto sought to recreate something of the Bombay film scene he had left behind after Partition.

Neither Usman Cheema nor Idris, freshly returned from half his lifetime in the Gulf, considered themselves part of the awaam—a communal or pejorative *people*, depending on the context of its use—or the elite. The Cheema family described themselves as "old Lahore," the same term they used for their family business and its lived connection to the lost heritage and multi-religiosity of pre-Partition Punjab. Although these men would never sit together over tea, Usman Cheema echoed Idris's proud cosmopolitanism in finding allegiance and nostalgia in the colonial era, particularly through the materiality of the grid line roads of the former-British military Cantonment area and the brickwork of early colonial buildings. After our first meeting, Usman sent me to go and look at one nearby example, threatened by the then-ongoing construction of the Lahore-based Orange Line Metro Train project, that took place less than a hundred meters from their building. Planned and financed in connection with the China–Pakistan Economic Corridor (CPEC), and constructed by Pakistani and Chinese firms, the project was delayed when protest groups argued that the planned route violated Pakistan's 1975 Antiquities Act and threatened protected sites such as the Mughal-era Shalimar Gardens. Many of the traders on Hall Road, who formed the support base of the then-ruling

PML-N party, led by steel magnate Nawaz Sharif, supported infrastructure megaprojects as the expression of an ambitious, modern, and business-minded Pakistan.

Their support was frequently tested. In the winter of 2017–2018, on the street adjoining Hall Road, all the trees were ripped up and what was left of the sidewalks was combed into dirt tracks where still-functioning businesses laid their wares. A deeply dug section connected to some already lain tubes recorded deep levels of built structures beneath the surface, leaving the bases of fluted columns of ambiguous antiquity strewn across the road like dusty cauliflower florets. Stray trenches dug for smaller pipes were left unfilled long enough that they became latrines, sending up plumes of mosquitoes visible in the early-evening light and smog, even at the height of dengue season. At the end of McLeod Road, the Lakshmi Building, a symbol of Lahore's pre-Partition Hindu heritage, was covered in a green tarpaulin to protect it from the ravages of the Orange Line. On the other side of the city the looming great overpass suddenly stopped as if in reverence at the Chauburji, a Mughal-era monument covered on all sides by another green protective tarpaulin.

Referring to an undefined other, Usman complained, "They are ruining the whole fabric of this city. They have shaved off the colonial goodness of that area." He told me, "Those buildings were not made by them." He went on, "Those buildings were owned by Hindus and Sikhs; those were the affluent people of those times. They were not the present class who have been hijacking the system." He added, for good measure, "No, we are not a *refugee* family over here," using the English word rather than the Urdu term *muhajir* more commonly used to describe the millions of Muslims forced to migrate from India in one of the largest population exchanges in history. "This is our landed area, our ancestral property," he concluded. For Usman Cheema the current state of Hall Road was a direct consequence of Partition. This he associated again with the "refugee element. The refugees that came during the exodus . . ." That he believed they continued to come either made his statement more of a class distinction rather than the result of a causal action, or a distinction that referred to the presence of Afghan refugees in the country on whom many social ills are blamed. "They don't own these places, they don't have any papers that tell them that this is theirs," he continued, "Everything on Hall Road is Hindu property, and still under their names." He said that since the current owners have acquired these properties, they have only torn them down to make plazas for rent and sale once the value is driven up. He added, "It reminds them of their past when they weren't allowed in such premises." I quizzed him on what he meant by this.

> Because they were all working-class people. I mean, I've got my own trade here. I have my workers in the back—they work over there, and I work with them. But you know, to preserve a good mahaul you cannot allow them to come over here and sit with us, can you? . . . Those people were never allowed in such structures, ever . . . And our ruling class is also from the refugee families. They're not from Lahore. They are not from Pakistan. No, they're not . . . You will not find such dialogue in the media because they themselves belong to that refugee mahaul. How can they talk about it?

Evidently, Usman believed that there once existed an urban cosmopolitanism in Lahore that existed alongside one's religious identity. "It was a very multicultural, elitist, settled city," he said, as if those things were indivisible elements of religious plurality. For him, even Lahore's traffic was "indigenous" and "refugee," when he recalled how quiet the roads were on Islamic holidays Eid-al-Fitr, Eid-al-Azha, and on the ninth and tenth of Muharram, when so many people return to their ancestral villages. The "refugee mahaul," an atmosphere that describes a difference in urban morality, membership, and attitudes towards built space, was antithetical to Usman Cheema's nostalgia for a Lahore of Parsis, Sikhs, and Hindus. His faith in this mahaul was even more remarkable for having no basis in lived experience, instead having been mediated by the oral tradition of his family and emanating from the absorptive nature of the postcolonial city. By siding with minorities and with long-departed adherents of other faiths Usman felt he was speaking truth to power, giving an ambiguous tinge to his disparaging views on the "refugees" he suggests have become the ruling class. His description of a "refugee mahaul" also cohered with ways in which architecture and the built environment have been central to the ways that the materiality and aesthetics of atmosphere are conceptualized in the arts and humanities, particularly in relation to notions of ruination and absence.[29]

In Usman's reading, plazas and the assertion of qabza over objects and spaces relating to the past were the result of the absorption and assimilation required by the traumatic early years of Pakistani history. Lahore's infrastructural unease was paralleled with anxieties over built heritage and the post-Partition allocation of evacuee property and a feeling, for Usman, that the property went to corrupt, socially inferior people. His was an entangled social class, neither the awaam nor the elite, who marked themselves out by having a direct, consanguineous, or experiential connection with social and religious hybridity. The creation and production of urban class values tied to being "old Lahore" hinged on the celebration of cosmopolitanism formed by creating a distinction against those who migrated to Lahore, either after Partition or more recently from surrounding towns and villages in Punjab. This was evinced in Usman's oral family history of cultural connection and peer networks built on education, business status, and class in pre-Partition Lahore. It was also evident in Idris's experience of cross-religious, transnational contact in Dubai, and to a certain extent in his kinsmen and colleagues, Durrani Electronics' status of longevity in the market allowing them to recall a time when international businesses and customers came to, or were stocked by, Hall Road.

"New Heritage"

For the first few months of my fieldwork in Lahore, the looming concrete flyovers of the nascent Orange Line lay interrupted, frozen mid-construction. The project had been halted by a stay order following numerous legal challenges from groups like Lahore Bachao [Save Lahore!] and an architectural heritage commission that included the Cheema family. In those early days researching the copying and retrieval of Pakistani media on Hall Road, I would spend my time flicking through and talking over racks of VCDs. With three or four films poorly compressed and squeezed into the capacious confines of one disc, the content would often glitch, introducing unwanted visual artifacts caused by compression to cause an inoperable error in encoding and playback. The half-finished flyovers reminded me of these persistent glitches, an external interruption to the signal, pointing to both the absence of resources for its continuation, or of an overload of data confined within too small a space.

A few months later, in late 2017, the tide swung in the government's favor and work restarted on the Orange Line. Over tea Usman Cheema told me about meetings he had attended during the campaign to halt the construction, and an incident with the then chief minister of Punjab,

Figure 5.5 The Orange Line Metro Train project under construction. Photo by author.

Shehbaz Sharif. The chief minister had been told by Usman and other conservationists about the threat posed to brick-built pre-Partition buildings by proximity to the railway tracks and the possibility of irreversible damage to local heritage. He shot back, with the promise, "I will build them *new* heritage sites." Perhaps because of the pithy, yet absurd, logic of the suggestion, I recalled hearing the story before. Other people involved in the campaign had reported sitting in the same meeting or told the story in the position of Usman.[30] There were other versions circulating in WhatsApp groups told in the form of news reports, that suggested that the terms of the China–Pakistan collaboration even had funds earmarked for the creation of simulated heritage sites. Usman may have come across the story this way, through one of the many "forward as received" messages that featured unverified news forwarded unchecked and unchanged as if from a legitimate source. Within hours, the velocity of the spread of such information can quickly become recognizably "public" news items. What was remarkable was that the source of this story was almost a year old at the time and originated on a satirical news site whose website was blocked by the Pakistan Telecommunication Authority shortly after its publication.[31] What was perhaps more remarkable was that Usman felt that this piece of satire possessed such critical force that he located himself within its retelling. The myth of "new heritage" seemed to hold some indelible truth about the logic of the absorptive city, about how unrestrained construction destabilizes the value of objects relating to the past by offering the possibility of scalable reproduction.

Like Qadeer's focus on a "hierarchy of circuits," the language of urban form that gave rise to the myth of "new heritage" operates at the fraught threshold of individual self-recognition and the categorization and hierarchization of others. The assertion that "new heritage" is believable for inauthentic persons is an active movement of the identification of fakeness in things to people. In this instance, "new heritage" is an imagined inauthenticity where its conception does not otherwise exist, wielding a notion of conceptual (and in the narrative, practically) foreign origin, to translate the more diverse practices of qabza, kacha, and pakka, into clear binaries of right and wrong, real and fake, old and new, authentic and inauthentic, within an infrastructural sphere in which they can be understood. That Usman and other concerned parties did this by placing themselves in a satirical narrative that exceeds the truth while remaining within verisimilitude underlines how integral these fuzzy boundaries are to Hall Road and Lahore's urban form. The materiality of these boundaries can also be seen in the heavily pixelated images of violence that illustrated the issue of the *Lahore Tajir Log* at the beginning of this chapter. The ambiguous aura of these images recalls the very produce of Hall Road: mass-copied films whose journeys across analog to digital formats and data-limits themselves test the thresholds of discernibility.

CHAPTER VI

The Master Copy

Atmospheres in Circulation

lways dressed in a crisp blue *shalwar kameez* topped with a tweed-patterned sports jacket, Adil started working at Durrani Electronics when he was seven to provide for his ailing father. A photograph of him in the shop as a child showed him in a similar outfit, as if his clothes had grown with him. As he was related neither to Idris nor Faisal, nor was he connected to their wider Pashtun Durrani tribe, he initially took on menial tasks before rising to the role of salesman. In those earlier days he lived in the residential houses that used to back onto Hall Road, against the facades of which groceries would be winched up with a system of elevated baskets to households living at the top. By the time of my fieldwork, these buildings had almost all been levelled to make space for new shopping plazas.

Adil winced when he remembered how, in 2008, the flimsy structures shook violently following several low-intensity blasts that targeted the floor above them in Zaitoon Plaza. These attacks, designed to maim and inspire fear, followed an anonymous bomb threat sent shortly before, prompting Hall Road's Anjuman-e-Tajiran, the official traders' union, to burn sixty thousand discs containing "pornographic" content on the street outside. While no group claimed responsibility for the threat, it came at a time of widespread violence, perpetrated by the Tehrik-i-Taliban Pakistan against the Pakistani state and armed forces and the Sipah-e-Sahaba, a terrorist organization responsible for atrocities against Pakistani Shi'a. The threat had also been preceded by a bomb attack on a nearby juice bar frequented by families and young couples. Those protective of the city's liberal reputation began to describe the destruction of media as the beginning of the "Talibanization of Lahore."[1] While traders saw this act as pragmatism rather than appeasement; others worried about the radicalization of the powerful merchant stratum that might soon infect society from its middle-class core.[2] At that moment Hall Road came to encapsulate Lahore's fragile liberalism, isolation, and its precarious immunity from the upheavals taking place in the rest of the country. The street—and all it stood for—had evaded the censors, copyright law, and the city corporation's planning department, but had responded to one anonymous letter and its accusations of immorality with a public bonfire.

Several Hall Road traders who had participated in the bonfire recalled to me that by 2008, when both videocassettes and low-cost VCDs coexisted in the market, it was low-value copies that were burned rather than the master cassettes from which reproductions were made. While the event bore similarities with the cinema-burnings that would follow a few years later in 2012 (chapter 1), it differed in many crucial respects. In his comments on the matter, Idris told me that while traders would have been reluctant to destroy their wares, they harbored no affective outrage or wounded sentiments. "They did not believe in what they were doing," he told me. Idris believed that this was the fulfilment of "public demand"; Hall Road traders felt that the anonymous threat was in tune with the prevailing moral mood of their public, their awaam. The resulting bonfire was a form of address, a message to would-be Sunni militants that Hall Road was not opposed to their interpretation of public morality. In this respect, the bonfire bore close resemblance to recent precedent. A few years before, in 2006, the Muttahida Majlis-e-Amal (MMA)—a coalition of religious parties that formed the regional government in Pakistan's province of Khyber–Pakhtunkhwa—cracked down on the ownership of electronics and recordings deemed impermissible; CDs, videocassettes, and playback hardware were burned on the directives of the provincial government.

The bonfire on Hall Road differed in an important respect. Firstly, it was traders burning their own wares, rather than material confiscated from others. Secondly, it was a bonfire of cheap copies, rather than the valuable master copies from which new material could be reproduced. Overlooked by many commentators at the time, understanding what made the bonfire simply a recognition of the potential tide of public affect, rather than a rupture that signalled a societal change, requires understanding the ways master copies form an interface between different hierarchies of value, authenticity, and legality. In the marketplace trade in Pakistani film and music, master copies have long played a central role in an economic model that allows for pirated as well as authorized reproduction. Situated at an ever shifting bottleneck of content that passes from analog to digital carriers, a master copy can be considered a kind of interface, a mode of relation between the social circumstances that these means of storage and communication afford.

Previous chapters have considered anxieties over the permissibility of secular media, periods of moral exception that coincide with religious commemorations, and the need to gage the sensorium of public demand. This chapter examines the material means through which Hall Road's traders navigate the moral atmospheres of media and their objectification. For my interlocutors, being alert to the moral qualities of a social atmosphere and benefiting economically from Pakistan's informal free market were two sides of the same coin. Hall Road's traders were also cautious about how their own atmosphere was perceived and keen to brand themselves in a particular way or promote in themselves virtues that the market rewarded. As the films they sold circulated, these reputations became entangled with those of others. A cheap disc of a film was no longer just a film but an interface between different times, places, and the ways other traders had read the moral qualities of a social atmosphere and remained alert to public demand. In this final chapter I argue that greater sensitivity to, what in the introduction I express through the words of Jack Goody as, the "situation of the interface" can usher in a methodological approach to the mediatic conditions of social, technological, and ethical systems experienced as relational and porous.[3]

The Promise of the Face

At the entrance to Hall Road, the faces of the leaders of the official traders' union competed for loyalty with those of the Khidmat Group (chapter 5) with the promise of the face as a legible guarantee of honor and integrity. In Pakistan the publicity of faces can act as ideograms that assert presence and power in a competitive and highly masculine sphere. Posters for Sunni Barelvi meetings were resplendent with the faces of pious orators and *ulama*, while VCD copies of majalis and Shi'i recitations (see chapter 4) evinced the variety of genres of devotional prayer through the assembled faces of popular reciters. In many Punjabi-language Lollywood films, narratives are driven by the villain's desire to avenge the scar [*nishaan*] made by the hero on his face. Older, more established businesses used whitened and retouched photos of their founders to appeal to public faith in the face as a portal to experience and knowledge. The publicity of the *imandar* [respectable] male face also serves to emphasize the seclusion of the *sharif* [pure, modest] woman. As earlier chapters have shown, on Hall Road, heavily gendered as it is by Sunni patriarchal priorities, women are discussed peripherally as makers and breakers of moral atmospheres, yet rarely appear in the flesh. These issues of masculinity, control, and power undergird its system of atmospheres in its processes of formation, evaluation, and renewal. On Hall Road, this system required one to be committed neither to the affects, nor the materiality of sexual or religious difference, but rather to cultivate a sense of distance and ambiguity. The publicity of the face is little to do with its physiognomy but is a site of ethical claims-making.

On Hall Road, the public image of a trader's face was formal and uniform, borrowing its aesthetic from the passport or identify card photograph. The photographic trade in Pakistan had shrunk in the 2010s from studios with experienced camera operators offering stylized shoots with elaborate backdrops to stalls that took simple passport-style photographs or printed out images from smartphone SD cards. At these photographic stores, I observed customers routinely ask to witness the images being deleted from the studio operators' hard drive before paying, fearing that their likenesses would be used in nefarious ways. When I asked people how exactly their images might be used, many cited fears around blackmail or composite, DeepFake pornography. One national news item that some referenced was the case of a Karachi university that disposed of unsuccessful application forms, complete with photographs, phone numbers, and personal details, to a *raddiwala* [scrap dealer]. Sold as scrap, these papers found their way to a vendor who used them to wrap *paan*, a mouth freshener made using sugared sweets, fennel, anise, coconut, coriander seeds, and sesame wrapped in a betel leaf. The *paan* vendor used WhatsApp to contact several of the female applicants to tell them that their photos were being "misused" throughout the city. This was not so far-fetched. In 2018 around 90 percent of claims in the Federal Investigation Agency's "Cybercrime Circle" related to harassment and blackmail, mainly to the non-consensual use of photos or images.[4]

Before arriving in Lahore to conduct research, I pieced together information about Hall Road from adverts on VHS covers sourced from the last Pakistani videocassette and videodisc rental libraries in English cities like Blackburn and Birmingham. One recurring distributor stood out. Haji Shams, the proprietor of Jibran Video House, would affix an ID-style head-and-shoulders photograph on the front cover of his releases, underwriting his guarantee of image quality with a human face. When I arrived in the city, I saw stickers and posters with passport-style photographs of election candidates, politicians, and union representatives, yellowed and faded across walls and down alleyways. Even Lahore's famous eatery Amristari Hareesa was advertised with the face of its founder. His face had been lightened, or maybe even colorized from black and white, so it remained present and luminous. The publicity of the face provided an interface between the force of public demand and individual values and virtues, in this case the longevity, trust, and reliability associated with a culinary stalwart. The face of Haji Shams or the watermark of a film collector variously appealed to the trust of those skeptical about the atmosphere of secular media, those devoted to the atmosphere brokered by their religious media, or those seeking the atmosphere of the media bazaar as a place of anonymity, desire, and mediation. In Urdu, the face does not possess the same window onto the soul as evoked by the English-language phenomena of being face-to-face with the other. Instead, one is *amnay samnay*, front to front. These are not faces that are read for emotion or depth, rather they absorb and homogenize hopes and anxieties.[5] It is the trace of a bureaucracy that is the sole guardian of access, and where the form and personhood of individual people mediate requests for retrieval from the Hall Road repertoire.

On Hall Road the face also promises proximity to the master copy, the root of the supply chain of media copies, the fixed referent around which a trade in retrieval and reproduction circulates. Unlike the publicity of the face, the agency of which absorbs rather than refracts, the master copy is a product of a wider contextual domain whose contingency lies perpetually on the threshold of media formats and moral atmospheres. The discussions that follow attempt to reach some conclusions on the coexistence of interdiction and reproduction in the Hall Road repertoire by showing how my interlocutors attempted to draw equivalence between the value of objects in circulation with virtuous characteristics and expertise in persons. In this way, virtue was located in the conditions of circulation rather than in objects themselves. As the virtues appended to mediation are usually not as emphatically foregrounded as they are on Hall Road, media objects in circulation are often subject to scrutiny over the extent to which the content is commensurable with cultural values in the networks through which they pass.[6] In short, it might be said that on Hall Road circulation creates and renews interfaces, whose situation allows people to communicate across atmospheres.

The Blood Line: Durrani Electronics

Unlike many of his peers, Idris was aware of the international language of media piracy. Pointing to those around him, he said, "If you ask these people, they wouldn't know anything about it. I remember when the cable [television] guys would send people with cameras into the cinema. The camera would capture the whole film and that *camera print* would come the next day on cable TV. In Pakistan, whoever has the stick owns the buffalo [*Jis ki lathi uski bhehns*]."

The camera print and the master copy have long been key terms in the vernacular terminology of Pakistan's trade in film copies, terms used by traders and customers alike. Many stores' racks were organized by these two categories, which in turn determined the value of the product. While still in use during my research, these terms were rapidly being replaced by the term "data"—in English—to describe digital audio and video content that had never had to traverse the bottleneck of analog to digital conversion. The relatively new arrival of this word in the vernacular came from the sale of both mobile phone and internet "data" and coincided with a more recent turn towards the replacement of indexical media forms with digital platforms for storage. Despite many businesses shifting their operations to other kinds of electronic hardware, I found that among many of my interlocutors, digital technology was changing little to do with the moral atmospheres of film. Instead, on Hall Road the relationship between digital and analog media was a complex and multifaceted one. Firstly, the residual power of analog media was a marker of reliability and early investiture. Master copies passed down through family businesses or in collections amassed by a single individual carried associations of trust in being provided a quality product. Secondly, on Hall Road, the shift to digital did not transform working practices but rather destabilized networks of lateral mediation.[7]

While magnetic audio- and videocassettes were highly prized as carriers of heritage media, disinterest in preserving celluloid film was such that Faisal at Durrani Electronics remembered a back alley of Hall Road dedicated to the sale of discarded strips of 35-mm Pakistani films, refashioned and sold as kinetic toys to be placed over night-lights for the entertainment of children. He compared this wider ambivalence about film heritage with that of Pakistani paper currency. "We don't remember when the ten-rupee note changed or when the five-rupee note came and what those notes looked like," he told me. "No one kept it safe in their pockets . . . I know they went out of circulation, but we could have kept it as a memento." In South Asia, banknotes are taken out of circulation by their Muslim bearers when found with the number set 786, the numerical value of the opening phrase of the Quran, "Bismillah ir-Rahman ir-Rahim," as per the Abjad decimal numeral system. In these instances, they are often framed and prominently displayed as a serendipitous omen in the impersonal flow and circulation of wealth. I was always struck by the way my interlocutors used paper currency as an example of how plucking objects from circulation and adapting them helped produce the moral standing, discretion, and reputation of their bearers.

Faisal spoke to me nostalgically of the days when he worked with the stockist Famous Video, the principal traders in Pakistani film master copies who operated from Tooting in South London. They were "respectable and principled people," he told me, "who favored print quality over everything else." They would buy a new celluloid film print from producers in Lahore's Royal Park, one fresh from the laboratory that had not done the rounds in cinemas, and have it transferred back in the UK. Such telecine technology—the ability to transfer direct from celluloid to another format without cinematic projection—was not available in Pakistan other than at the partly state-run Shalimar Recording Company. For Faisal, the decline of firms who prioritized the surface quality of the image and sound over providing cheap and low-quality forms of access, coincided with the diffusion of value to "public demand." He also perceived that the increase of traders and materials with which to trade had occurred in tandem with a decline in moral values. For him, this was exemplified one day when the store opposite theirs closed for a day to attend the funeral of their founder, whose business started at much the same time as Durrani Electronics. Faisal had observed the custom that neighboring stores should also close for a day, both out of respect for their peers and to ensure that no extra capital was earned at the expense of others' mourning. Faisal and Idris, for once united in disgust on an issue, were furious to find out that many of the newer stores on their basement floor had remained open that day. Idris pointed outside to one of the visible faces of the traders' union on a banner and suggested he should run for office to restore decency among the community of traders.[8] As Faisal rapped his fingers impatiently on a stack of boxed DVD players, I asked Idris what he would change if he was Hall Road's union president.

IDRIS: You've heard the name Genghis Khan, right? When he became king, he made all Mongol people come to hear his speech. He had a horse-cart wheel . . . and he said, "One-by-one you will walk past this cartwheel. If just 1 percent of your height is below the wheel, you are to be beheaded." So, all Mongols are tall now. If you want a good Pakistan, then this is the formula.

TIMOTHY: Bring in the cartwheel?

IDRIS: Not a cartwheel, a table like this. [*He gestured to a table two feet off the ground.*] The smallest ones, the children, you can spare . . . but me, them [*pointing to Adil and Faisal*], all other people would be killed. These children will grow up and they will know everything, because they would have been shown an example. Pakistan doesn't have any example. France had their revolution. They killed their king, their queen, and all their household; everything they destroyed. After that a good France could rise, and it did. You need blood."

Idris's overextension of the duties of the president of the Traders' Union also borrowed some creative license in regaling the "measuring against the lynchpin" story of Genghis Khan, portraying both a preoccupation with overpopulation and an anxiety about the manners and morals of his generation. That he turned the story into one about selective breeding to create a future race of taller Mongols, rather than a parable about murdering those in conquered territories capable of committing revenge attacks, showed confidence in a future that might be able to correct the wrongs of the present. It also reflected the reputation Durrani Electronics had nurtured as guarantors of the purity of a film transfer, the mediators of a film's genealogy.

A Prehistory of Compression

On Hall Road the trade in reproducing and remediating content used two key terms to describe the origin of the material, and the audio, visual, and surface quality that the buyer could expect. The English words master copy and camera print referred to the template or prototype from which to duplicate copies. While the content of the carrier might be a particular film, made by a director, starring actors, and released into cinemas, the master copy and camera print refer to the indexical relationship with the film in reproduction. A master copy was a print made in close proximity to a particular carrier—such as a celluloid film, an audiocassette, or a vinyl record—considered to be the earliest or most unblemished extant recording. In the case of Pakistani films, this often described a VHS copy telecined in the 1980s by the Shalimar Recording Company. Before widespread internet connectivity, the trade in master copies was a costly business as far as the acquisition of newly released Indian films was concerned, which operated through smugglers and across borders. Because of the economic value associated with this trade, the master copy emerged as a mark of distinction in terms of image quality, as well as a bloodline, a guarantee of provenance in Hall Road's wholesale film trade.

This system finds echoes in William Ivins's history of printmaking. Ivins's study of painted woodcuts, engravings, etchings, and lithography, and the impact and complexity of the "exactly repeatable pictorial statement," looked at prints not in terms of their artistic content but their use in disseminating knowledge.[9] He argued that the benefit of the repeatability of pictorial statements outweighed the inaccuracy of their rendering, their relation to their origin, or their place in a chain of authorized reproduction. There are many parallels between the repeatable "pictorial statement" explored by Ivins and the repeatable editions of Pakistani films on Hall Road. As with printmaking, the syntactic elements of Pakistani film-copying do not allow themselves to be infinitely repeatable in perfection. One might assume that proximity to the master copy will make infinitely precise copies, but with inter-media transfer, such as between VHS to DVD, the marketplace entails data loss. Ivins, however, was stimulated by the theoretical question of how much historical knowledge was known first-hand and how much through reproduction.[10] Following the arrival of the first books with instructional or informational prints, later material written or compiled from this base material attempted to replicate illustrations until they had become warped, adapted, shrunken, and marked by "degradation and distortion" into decorative motifs.[11] Grappling with the circulation of knowledge known only through reproduction, Ivins compared words and visual images to a fishing net. The existence of fish in a bay on a given day for a fisherman are those big enough and small enough to get caught in his net. He went on, "So far as the fisherman is concerned fish are only such creatures as he can catch in his net. In the same way words and visual images catch only the things or qualities they are adequately meshed for."[12] What, then, are the ethnographic and ethnosocial conditions of the containers of Pakistani media "adequately meshed for?"

It might be easier to answer this question if the master copy and the copies it engenders were considered an interface. I understand the term as a point of connection between two forms or phases of activity, or the common overlap between two otherwise separate practices. As opposed to the discussion earlier on the publicity of the face, which absorbs reputations and trust, an interface is porous to communication between human and non-human forms. These overlaps characterize Hall Road's residual film trade, in which the master copy secured its presence in the marketplace as a genealogical link through trusted mediators who could guarantee the best image quality in a marketplace of largely poorly transferred copies. It is Marshall McLuhan who is widely acknowledged to have been the first to have brought the term *interface* into use in relation to technological systems. He used the term to describe how "two cultures or technologies . . . pass through one another without collision; but not without change of configuration."[13] McLuhan was interested in the "meeting and metamorphosis of two structures" as historically, as well as culturally, conditioned by print media.[14] Carlos Alberto Scolari charts the word's semantic shift to the arrival of personal computing.[15] From its original meaning of a surface that allows volumes or spaces to possess a common limit, the term *interface* retained the degree to which elements can pass through a threshold by describing how devices can exchange information between users and machinic systems. This led to studies in "encounters at the interface" of human–machine interaction and social exchange necessitated by obligations not inbuilt in an interface's design.[16] In these studies, the interface is that which creates "generative friction between different formats" and the dispositions they afford in their users.[17]

Classical film theorists might have located this generative friction in the medium. For many formative figures in this field, film most lived up to its ontological possibilities when its indexicality, its physical connection to the moment of its impression, was foregrounded.[18] Due to the materiality of this encounter, indexicality in film has often been closely connected with epistemologies surrounding medium specificity. For film theorist Mary Anne Doane, the digital era spelled the "annihilation of the concept of a medium . . . a dream of immateriality, without degradation or loss," taking with it the certifiability of the celluloid imprint.[19] Such a damning indictment of the digital era held by many film theorists in the early twenty-first century echoed the logic of planned obsolescence driven by Euro-American technology companies. Removing the possibilities of indexicality and the temporal markers of this most durational medium simply made digital film not film. For traders in Pakistan's media markets, the systems of valuation defined by mediation resituate the indexicality of the copy outside the film "text." Instead, the copy's physical, existential connection—and the value that it accrues—is underwritten by the expanded backdrop of its storage and reproduction, to the situation of its interface.

In current usage, the inferior relative of the master copy, the camera print, has come to mean a poorly compressed copy of another poor copy. As Idris mentioned, the term first referred to a recording made of a cinema screen by a bootlegger. In the present, camera prints describe the ease with which such material can be acquired and then copied. A request for a particular film may prompt a trader to download it from YouTube and write it onto a disc for sale. That would be described as a camera print. If the customer then made copies of that copy, those too are camera prints. If, in the years that followed, that film fell out of circulation and suddenly found itself in demand, perhaps the customer's copy might be elevated to the status of master copy in the absence of other legible origins. In qualitative terms, film copies sold as camera prints are those deemed unintentionally porous to the infrastructural conditions of their transfer rather than in relation to any regime of authenticity.

Camera prints are reminiscent of what contemporary artist and essayist Hito Steyerl has called a "class society of images."[20] Resisting the dominance of technologies of reproduction that largely decide on what should pass through the analog–digital bottleneck, Steyerl calls for appreciation of the aesthetic value of a widely circulating carrier as that shaped not by image resolution or sound quality, but by "velocity, intensity, and spread."[21] Steyerl's influential essay largely addressed itself to the world of contemporary art, acknowledging only briefly images of urgency or actual poverty, calling for resistance to such an aesthetic hierarchy by dwelling proudly among its lower rungs. Where Steyerl's work is important for considering the situation of an interface is the proposition that the poor image brings to the surface its own material thresholds, particularly the visible marks of data transfer which so richly characterize the camera print. In the language of signal processing, these errors in the manifestation of visual information introduced by the very technology used to reproduce it are known as artifacts. A compression artifact is an anomaly in the representation of data in which the machinations behind the presentation of a signal become visible through malfunction. What is known as "lossy" compression occurs when data is shed so that audio and visual media can be simple enough to store on restricted disc space or transmitted on smaller bandwidths. The lost data that cannot be reproduced in the same way as the original introduces a kind of inscribed noise. As the rest of this chapter argues, this noise has its own aesthetics, social histories, possibilities, and ethics that afford it certain opportunities and obstacles that follow its position within hierarchies of image value.

Keeping Steady: Kasur CD House

As soon as Hall Road opened again after the Day of Ashura, the Shi'i discs that Qasim appropriated from traders like Hasan Mir (chapter 4) were nowhere to be found. Demand, he told me, quickly dries up. The perceived waning of demand had caused hundreds of traders like him to permanently switch their businesses from trading in film copies to mobile accessories, televisions, drones, and even virtual reality headsets. As a result, the older stalwarts of the videocassette era had been pushed to the basement of the Dar-ul Rehmat Plaza, having once run street-facing shops. In his basement store, Qasim showed me the new passport photograph his father had glued onto the DVD racks at eye level. To 1960's, 1980's, and 2000's photos he had added another since our last meeting, perhaps uncertain if the family business would exist for much longer. Even Qasim's grandfather worked

Figure 6.1 Two photographs of Kasur CD House six months apart. (Photos by author.)

Figure 6.2 Cover of a videodisc release of *Haseena Atom Bomb* (1990). (From the author's collection.)

on Hall Road, establishing one of the first radio repair shops, Kasur Radio House. Now his store shared space with the rest of the remaining VCD stores who decided to sell off their master copies and deal in cheaply copied reproductions sourced from private collectors in Lahore and beyond. They sold "box-sets" of three Pakistani films on one disc, poorly compressed and roughly pixelated, and curated around a certain theme, actor, or director. Thus, *Aurat Raj* [Women's Rule] (1979) was packaged with *Wehshi Aurat* [Wild Woman] (1995) and *Zakhmi Aurat* [Injured Woman] (1989), together stacked beside pirated computer software and na'at recitations.

Already bald in his early twenties, Qasim exuded a discretionary confidence in himself and his business, as well as an immediate knowledge of the other traders who had once dominated Hall Road. Their station in the downstairs hall still saw a lot of life. Customers wandered the windowless corridors, while drug addicts with pronounced tics and bored men flicked through the racks of DVDs with no intention of buying. A transgender individual paid daily visits, arm in arm with their boyfriend, asking Qasim

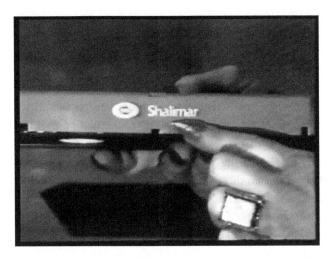

Figure 6.3 A still from an infomercial on Shalimar Recording Company videocassettes. The consumer is shown the process of celluloid to videocassette transfer, tutored in methods of storage and preservation, and directed to the quality mark indicating a genuine product. (Still from a videocassette from the author's collection, early 1980s.)

for his latest recommendation for a violent, blood-soaked Lollywood film. While most had never met someone from abroad, none of the traders seemed surprised to see me; in their all-weather urbanity, surrounded by pornography and devotional Qawwali performances from local shrines, they exuded a cosmopolitanism common to those tuned in to public demand. An untrained voice delivered the azan through a loudspeaker wired from the mosque above them to the market hall, its aural terrain proximate and immediate. Amongst these traders, film did not have a poisonous residue; Hall Road had its own mahaul, like a free trade exclave outside moral and legal authority.

When the international trade in master copies became established in the 1980s, a more diffuse trade began in Karachi with the opening of the Rainbow Centre, a large market plaza with an array of modular units selling films in copy. In spaces such as this and the downstairs market hall in the Dar-ul Rehmat Plaza, competition was fierce, but the traders still operated within a recognizable space of a commons. When Qasim could not provide me with a film I'd asked for, he would shout across the hall to his friend. If his friend had a master copy—or even a heavily pixelated camera print—he would let Qasim make copies of it for a small fee. In other films, the opening titles often asserted that additional mastering had been done by a Hall Road trader, giving a film a second life through sound levelling or image grading. These interventions followed on from the videocassette era, when Pakistani films were disassembled as raw material for other things, as compilations of song numbers or fight scenes.

Early on in my research I would compose questions using the verb *mahfuz karna*, "to keep safe." Instead, traders like Qasim used the verb *sambhalna* to describe the act of ensuring the continued accessibility of older Pakistani films. In its usage this multifaceted Urdu verb pertained to the act of keeping steady or described steadying one's balance. The act of keeping steady operates on the assumption that the object in question is already in motion and the agential and ethical responsibility of someone else. As with the force of public demand, in this sphere of mass-mediation traders asserted themselves as ethically neutral conduits. Fittingly, Qasim corrected my assertion that they have kept anything safe. "We have kept it in circulation," he told me. Comparing the absence of a Pakistani national film archive with the absence of centralized ownership, Qasim told me, "Over here, when someone makes a film, you'll hear in a few days that they have sold the film to someone else. In this cycle, sometimes the film goes into ten people's hands. What interest would these people have to keep the negative or the film safe? It is like property."

For Qasim, property (and thus, piracy) was not a salient category of knowledge in his trade. The kind of circulation he described did not require films to have a fixed referent held by an archive or the producer. The Hall Road repertoire allows media to survive its immediate release through retransmission if it attains a social life within the community. If, as detailed in chapter 4, Tahir Jafri described his acts of preservation and retrieval as "guardianship on behalf of the community"—which itself carries religious connotations to shrines, mosques, and devotional practices—on Hall Road "keeping steady" described an act not of storage but of continuity and participation, of maintaining the kinetic energy powering a mobile, circulating object in order to squeeze as much economic value out of it before its trajectory wanes.

Home Video

Before I began following my interlocutors' interest in the moral atmospheres of media, the initial subject of my research in Pakistan examined how, in the absence of a national film archive, the extant traces of historic Pakistani film owed much of their existence in the present to these dynamics of informal circulation. In Pakistan, a "National Film and Filmstrips Lending Library" was set up in Karachi in the 1950s by the Ministry of Information and Broadcasting from various 16-mm and 35-mm shorts left-over by British and U.S. Information Services departments.[22] This pedagogic archive—which I'd heard through rumors to still exist in a Karachi library—was the only one of its kind the state possessed. Of the approximately 4,500 films made over seven decades in Pakistan many have been lost.[23] For countries with whom Pakistan shared a border or entangled histories, film archives became formative decolonial events. The Bangladesh Film Archive was established in 1978, just seven years after independence from West Pakistan, while the archives of national development body Afghan Film in Kabul were famously saved from a Taliban raid when two workers risked their lives bricking up the most precious reels in an office storeroom.[24] For Pakistan, it seemed, the bad mahaul of film was too contingent a contaminant for bureaucrats to risk muddying their hands with it.

The only exception was the National Film Development Corporation (NAFDEC), established in 1973 by the government of Zulfiqar Ali Bhutto and closed in the late 1990s. While by no means an archival initiative, the most transformative shift in the continued existence of Pakistani films in copy can be said to be the arrival of home videocassette technology. In 1974, shortly after the establishment of NAFDEC, the Shalimar Recording Company (SRC) was established by the Government of Pakistan. I owe the account of the SRC that follows to correspondence with Rashid Latif Ansari, a long serving managing director of the company. As a business, SRC was unique; Pakistan Television Corporation (PTV), Pakistan Broadcasting Corporation (PBC), NAFDEC, and the Arts Council of Pakistan were its public shareholders, and its private shareholders were poets, music composers, singers, and film producers. Perhaps eager to compete with his predecessor Zulfiqar Ali Bhutto—who hosted the second Organization of the Islamic Conference (OIC) in Lahore in 1974—General Zia-ul-Haq was eager for the public to consume his own speech at the Fourth Islamic Summit in Casablanca, Morocco, in early 1984. He set his right-hand man, Lieutenant General Mujeeb-ur-Rehman, the task of producing and circulating videocassettes of that speech among the population.

Before 1983, videocassette recorders (VCRs) had been illegal to import into Pakistan, but home viewership thrived on hardware brought back by

Gulf expatriates like Hasan Mir (see chapter 4), those associated with contingents of the Pakistani army in Saudi Arabia, or from the diaspora in the West. Many expatriates came from and returned to economically deprived villages, making them an example of what one survey of the videocassette-era described as "the complex interplay between the migrant, his VCR, and his government."[25] Perhaps following the influence of the new Islamic Republic in post-revolution Iran, which banned videos and videocassette recorders, and Saudi Arabia, who closely regulated circulation and closed all public cinemas, the Zia government were initially hesitant about hardware for home recording and viewing.[26] But with Zia's prompt, SRC—which was already producing audiocassettes—were ordered to produce and distribute a few thousand free copies of his OIC speech.

Soon afterwards, all extant Pakistani films, regardless of language, whose producers agreed to release their films on VHS were transferred from celluloid to videocassette and released by SRC. Despite his conservative public face, Zia stipulated that one copy of each film transferred onto VHS be sent to him fresh from the factory. SRC's tapes provided the raw materials for the establishment of a new trade in the copying and reproduction of Pakistani films, joining a burgeoning informal trade in Indian films. The families of expatriates in the Gulf who had sent back or returned with VCRs supplemented their income by giving local film showings of SRC videocassettes and Indian films. The impact on Pakistani film was rapid. A pervasive appetite for Bollywood films available on videocassette took urban family audiences away from Urdu-language film, resulting in the closure of cinemas and the decline of film production in Urdu. Punjabi and Pashto-language films filled the gap, made for the tastes of male workers arriving in cities from surrounding rural areas. These films further alienated middle-class and female cinemagoers, encouraging them to consume film at home or through programs broadcast on PTV.

At the beginning and end of SRC videocassette releases, a short introductory clip was illustrated with stills of Shalimar's all-female technicians working at the telecine technology imported from German company Bosch. The voiceover advised, "To protect you from buying an inferior, illegally copied cassette, all genuine Shalimar cassettes have brown tape guard with Shalimar embossed on it." After the film finished, another short clip brought the viewer into the science of conservation, with advice on handling and storage. Cardboard inserts on audio- and videocassettes also reminded the user that the recorder head should be kept clean, that cassettes should be kept out of excessive humidity and away from magnetic fields, and to remove the anti-erasure plug to preserve valuable or prized recordings. Such informal training in conservation science both inculcated passion for the seriality of collecting and fostered archival knowledge in non-archival systems of viewership and consumption.

Power and Provenance

Following a downturn in the activities of SRC in the 2000s, officials saw the original master copies telecined from celluloid reels as unnecessarily occupying shelf space and sold them and master sound recordings to scrap dealers.[27] Despite this, the continued existence of Pakistani films was aided by their mass transferal in the 1980s, which saw copies and recordings stand in as multiple surrogates for an absent national archive. The creation and storage of SRC master copies was a source of pride for market traders on Hall Road. Faisal from Durrani Electronics told me, "None of the filmmakers have their own films. They would come to us to watch what they had made." Other films did not pass through the SRC-bottleneck and required transfer onto new formats through rudimentary telecine technology. This process, in which a celluloid film is projected in a dark room and recorded with a fixed videocassette camera, achieved something closer in quality to a camera print, although due to its proximity to the base version would be referred to as a master copy. These films would often have aged and decomposed due to improper storage conditions or following their long exhibition in cinemas. It is for this reason that many Pakistani films in the marketplace did not have what my interlocutors described as *taaqat* [power], by which they meant image clarity, quality, and sound continuity, but also strength and influence. Due to the unavailability of telecine technology the disentanglement of Pakistani films from their formats took on the qualities of authorship. This led to the development of prized reputations, such as that of Famous Video or of particular private collectors.

In this sphere of activity, the master copy—combined with the influx of capital from the Gulf—became a valuable, transformative object. The exorbitant prices paid for valuable master copies, such as those smuggled from India to Dubai for copying and release in Pakistan, was often entangled closely with the *hawala* or *hundi* money transfer system, an informal system of transferring wealth or value through an expansive network of brokers. *Hawala,* meaning "change" or "transformation," comes from the same Arabic root *h-w-l* that gives us the word *mahaul.* In its deployment in Urdu, it has closer connotations with "trust."[28] To be involved in the process required one to sustain a lasting relationship with the broker. While formal systems have penalties and easy recourse to lawsuits if financial protocol is not maintained, hawala is based on trust on the *hawaladar* [broker], the relationship with whom is defined by already existing codes of trust and reliability within a given economic community. Each year billions of dollars are transferred through these systems, known in the parlance of international finance as Informal Value Transfer Systems (IVTS). These systems often predate their formal counterparts and are most frequently used in South Asia because of the ease of implanting the value transfers within existing trans-local networks of trust and kinship groups. Like hawala, the informal transfer of film has no specific center other than its multiple master copies.

The *bidaderi* system of extended kinship networking in South Asia wields a powerful influence over many established merchant communities. Rather than being contingent on caste, rural livelihood, or tribal identity, the bidaderi system is a key element in social organization in urban Punjab, which structures dispute regulation across different social strata.[29] While the spread of both formal and informal marketplaces has allowed for class divides to emerge through the accumulation of capital rather than land, the cultural capital accrued in possessing and transferring master copies often operates as an individual mode of distribution that does not erect any boundaries to its dissemination. These are not methods of conservation that function by keeping things within a given community but through unfettered reproduction and spread. Moral, rather than kinship, boundaries are perceived in the reception of media rather than in preordained rules. Perhaps this is why I found the bidaderi system less evident in working practices on Hall Road; due to the ease of reproducing digital media, and so as to maximize profits, film traders usually preferred to operate alone.

However, the economic model of the master copy was one that was intentionally porous to local systems of trade, competition, and risk, and thereby brokered a sense of kinship with other technological systems. As with the assertion of qabza at the threshold of kacha and pakka phenomenology and transformation (see chapter 5), the master copy as concept contains within it the interrelation of authorized, informal, and pirated procedures. In the case of films released into the market with the permission of producers, after three months screening in cinemas the master copy would be auctioned on a limited number of videocassettes, with bids ranging from 25,000 PKR to as high as 150,000 PKR for each. At the same time in the Western art market of the 1980s and 1990s such a "limited edition" model allowed for the sale of videocassettes as an art object. In the case of pirated Indian films, the auction would usually take place in Dubai, with bids taken over the telephone from Pakistan. The aim of the producer, distributor, or pirate would be that the combined bidding would, at the very least, match the cost of the film's production or the cost of its smuggled transit. Once the bid was won the challenge for buyers was making copies of the film in time for a coordinated release with other traders, a date incorporated in the terms of the sale. Durrani Electronics' recording room was offsite, a large hall where three hundred VCRs were hooked up and manned by two or three young workers. Idris's insight was correct: the trade in Pakistani film did not cohere with the international discourse of media piracy.

Buyers purchased both proximity to the celluloid print and the ability to release the copy first into their requisite areas. During the videocassette era a dozen respected traders would buy copies from Durrani Electronics specifically to make their own copies. Sometimes traders could pay a premium for a transfer without any watermarks so that they could affix their own, usually if these were to circulate in other cities beyond the demographic reach of the winning bidder. If these terms were not in place, they would simply overlay the film copy with their own claim and obscure the original. As such, the master copy was always contingent on the production and advertisement of provenance.

The Middleman: Haji Shams

To my early enquiries, Qasim responded to my list of old videocassette-era stalwarts with the words, "Dead, all dead." But eventually, towards the back of Rafi Plaza, beside a gangway cleaved in the side of the building that dangled precariously over Yaseen Street, I found Haji Shams sitting in the dark of that hour's scheduled loadshedding. The Haji prefixed to his name not only denoted his completion of pilgrimage to Mecca, but also served as a reminder of a period in the 1980s when his business operated from Saudi Arabia and prospered on expatriate labor capital. It was a strange and euphoric experience, meeting this man whose face took me from northern England to Hall Road, once the only identifiable human in an otherwise invisible trail of mediators.

Haji Shams would arrive for work a few hours earlier than any of his neighboring store-holders on the first floor of the Rafi Plaza, when the building below was dusty, and the hallways echoed quietly. By the time the first traders arrived and gave their greetings to Shams, he was already dealing with a collector or trader buying discs from him wholesale. The late-morning clatter of ascending metal shutters gave way to the sounds of tinny speakers playing film songs and the young son of the trader next to Shams whispering in recitation from a Quran bound in emerald-green felt. As he did every day, a gaunt, elderly man arrived at midday to open his tiny DVD store, shouldering the weight of a large pot full of his wife's *biryani* that he sold to his fellow traders to supplement his income. At first glance, Haji Shams's modular trading unit was like that of many others, but this uniformity hid an intricate, ordered, and ergonomic arrangement. The front and side customer-facing counters were topped with a rack of DVDs to flick through at chest-height that was matched to the bodies of customers and stallholders. These wheeled units boxed Shams into his stall but allowed for the internal storage of materials, discs, ledgers, bags, and teacups. In all visible spaces around the eyeline of the customer were front-facing DVDs, usually cardboard-boxed cases with colorful designs, behind which were the plastic-wrapped and printed reproductions which the buyer was given when they made a transaction. Directly behind Shams's head there was a fan, and to the right of that a wall-mounted television used to test and preview discs. Every adjoining unit was panelled with mirrors or reflective glass to give the illusion of depth and to magnify the little light that crept in from the gangway over Yaseen Street. Display stands on the front racks boasted curated choices, showing Shams's evident love of Lollywood excess, grouping together films like *Miss Hippy* (1974) and *Sharaabi* [Drunkard] (1973).

Haji Shams started selling film music on vinyl in 1975 from his family convenience store set into the back of Lahore's upscale Liberty Market. When videocassette hardware crept into the country at the start of the 1980s, his store became a hub for the informal exchange of videocassettes. He remembered,

In those days you couldn't just go and buy a film but rather had to use our store as a *middleman* [in English]. Customers and friends would come to us and say, "I have an Indian film, called *Sholay* [1975], which I bought from India. Write my name down. If someone comes with another film, I would like to exchange." Another man would come and say that he has an Indian film called *Bobby* [1973]. I put them in touch and helped them exchange the films, and like this our network began.

When SRC began selling videocassette transfers of Pakistani films, Haji Shams's store in Liberty Market was one of the first official stockists in Lahore. As the videocassette trade became more saturated, Shams decided to build up a reserve of materials, either by transferring the vinyl records that were being eclipsed by audiocassettes in his store, or by recording television transmissions and drama performances, spectacles previously only experienced live. As PTV drama serials on television gained in reputation and respectability, even the writers and producers of the shows would come to Shams to buy keepsakes of the recordings that had not been archived by the station. But it was the trade in recording Punjabi stage dramas that made it financially viable for him to relocate to Saudi Arabia for the best part of a decade, where he joined his business partner who was already working in the Gulf. Together they opened three outlets selling a mixture of live recordings, informal copies, and authorized material to the large expatriate labor population. Finding an absence of recordings of Punjabi-language stage shows he began acquiring licenses to record more live spectacles back in Lahore and distributed them among the diaspora in the Gulf.

When he returned to Pakistan in the mid-1990s, Haji Shams found Hall Road a much more profitable commodity zone for film than Liberty Market, which had by then become widely associated with women's shopping and public leisure. He faced a quandary: Pakistani film during the Zia-era had become increasingly lurid and sexually suggestive, and the advertising material on show on Hall Road had put many women off visiting. However, with commercial rents skyrocketing, the varied and expansive reserve of materials he had collected over the years could allow him to keep master copies offsite and operate a small store producing copies struck from his base versions. The reputation he had gained in the Gulf was not based on legality or legitimacy but on quality and provenance, particularly proximity to the master copy, the urtext of the Pakistan videocassette and videodisc trade. When I met him, Haji Shams mourned how the ease of accessing knowledge on smartphones had reduced the need for middlemen like himself. Rarely anymore was he called upon to assist in retrieving something that previously only the video shop would have been able to access. He claimed his was the first shop in all of Punjab to develop a style of trade in which authority was associated with intimacy with the material, "All these shops you see in Lahore and Punjab, they all used to be our employees. We trained them." Wedged into an orange chair, with his impeccable black moustache and two gold signet rings taking up half of his left hand, Shams maintained his self-respect by reminding others of what marked him out. He felt he was selling a different product to his peers—prized, rare, and highbrow works that without him and his early investiture and faith in Pakistani moving-image media would not have survived.

His reputation, long cultivated, continued to pay dividends. He was one of the only film traders on Hall Road to whom women visited, as well as rarely visible minorities such as members of the small Hindu community centered around nearby Nila Gumbad. Haji Shams unwrapped the discs that were stacked in categorized bundles and dealt them in front of the buyer like a deck of cards. Having appraised his customers' sentiments, he might offer them Shiʻi discs illustrated with a selection of images that concealed the face of Imam Hussain with an ethereal white light.[30] Such repeated visits, as well as my own, only further strengthened his prestige amongst the other retailers. Being *imandar* or fostering a reputation for being *sharif* was an important part of a line of work which relied on the navigation of the potentially transgressive mahaul of film. The head-and-shoulders photographs that he and so many other established traders affixed to the cover of their discs was an avatar of this appeal to reliability. Shams told me, "I print my photo because everybody should know the middleman by his face. People should know the face of the person who has released the film."

Building on Emmanuel Levinas's philosophy of being face-to-face with difference, media theorist Roger Silverstone proposed the notion of "proper distance" as the foundation of media ethics.[31] "Proper distance" was predicated on the notion that only the separation of self and other allows for the formation of responsibility. What was for Silverstone, at the time of writing, "new media," such as the internet, bore a transcendent character, requiring the "personalization of the other" with whom one communicated but who was outside of immediate perception.[32] For Silverstone, technological mediations "destabilize . . . the proper distance that we must create and sustain if we are to act ethically."[33] This was the issue that stimulated my interlocutors in Lahore to express atmosphere as a way of putting a degree of distance between themselves and others. Yet the habit of using the face of the "middleman" as a mark of authority did not destabilize technological mediations in Lahore but rather helped Hall Road traders bring them into a wider sphere of commensuration and economic exchange. The face of Haji Shams was also a more personified version of the identifiers that Hall Road traders placed at the point in each film that features the most notable song or, more recently, the segment most likely to be extracted and uploaded to YouTube.[34] Like Hasan Mir's video identifiers of ritual flagellation (see chapter 4), the photographs of vendors' faces functioned somewhat like a watermark, a guarantee of trustworthiness, an appeal to repeat custom, but also as attempts to fix moral atmospheres and thresholds, by designating through whom the content generates value and to whom one can attribute responsibility.

The Threshold of the Copy

Unlike paper currency whose value is essentially redemptive, the circulatory dynamics of the Hall Road repertoire are accumulative in the patinated traces of those who mediate its movement through the morality of exchange. In the cases explored in this chapter, it is important to consider the material accumulation of patina as a result of media circulation. Typically, it is understood that agency can only be that of the subject or the object. The patina of Pakistani media in the Hall Road repertoire points to a third possible way whereby the materiality of the object becomes visible through marks made by the mediator, often occurring when objects in motion fuse with the hands through which they pass.[35]

As the first half of this book argued, in religious, state-secular, and individual moral worlds film holds an ambiguous place. As a crucial hub of urban political power Hall Road has its own mahaul, through which it forms a space for the reproduction of technology and capital—with film as just one of its instantiations—as well as the continuity of social reproduction. The 2008 bonfire on Hall Road was explicitly related to a hierarchy of copies and origins, such that value could be withheld at the expense of the destruction of iterations of offense, rather than its ultimate source. In the marketplace circulation of Pakistani film these master copies were not a gateway to an original but a superficial surface upon which trades and services were propagated and made respectable. Mediators, known by their names and faces, strived to indicate personal, existential contact with a master copy of quality and distinction. In this sense, re-copied Pakistani films on Hall Road were not indexes of their celluloid originals but of the space and contact of their transferal and the situations that characterized their interfaces. Morality, like that of the business of Hall Road traders, is an art of recording, retrieval, and reproduction. In this master-copy economy there were no perfect copies, but approximations blurred by the incisions and excisions of their mediators, and by the atmospheres between which interfaces allowed communication. This provides an answer to the question, what are the containers of Pakistani media "adequately meshed for?" While the master copy and the camera print retain a trace of the film, its simulated colors, the grain of its encounter with videocassette and dispersed pixels, they also catch the individuation of the transferrer.

In the last chapter, I suggested taking a more nuanced approach to the language of informality, to explain how not all the dynamics operating herein are reconcilable to the poles of state and non-state or authorized and illegitimate. Instead, the local terms kacha and pakka motion towards engagement and temporary consensus in the former and fixity and permanence in the latter. Kacha phenomenology is formed through communal use. A kacha road over an undeveloped plot of urban land turns back into scrubland if the tyre marks that demarcated it are not renewed. If a pakka road is desirable, the prior creation of a kacha road might be an effective strategy that can often lead to it. This might have been what Mubaraka had in mind in the Punjab Archives (see chapter 2) when she suggested that if the public at large have little understanding of what an archive is, or even that documents relating to the past can be useful or valuable, then the archive should open itself up, radically and irreversibly. "Give it to the public, send it to the market," was how she put it. This is exactly what has happened with the circulation of Pakistani media on Hall Road. Whether by accident or design Pakistani film has been allowed far wider circulation than other forms of image-making or sound, pertaining to languages, practices, and bodies that if broadcast on state media or the internet might have been subject to stricter control. If to be kacha is to be communal and unplanned, in the pakka lies the dangers of being accommodated by governing regimes of visibility and permissibility. Due to the multitude of perspectives over the epistemology and ontology of moving images in the public sphere, in turning film pakka lies a double-edged sword. My interlocutors found it better to "send it to the market," to let it age, develop a patina, fall out of view, return, revive, and disappear once again. In its atmospheres, thresholds, and interfaces, the circulation of film and video in Pakistan reminds us that mediation is not just a bulwark for transmission. Instead, mediation, like atmosphere itself, can be a container for the debris that cannot pass through the bottlenecks of time, materiality, and morality.

Epilogue

Towards the end of my time in Lahore, the relationship between Faisal and Idris at Durrani Electronics had soured. Idris became a more subdued version of himself, evidently muted by the frequent criticism from his uncle of his often ambivalent attitude to his work. Idris's eagerness to develop a standpoint on theological issues, something not expected of him in his former life in Dubai, also served to homogenize him to his environment. In searching to define moral atmospheres, he quickly became engulfed by them. However hard Idris had attempted to find ways to chip away at social norms and bring something of his life as an expat back with him, he found that Hall Road's merchant community mercilessly absorbed any kind of difference. I later learned that Idris had soon parted ways with Durrani Electronics and took up the family trade in taxidermy. Through a burst of WhatsApp messages with images of stuffed ibex, chukars, and pheasants, I got the impression he was satisfied with his work. That Idris had asserted too much individualism to thrive among Hall Road's traders was itself puzzling. It was my impression that the value of the master copy operated by highlighting the place of individual mediators of a film's genealogy while remaining porous to future users, technological affordances, and appropriations. Yet in the new form that Hall Road's media environment had taken—as a place of digital hardware, internet data, appendages, and spare parts manufactured in bulk and sold cheaply—the entangled materiality of persons and things felt precarious. Its sense of precarity was amplified by the destruction of Karachi's Empress Market in 2018 in a government anti-encroachment drive, leaving Hall Road's labyrinthine alleyways vulnerable to similar clearances.

One might argue that the close entanglement between film and public morality that I have traced in this book is not unique to Pakistan. In the United Kingdom from where I write this, the Obscene Publications Act of 1959 still requires those accused of releasing a film deemed obscene to argue that its exhibition is justified as a positive contribution to the "public good."

Yet the way I found people speculate on the mahaul that surrounds film culture and experience in Pakistan provides a way of understanding atmosphere in a new light. When people give a name to disquiet, unease, and awe, they also give name to the collective as well as the individual who perceives it. For a country shared by various faiths, ambient interruptions, offending images, and competing soundscapes, to name an atmosphere is to describe possible cohabitants as well as strangers. Mahaul describes a sense of immersion in the moral and social qualities of an environment. This sense of immersion acknowledges that there are moral worlds other than your own, and that they have atmospheres too. Nida Kirmani is right to suggest that when a community that one can find membership within does not present itself, many look to mahaul as a concept that holds together and sets apart persons, things, and ideas.[1] This also leaves us with a question for future research. If the community affords collective action, what forms of solidarity do atmospheres afford?

Atmospheres make demands of you. These demands provide instructive but fluctuating ideas about how to act in the immediate or assumed presence of others. For the interlocutors with whom I discussed these matters and more, mahaul was many things. It was an ever changing ecology formed in the commensurate and non-commensurate sphere in which film, music, images, and entertainment move; an aura that emanates from the very distributed object-hood of a film that changes with the hands through which it passes; an esoteric quality that gives pious sentiment to affective experience; and the felt dynamics of market demand. The local concept of mahaul serves as a call to recognize the moral character that atmospheres can take, particularly at the interstitial friction between religious coexistence and a secular free market shot through with the overarching influence of majoritarian faith. In this way, mahaul is closer to the idea of atmospheric citizenship suggested by Patrick Eisenlohr as a form of place-making and claims-making.[2] Yet when the means of circulation is primarily restricted to a male domain, the ability to influence the mediatic conditions of a particular moral atmosphere remains patriarchal. This does not mean that atmosphere will always be coercive; this would be to miss the speed with which its character can dissipate and be taken over by other ways of receiving, participating, and finding meaning in media cultures.

Having begun my research as a study of the circulatory dynamics of film in Pakistan I soon found that consensus and dissensus over what constitutes an accurate copy of a film, the place of film experience in the public sphere, and what is and is not film have been collapsed into a perceptible focus on moral thresholds, rather than their aggregation to binaries of right and wrong. In what I have called the Hall Road repertoire, circulation does not only determine economic value through rarity. The free market, acting in its more coercive dimensions as a censorial regulator of public morality, also makes palpable the shifting moral thresholds that define others' sentiments about right and wrong. Knowing these thresholds as the result of countless value decisions is also to come to grips with a sense of moral consensus produced dialogically between those present to one another face-to-face. This is not to say that the result is radical or emancipatory, but rather that it highlights the ways in which people become aware of how to avoid hurting the sentiments of others. Here resides the kinds of knowledge it is possible to attain by talking about thresholds as magnitude, as a level of intensity before something becomes manifest, rather than the traditional anthropological understanding of the threshold as a line of ritual crossing. Another way of reading someone like Victor Turner's exposition of the figure of the threshold is as a particle of moral experience, an unassigned phenomenon resistant to aggregation into moral norms. Somewhat in keeping with Turner's language of social drama, I studied these thresholds through their repertoires.

By coming to grips with atmospheric phenomena such as blurred edges, thresholds, and moral moods this book has tried to better understand how film and media become objects around which forms of religious life are contested. In the marketplace circulation of film in Pakistan, these atmospheric forms are characterized by the mutual coexistence of conflicting, often opposed viewpoints which evince a disjuncture between how people feel about popular entertainment and how they act. The introduction characterized this as the coexistence of interdiction and reproduction in the circulation of media. In these terms reproduction refers to the mechanical production of duplicate containers of media content or their digital transformations. Interdiction refers to a discursive and sensory realm that might be called the permissible. The coexistence of interdiction and reproduction in the practices of film traders is indicative of a wider shift to forms of public morality guided *by the people*.

Such residual populism instantiates what William Mazzarella calls "the moments in which the affective and corporeal substance of social life makes itself felt as an intensification that exceeds or has fallen out of alignment with prevailing institutional mediations."[3] This line of thinking finds echoes in Siegfried Kracauer's conception of modernity as material culture in a state of evaporation. His notion of the "mass ornament" was driven by the idea that through surfaces, or surface-level expressions, it is possible to grasp the logics that systems aspire to produce through the spasmodic "aesthetic reflex" manifested as the emanations of objects.[4] In the proliferation of master copies, the resultant patinated palimpsest, and the unstable origins registered on the surfaces of Pakistani media objects, the degraded image reveals the aspirations and anxieties of a "people" understood to be the arbiters of public morality.

In my ethnography the movement of the three central concepts took the following form. Thresholds arise when the surface tension of public affect is made taut by feelings of alliance, disavowal, and ambivalence that radiate between felt bodies and moral others. Tethered to subjective ideas like proper conduct or a common good, thresholds have a vaporous quality. Yet in a state of saturation, they precipitate a crisis, such as in a public sphere saturated with anxieties or affinities towards film experience. Poured out into a shared volumetric space—that is, space enclosed by a common boundary—thresholds come together like clouds. As both airborne media and discursive frames, atmospheres turn thresholds into objects of moral perception, giving them stakes like membership and exclusion, public decency or decay. I call the boundaries between atmospheres *interfaces*, describing planes of connection and communication that are recognizable by a common metric, such as how the master copies used by Hall Road traders are porous to virtues like trust, guardianship, or image quality.

To go through the cycle again in different categorical terms, thresholds are poured into volumetric space and form atmospheres in the realm of opacity, where somatic forms of membership and exclusion remain latent. This atmospheric space is also the domain of affinity, of abjection, and of uncertainty. Coexistent atmospheres, some drawn from the same thresholds, also tip into the realm of legibility, a semiotic realm of membership and exclusion which is primarily the domain of alliance, disavowal, and ambivalence. Whether by accident or design, interfaces emerge that form a wedge between atmospheres and the domains of the opaque and the legible. An interface also serves to reflect the atmosphere back to those whose bodies are first to recognize them, at the same time as providing a readable surface for those on the outside. This latter form of legibility also disciplines the atmosphere at the same time as fixing blurred lines between atmospheres. The triangulation of interfaces makes them able to assume the appearance of moral injunctions and proscriptions. Finally, the circulation and interaction of these concepts retune and retighten the surface tension of public affect, making a variegated situation through which people perceive one another's moral character.

This book has also highlighted the different kinds of moral stakes that come together in a media marketplace that has thrived through its traders' intervention in the space of the commons. Idris's prompt to explore the mahauliyat of media led me to engage with the force of market demand. On Hall Road demand can act as an alibi, such that whatever is in circulation is not one person's will and thereby renders mediators neutral conduits in relation to potentially transgressive content. Demand is also predicated on the assumed values of others and is therefore predisposed to wider moral thresholds. As a constellation of moral choices and value decisions, what I have called the Hall Road repertoire is an accumulated inventory of media affects. To focus on media repertoires, their contents, omissions, and mediation, is also to explore the ways in which other kinds of repertoire should be approached and the choices that follow such reflection. These choices could include whether to look or avert one's gaze, to become accustomed to music beside a pious space or tune out altogether, or whether to delete a dubious news item or circulate it further.

As I have already mentioned, Pakistan's electronics and media marketplaces can act like free trade exclaves outside moral and legal authority, in which pirated or copied materials come to form a commons due to a historic lack of copyright enforcement. This sits in stark contrast to many of the country's bureaucratic records offices and archives. As a counterpoint to the impenetrability of the bureaucracy, its inverse, the trade in and transfer of moving-image media, has been largely permitted free reign. The Hall Road repertoire is formed directly by the levels of intensification that exceed the country's censor boards, archives, or legal enforcement. Further study of moral thresholds might help to locate these forces of affective presence in the spaces between institutions, infrastructures, and agency.

As communication and social media technologies become ever more constitutive in shaping the environmental conditions of everyday life, many strive to demarcate their own frontiers and limits. As a physical site that shapes the elemental conditions of media technology, Hall Road is also a sphere of anonymity and moral ambivalence. Traders of religious media who find themselves unintentional stockists attempt to define moral thresholds for their content as it circulates beyond their own proximate boundaries of kin and faith. These boundaries come together in periods of abeyance such as Muharram, in which the contours of how to disturb and how to endure are widely perceptible, if not immediately knowable. As information flows, halts, and disturbs in myriad ways, borders and frontiers manifest themselves in productive friction with normative approaches to piety or power. The sensual and atmospheric boundaries manifested or transgressed by the spread of music, film, rumor, news, and energy, or the recording and retrieval of sounds, images, and data, call for engagement with the ways in which the making and breaking of affective boundaries operate through media, its digital flows and unruly circulation.

As the fearful bonfire of pornography in 2008 showed, tipping points are not necessarily material states of affairs that exist in the world, but the felt force of a threshold which might be driven by the magnitude of public sentiment. If pornography is the limit to a good moral atmosphere, such that a public bonfire serves to make the boundary more explicit, these come coded with gendered forms of sociality and violence attached to them. Whether predicated as its corporeal limits or remaining on the outskirts of this system of atmospheres, women are intimately linked to the risks and dangers that are kept at bay through a heightened sensitivity to moral thresholds. Yet the means of accessing this ambient and discursive sphere, in which the surface tension of public sentiment is felt and revised, is ultimately the preserve of majoritarian, masculine agents.

In this patriarchal sphere, the technologized commons of films, songs, atmospheres, moods, and saints becomes a source of promise or anxiety when combined with the awareness of the presence of mediation and retrieval that must necessarily bring such things out of storage and provide interfaces for their materialization. Lahore's urban visual culture is a space transformed by the ways in which capacious media perpetually brings its latent contents to the surface as interface. The anxieties that surround technological systems of recording and containment turn them into interfaces for protean objects capable of other lives. The result is an aura of holiness, profanity, or ambiguity, that makes one brace before the patinated image or the materiality of a well-worn film and its various layers of age, overpainting, and retouching, and that speaks of atmospheres inherited, subsumed, contested, and shared. Rather than marking the presence of the divine, the mahaul of sites such as Hall Road and its repertoires are made up of the combined presence of primarily male moral selves, receptive to one another. As mediation has come to be seen as central to the material and immaterial dimensions of faith and piety, such atmospheres are as entangled in urban and informal topographies as they are in practices of representation. The surfaces and interfaces of media objects that can be experienced as superficial, porous, or deep in meaning are another way of feeling and animating the thresholds that manifest change. Studying atmospheres in this way is to glimpse ethical conduct grounded on the proximity and presence of a stranger who is also, potentially, an equal.

Glossary of Frequently Used Terms

AHL-E BAIT: The family of the Prophet Muhammad.

ALIM (sing.) / ULAMA (plural): A figure of Islamic learning.

ASHURA: The tenth day of the Islamic month of Muharram.

AWAAM: The people or public.

AZADARI: Communal mourning for Imam Hussain, but also the Twelve Imams and Ahl-e Bait.

AZAN: The Muslim call to prayer.

DVDWALLA: Medium-specific term for a film trader.

FILMI: Related to or characteristic of a South Asian film industry.

HADD (sing.) / HUDOOD (plural): The social location of divine boundaries.

KACHA: Temporary.

KHIDMAT: Religiously infused service or the provision of welfare.

MAHAUL: Moral atmosphere.

MAHAULIYAT: Environment; system of atmospheres.

MAJLIS (sing.) / MAJALIS (plural): A program of oration attended by Shi'a Muslims.

MAZHAB: Jurisprudential school of thought.

MOHALLA: Neighborhood.

MUHARRAM: The first month in the Islamic calendar. Also a shorthand for the first ten days, when the trials of the Battle of Karbala and the death of Imam Hussain are commemorated.

NA'AT: A recitation in praise of the Prophet Muhammad.

PAKKA: Fixed.

QABZA: Occupation, possession, or encroachment.

RAMADAN: A month of fasting and contemplation that culminates in Eid-ul-Azha.

TAUBA: Repentance or renunciation.

Notes

Introduction

1. Cressida Jervis-Read, "Frontier Town: Marking Boundaries in a Delhi Reset-tlement Colony 30 Years On," in *Sarai Reader 07: Frontiers*, ed. Monica Nerula, Shuddhabrata Sengupta, Jeebesh Bagchi, and Ravi Sundaram (Delhi: Sarai Media Lab, 2007), 519; Anita Weiss, *Walls Within Walls: Life Histories of Work-ing Women in the Old City of Lahore* (Colorado: Westview Press, 1992), 155.

2. Nida Kirmani, *Questioning the "Muslim Woman": Identity and Insecurity in an Urban Indian Locality* (London: Routledge, 2016), 50.

3. Leo Spitzer, "Milieu and Ambiance: An Essay in Historical Semantics, Part I," *Philosophy and Phenomenological Research* 3, no. 2 (December 1942): 169–218.

4. Anthropologists often describe their mode of description as holistic, that is, embedded in an assumption that even the smallest parts of a relationship, envi-ronment, or object are interconnected parts of a wider whole. Holism allows anthropology to balance its contributions to both the general and the particu-lar. This interpretation is closely associated with the work of Louis Dumont, who argued that the tension between holism and individualism, where a person forms their own moral whole, is present in many societies. However, as Katherine Pratt Ewing has argued, even within a single individual, the experience of wholeness can be contingent and inconsistent. Louis Dumont, *Homo Hierarchicus: The Caste System and Its Implications* (Chicago: University of Chicago Press, 1980); Katherine Pratt Ewing, "The Illusion of Wholeness: Culture, Self, and the Experience of Inconsistency," *Ethos* 18, no. 3 (Sep-tember 1990): 251–278.

5. In this way, it has much in common with *mana*, the Polynesian concept which sees persons, places, and things imbued with a force of prestige or authority. The force of *mana* has animated works from Émile Durkheim's *The Elementary Forms of the Religious Life* to William Mazzarella's illuminating work on political populism and mass mediation. Émile Durkheim, *The Elementary Forms of the Religious Life*, trans. Joseph Ward Swain (London: George Allen and Unwin, 1964); William Mazzarella, *The Mana of Mass Society* (Chicago: University of Chicago Press, 2017).

6. Annabelle Sreberny and Ali Mohammadi, *Small Media, Big Revolution: Communication, Culture, and the Iranian Revolution* (Minneapolis: University of Minnesota Press, 1994), 178.

7. Alamgir Kabir, *The Cinema in Pakistan* (Dhaka: Sandhani, 1969), 98.

8. Kabir, 98.

9. For the purposes of a rough chronology, videocassettes were used as the primary means of moving-image media distribution on Hall Road between 1980 and 2008, while videodiscs have been used between 2000 and the present (2023 at the time of writing). Digital data files, loaded onto USB or microSD cards, became a means of sale between the beginning and middle of the 2010s.

10. Ravi Sundaram, *Pirate Modernity: Delhi's Media Urbanism* (London: Routledge, 2009).

11. Ravi Sundaram, "Uncanny Networks: Pirate, Urban, and New Globalisation," *Economic and Political Weekly* 39, no. 1 (January 2004): 67. It should not be assumed that the subalterneity of labor practices and the content of informal media coalesce. Take, for example, contemporary artist and media scholar Farida Batool Syeda's study of sexually suggestive *mujra* dance recordings and their journey across formats and audiences, which sees Hall Road become a site in which to study material, moral, and responsive discourses on performance culture. Farida Batool Syeda, *New Media, Masculinity and Mujra Dance in Pakistan* (diss., SOAS, University of London, 2015).

12. Lenart Škof and Petri Berndtson, "Introduction," in *Atmospheres of Breathing*, ed. Lenart Škof and Petri Berndtson (New York: State University of New York Press, 2018), xv.

13. Hazrat Inayat Khan, *The Music of Life* (New York: Omega, 1988), 15.

14. Khan, 17.

15. Khan, 17.

16. In the words of John Durham Peters, then as now, communication can be both "bridge and chasm." John Durham Peters, *Speaking into the Air: A History of the Idea of Communication* (Chicago: University of Chicago Press, 1999), 5.

17. Hermann Schmitz, Rudolf Owen Müllan, and Jan Slaby, "Emotions outside the Box: The New Phenomenology of Feeling and Corporeality," *Phenomenology and the Cognitive Sciences* 10, no. 2 (June 2011): 247.

18. Gernot Böhme, "Atmosphere as the Fundamental Concept of a New Aesthetics," *Thesis Eleven* 36, no. 1 (August 1993): 121.

19. Gernot Böhme, *Atmospheric Architectures: The Aesthetics of Felt Spaces*, ed. and trans. A.-Chr. Engels-Schwarzpaul (London: Bloomsbury, 2017), 162.

20. By referring to theories and philosophies of atmosphere that have gained currency in Euro-American academia, I aim to highlight the importance of empirical research on the subject as a necessary contribution to what can, to some, seem to be nebulous or apolitical scholarly debates.

21. Patrick Eisenlohr, *Sounding Islam: Voice, Media, and Sonic Atmospheres in an Indian Ocean World* (California: University of California Press, 2018), 3.

22. Patrick Eisenlohr, "Atmospheric Resonance. Sonic Motion and the Question of Religious Mediation," *Journal of the Royal Anthropological Institute* 28, no. 2 (June 2022): 617.

23. Patrick Eisenlohr, "Atmospheric Citizenship: Sonic Movement and Public Religion in Shi'i Mumbai," *Public Culture* 33, no. 3 (September 2021): 371–392.

24. Lauren Berlant, *Cruel Optimism* (Durham, NC: Duke University Press, 2011), 231.

25. Matthew Engelke, *God's Agents: Biblical Publicity in Contemporary England* (Berkeley: University of California Press, 2013), 37.

26. Engelke, 50.

27. This is not to dispel the premium James Laidlaw puts on the freedom to reflect and adjudicate on one's position in the world as a prerequisite for ethical action, but to argue that reflection can take place while pressing oneself up to the surface tension of public sentiment. James Laidlaw, *The Subject of Virtue: An Anthropology of Ethics and Freedom* (Cambridge: Cambridge University Press, 2013).

28. Søren Kierkegaard, *Either/Or: A Fragment of Life*, trans. Alastair Hannay, abridged version (London: Penguin, 1992).

29. Mariam Ali Baig, "The Pakola Tale," in *Mazaar, Bazaar: Design and Visual Culture in Pakistan*, ed. Saima Zaidi (Oxford: Oxford University Press, 2009), 158.

30. In *Pandora's Hope*, the French anthropologist Bruno Latour uses the simile of a broken projector to argue that the disposition of technological artifacts only becomes apparent when they break down. Bruno Latour, *Pandora's Hope: Essays on the Reality of Science Studies* (Cambridge, MA: Harvard University Press, 1999), 193.

31. Gernot Böhme, "A Matter of Taste? On the Significance of Aesthetic Judgement for Morality," *Senses and Society* 16, no. 3 (2021): 352–353. See also Constantine V. Nakassis, *Doing Style: Youth and Mass Mediation in South India* (Chicago: University of Chicago Press, 2016).

32. Ali Nobil Ahmad and Ali Khan, "Special Issue: Pakistani Cinema," *BioScope: South Asian Screen Studies* 5, no. 2 (July 2014); Vazira Fazila-Yacoobali

Zamindar and Asad Ali, eds., *Love, War, and Other Longings: Essays on Cinema in Pakistan* (London: Oxford University Press, 2020); Gwendolyn Kirk, *Uncivilized Language and Aesthetic Exclusion: Language, Power, and Film Production in Pakistan* (diss., University of Texas, 2016); Iftikhar Dadi, "BioScopic and Screen Studies of Pakistan, and of Contemporary Art," *BioScope: South Asian Screen Studies* 1, no. 1 (January 2010).

33. Omer Shahab, "One of Pakistan's Oldest Cinemas in a State of Shambles, Plays Vulgar Films All Year Round," *Daily Times*, August 12, 2018, https://dailytimes.com.pk/282069/one-of-pakistans-oldest-cinemas-in-a-state-of-shambles-plays-vulgar-films-all-year-round/.

34. C. Jason Throop, "Moral Moods," *Ethos* 42, no .1 (March 2014): 70. Throop's work has sounded an important call for cultural phenomenological approaches to moral experience, at the same time providing theoretical insights into how the kinds of moral sensibilities that produce value aspirations are closely buffered by negative sentiments. C. Jason Throop, "Moral Sentiments," in *A Companion to Moral Anthropology*, ed. Didier Fassin (London: Wiley-Blackwell, 2012), 150–168.

35. Laura U. Marks, *Touch: Sensuous Theory and Multisensory Media* (Minneapolis: University of Minnesota Press, 2002); David MacDougall, *The Corporeal Image: Film, Ethnography, and the Senses* (Princeton, NJ: Princeton University Press, 2005); Birgit Meyer, *Sensational Movies: Video, Vision, and Christianity in Ghana*, (Berkeley: University of California Press, 2015); Ravi Vasudevan, "In the Centrifuge of History," *Cinema Journal* 50, no. 1 (Fall 2010): 135–140; Sudhir Mahadevan, *A Very Old Machine: The Many Origins of the Cinema in India* (New York: SUNY Press, 2015); Anand Pandian, *Reel World: An Anthropology of Creation* (Durham, NC: Duke University Press, 2015).

36. Joel Robbins, "Dumont's Hierarchical Dynamism: Christianity and Individualism Revisited," *HAU: Journal of Ethnographic Theory* 5, no. 1 (Spring 2015): 175.

37. Author's translation, S. M. Shahid, *Film Acting Guide* (Lahore: Aleem Publishers, 1994), 5.

38. Naveeda Khan, *Muslim Becoming: Aspiration and Skepticism in Pakistan* (Durham, NC: Duke University Press, 2012), 146.

39. Veena Das, "Moral and Spiritual Striving in the Everyday: To Be a Muslim in Contemporary India," in *Ethical Life in South Asia*, ed. Anand Pandian and Daud Ali, (Bloomington: Indiana University Press, 2010), 376; Das's vision of "ordinary ethics" is one divorced from "grand projects of redemption" and instead wedded to showing how "small quotidian acts stand up to the horrific." Veena Das, "What Does Ordinary Ethics Look Like," in *Four Lectures on Ethics*, ed. Michael Lambek et al., 53–126. (Chicago: HAU Books, 2015), 70.

40. Das, "Moral and Spiritual Striving," 233.

41. In Michael Lempert's critique of "ordinary ethics," ethics should never be presumed "immanent" in everyday life but should be sought in events and disruptions that themselves must be mediated to become wider objects of communicative practice. Michael Lempert, "No Ordinary Ethics," *Anthropological Theory* 13, no. 4 (December 2013): 370–393.

42. For Joel Robbins, the rejection of transcendence in ordinary ethics excludes religious subjects from participation in the ordinary, and from ethical life as a whole. Drawing on the work of Alfred Schutz, Robbins points to different taxonomies of transcendence, "little transcendencies . . . in which the transcendent item is presently beyond our immediate perceptual experience," and "middle transcendencies," the inner lives of others that we feel that we might share although might never fully know. By this logic of little and middle transcendencies, "we are entangled in transcendence all the time." Joel Robbins, "What is the Matter with Transcendence? On the Place of Religion in the New Anthropology of Ethics," *Journal of the Royal Anthropological Institute* 22, no. 4 (December 2016): 772.

43. Amira Mittermaier, "Dreams from Elsewhere: Muslim Subjectivities Beyond the Trope of Self-cultivation," *Journal of the Royal Anthropological Institute* 18, no. 2 (June 2012): 258.

44. Amira Mittermaier, *Dreams That Matter: Egyptian Landscapes of the Imagination*, (Berkeley: University of California Press, 2010), 56. In pursuit of a positive theorization of atmosphere, we might also look to the kind of social phenomena that Rupert Stasch finds rooted in forging ties through differences rather than likenesses, "otherness as a relation." Rupert Stasch, *Society of Others: Kinship and Mourning in a West Papuan Place* (Berkeley: University of California Press, 2009), 7.

45. Teresa Brennan, *The Transmission of Affect* (Ithaca, NY: Cornell University Press, 2004), 1.

46. Equally influential to me was Yael Navaro Yashin's work on post-war Cyprus, in which an affective sphere undergirded by the lingering presence of departed others, and the material residue of being othered, erects ambient boundaries that shape political subjectivities. Yael Navaro-Yashin, *The Make-Believe Space: Affective Geography in a Postwar Polity* (Durham, NC: Duke University Press, 2012).

47. Paolo Cherchi Usai, *The Death of Cinema: History, Cultural Memory and the Digital Dark Age* (London: Bloomsbury Publishing, 2001), 7.

48. Walter Benjamin, *The Work of Art in the Age of Its Technological Reproducibility, and Other Writings on Media* (Cambridge, MA: Harvard University Press, 2008).

49. Ali Nobil Ahmad and Ali Khan, eds., *Cinema and Society: Film and Social Change in Pakistan* (Karachi: Oxford University Press, 2016); Ali Nobil Ahmad and Ali

Khan, eds., *Film and Cinephilia in Pakistan: Beyond Life and Death* (Oxford: Oxford University Press. 2020).

50. Javed Jabbar, "Passion in the Pakistani Cinema," in *Snapshots: Reflections in a Pakistani Eye*, ed. Javed Jabbar (Lahore: Wazidalis, 1982): 149.

51. Brinkley Messick, *Shariʿa Scripts: A Historical Anthropology* (New York: Columbia University Press, 2018); Morgan Clarke, *Islam and New Kinship: Reproductive Technology and the Shariah in Lebanon* (London: Berghahn Books, 2009).

52. Maulana Mufti Muhammad Shafi, *Alat-e Jadida ke Shariʿi Ahkam* [The Orders of the Shariʿa on Modern Inventions] (Karachi: Idarat-ul Maruf, 1996), 223.

53. In thinking through the thresholds that arise at the interstice of media and public morality, I owe a substantial debt to over two decades of scholarship on film and media in South Asia. Central to this has been the research emerging from the Sarai group, which began in 2000 focusing on the relationship between media, urbanity, and the public sphere in India, founded by Ravi Vasudevan, Ravi Sundaram, and contemporary art practitioners the Raqs Media Collective (Jeebesh Bagchi, Monica Narula, and Shuddhabrata Sengupta). The latter's 2010 text *Seepage* can be seen as a manifesto for a new way of engaging with media, driven by pirate infrastructures, practices, and market methods that magnify the bleeding edges between formats and moral standpoints. Raqs Media Collective, *Seepage* (Berlin: Sternberg Press, 2010); A volume by Joshua Neves and Bhaskar Sarkar evocatively deploys the image of the penumbra, the transforming threshold between light and dark during an eclipse, as a way of understanding Asian video cultures whose emergent ethics resist their smooth aggregation into global flows. They write, "Penumbral forms and practices comprise much of the mainstream and *seem* marginal only because something opaque comes in the way of their legibility," succinctly describing the way I observed moral thresholds emerge in relation to media objects and their circulations. Joshua Neves and Bhaskar Sarkar, "Introduction," in *Asian Video Cultures: In the Penumbra of the Global*, ed. Joshua Neves and Bhaskar Sarkar (Durham, NC: Duke University Press, 2017), 1–34.

54. Long predating the ethical turn in contemporary anthropology, Katherine Pratt Ewing examined the unresolved tension that rises in the spaces between ambiguity, religious authority, and everyday conduct. Katherine Pratt Ewing, "Introduction: Ambiguity and Sharīʿat—A Perspective on the Problem of Moral Principles in Tension," in *Sharīʿat and Ambiguity in South Asian Islam*, ed. Katherine Pratt Ewing (Berkeley: University of California Press, 1988), 1–22. These ideas have also been examined more recently in Thomas Bauer's argument that the lived heterogeneity of Islamic faith provides an "intensive training in ambiguity" which delineates in its followers' plurality of responses and responsibilities a sign of divine grace. Thomas Bauer, *A Culture of*

Ambiguity: An Alternative History of Islam, trans. Hinrich Biesterfeldt and Tricia Tunstall (New York: Columbia University Press, 2021), 260.

55. Similarities with Barelvi Islam and Shi'ism can be found in the celebrated presence and personhood of the Prophet Muhammad, the celebrated role of Ali as an important exemplar, and attendance at shrines, many of which hold the Barelvi and Shi'a as their most ardent visitors.

56. In his calls for a philosophy of elemental media, John Durham Peters draws attention to how digital media has amplified the presence of the "stranger." John Durham Peters, *The Marvelous Clouds: Toward a Philosophy of Elemental Media* (Chicago: University of Chicago Press, 2015), 6. A similar sentiment is evident in Böhme's writing on atmosphere. In a dialogic sense, minor shifts in tone might cause disturbances, or the *"tearing open"* of an atmosphere communally produced yet traversable by outsiders. Indeed, the "appearance of a stranger" turns an atmosphere into a more perceptible human infrastructure. Böhme, *Atmospheric Architectures*, 107. Jarrett Zigon might describe the situation Böhme and Peters identify as a potential "moral breakdown" in which an event or an individual forces the deliberative action of an ethical response. Jarrett Zigon, "Moral and Ethical Assemblages," *Anthropological Theory* 10, no. 1–2 (March 2010): 3–15.

57. Simone Dennis, *Smokefree: A Social, Moral and Political Atmosphere* (London: Bloomsbury Publishing, 2016), 32.

58. See Bhrigupati Singh, "The Headless Horseman of Central India: Sovereignty at Varying Thresholds of Life," *Cultural Anthropology* 27, no. 2 (May 2012): 383–407.

59. Melody Jue and Rafico Ruiz, "Introduction," in *Saturation: An Elemental Politics*, ed. Melody Jue and Rafico Ruiz (Durham, NC: Duke University Press, 2021), 3.

60. Melody Jue, *Wild Blue Media: Thinking through Seawater* (Durham: Duke University Press, 2020), 53; Jue, 69.

61. It was also informed by the creation of four ethnographic films set in Pakistan and the first international retrospective of Pakistani film at the British Film Institute that I co-curated with Ali Nobil Ahmad. The retrospective examined the work of Jamil Dehlavi and was held in London in August 2018.

62. Kuhu Tanvir argued that "pirate histories" can sustain the memory of peripheral and marginal film cultures in ways that challenge the discursive underpinnings of formal repositories. Kuhu Tanvir, "Pirate Histories: Rethinking the Indian Film Archive," *BioScope: South Asian Screen Studies* 4, no. 2 (July 2013): 115–136.

63. John R. Bowen, *Islam, Law, and Equality in Indonesia: An Anthropology of Public Reasoning* (Cambridge: Cambridge University Press, 2003), 7.

64. Diana Taylor, *The Archive and the Repertoire: Performing Cultural Memory in the Americas* (Durham, NC: Duke University Press, 2003), 20.

65. Dadi, "BioScopic and Screen Studies," 13.

66. Iftikhar Dadi, *Lahore Cinema: Between Realism and Fable* (Seattle: University of Washington Press, 2022).

67. Nadia Fadil and Mayanthi Fernando perceive the divide between these two approaches to be reliant on Islamic piety movements acting the role of antagonists that produce a normatively inverted sense of the ordinary. Nadia Fadil and Mayanthi Fernando, "Rediscovering the 'Everyday' Muslim: Notes on an Anthropological Divide," *HAU: Journal of Ethnographic Theory* 5, no. 2 (Fall 2015): 80.

68. Talal Asad, *The Idea of an Anthropology of Islam*, Occasional Papers Series (Washington, DC: Institute for Contemporary Arab Studies at Georgetown University, 1986); Saba Mahmood, *Politics of Piety: The Islamic Revival and the Feminist Subject* (Princeton, NJ: Princeton University Press, 2006).

69. Charles Hirschkind, *The Ethical Soundscape: Cassette Sermons and Islamic Counterpublics* (New York: Columbia University Press, 2006), 26.

70. Lalitha Gopalan, *Cinema of Interruptions: Action Genres in Contemporary Indian Cinema* (London: British Film Institute, 2002), 28.

71. In a wider philosophical trajectory that might be read in parallel with this book's argument, Michel Foucault looked to understand discontinuity through the figure of the threshold. This text, which is largely limited in focus to the archaeology of discourse in the sciences, borrows the term threshold from Gaston Bachelard's *The Poetics of Space*, which inspired Foucault to direct his attention away from the smooth reproduction of knowledge and towards the "incidence of interruptions" that causes epistemological systems to pivot and veer off course. Michel Foucault, *The Archaeology of Knowledge*, trans. A. M. Sheridan Smith (New York: Pantheon Books, 1972), 4; Gaston Bachelard, *The Poetics of Space*, trans. Maria Jolas (Boston: Beacon Press, 1994).

72. James George Frazer, *Taboo and the Perils of the Soul* (London: Macmillan, 1911), 224.

73. Dominic Boyer, "Digital Expertise in Online Journalism (and Anthropology)," *Anthropological Quarterly* 83, no. 1 (Winter 2010): 87–88.

74. Birgit Meyer et al., "An Author Meets Her Critics: Around Birgit Meyer's 'Mediation and the Genesis of Presence: Toward a Material Approach to Religion,'" *Religion and Society: Advances in Research* 5, no. 1 (September 2014): 205–254. As Bruno Reinhardt rightly argues, the atmospheric presence that believers associate with technologies should not only be seen in attempts to mediate divine presence but also as a means of staying alert to the guises through which the divine might make itself known. Bruno Reinhardt, "Atmospheric

Presence: Reflections on 'Mediation' in the Anthropology of Religion and Technology," *Anthropological Quarterly* 93, no. 1 (Winter 2020): 1532.

75. Brian Silverstein, "Disciplines of Presence in Modern Turkey: Discourse, Companionship, and the Mass Mediation of Islamic Practice," *Cultural Anthropology* 23, no. 1 (February 2008): 141.

76. Katherine Pratt Ewing, "Introduction: Ambiguity and *Sharīʿat*—A Perspective on the Problem of Moral Principles in Tension," in *Sharīʿat and Ambiguity in South Asian Islam*, ed. Katherine Pratt Ewing (Berkeley: University of California Press, 1988) 2.

77. Katherine Pratt Ewing, *Arguing Sainthood: Modernity, Psychoanalysis, and Islam* (Durham, NC: Duke University Press, 1997), 5.

78. Khan, *Muslim Becoming*, 12.

79. Jack Goody, *The Interface Between the Written and the Oral* (Cambridge: Cambridge University Press, 1987), 78.

1. Cinema Itself: Film and Faith in Pakistan

1. The Pakistan Penal Code contains several strictures that guard against religious offense, which together are often referred to as its "blasphemy laws." Often this is implicitly referring to Section 295C.

2. Hall Road traders voted in large numbers for the Tehreek-e-Labbaik Pakistan (TLP) in the September 2017 by-election in the parliamentary constituency of NA-120 in which the market falls, helping them earn 5.7 percent of the vote. The rise of Barelvi protest groups like the TLP is indicative of the cooperation between entrepreneurial trade, Sufic devotional piety, and the state. See Katherine Pratt Ewing and Rosemary R. Corbett, eds., *Modern Sufis and the State: The Politics of Islam in South Asia and Beyond* (New York: Columbia University Press, 2020).

3. Faiz Ahmad Faiz, "What Would You Have?," in Faiz Ahmed Faiz, *Culture and Identity: Selected English Writings of Faiz*, ed. Sheema Majeed (Oxford: Oxford University Press, 2005), 120.

4. Faiz, 120.

5. Faiz, 120.

6. Mushtaq Gazdar, *Pakistan Cinema, 1947–1997* (Karachi: Oxford University Press, 1997), 127–128.

7. Iqbal Sevea, "'Kharaak Kita Oi!' Masculinity, Caste and Gender in Punjabi Films," *BioScope: South Asian Screen Studies* 5, no. 2 (July 2014), 133.

8. Stephen Putnam Hughes, "Music in the Age of Mechanical Reproduction: Drama, Gramophone, and the Beginnings of Tamil Cinema," *Journal of Asian*

Studies 66, no. 1 (February 2007): 3–34; Kaushik Bhaumik, "Cinematograph to Cinema: Bombay 1896–1928," *BioScope: South Asian Screen Studies* 2, no. 1 (January 2011): 41–67; Manishita Dass, *Outside the Lettered City: Cinema, Modernity, and the Public Sphere in Late Colonial India* (Oxford: Oxford University Press, 2016).

9. Lakshmi Srinivas, *House Full: Indian Cinema and the Active Audience* (Chicago: University of Chicago Press, 2016).

10. Farina Mir, "Urdu Ethics Literature and the Diversity of Muslim Thought in Colonial India," *American Historical Review* 127, no. 3 (September 2022): 1163.

11. Akhlaq literature understood these relationships as predicated on *huquq*, rights that rely on the mutual bonds endemic in one's relationship to others, to which one was exposed in everyday life through family duties or learning from the tensions borne out of this intimacy. Asiya Alam, *Women, Islam and Familial Intimacy in Colonial South Asia* (Leiden, NL: Brill, 2021), 35–36.

12. Lotte Hoek, *Cut-Pieces: Celluloid Obscenity and Popular Cinema in Bangladesh* (New York: Columbia University Press, 2013), 3.

13. Hoek, 92.

14. Greater access to new media outlets, private television networks, and social media were in large part responsible for the diffusion of these regimes of permissibility. In her work on religious programming on Pakistani television, Taha Kazi studies how talk shows that represent the diversity of Islamic thought offer viewers guidance on modes of correct comportment. These formats and modes of production encourage viewers to question traditional sources of authority and bring religion into the sphere of competitive politics. Taha Kazi, *Religious Television and Pious Authority in Pakistan* (Bloomington: Indiana University Press, 2021).

15. Ali Nobil Ahmad's work has examined how "cinephobic" ambivalence and animosity towards film has come to underpin discrete elements of Pakistani public culture. In her review of Ali Khan and Ahmad's edited volume of essays on film and social change in Pakistan, Salma Siddique takes issue with Ahmad's conception of cinephobia and its relationship with religious sentiment. While I agree with Siddique's point that one should not presume that lascivious aesthetics are a response to repressive attitudes to public piety, the idea that addressing cinephobia "eclipses the complexity of 'cinephilia' in Pakistan" ignores the affective possibilities of the medium and the genesis of these terms in early film history. While cinephobia, cinephilia, and other possible offshoots can help scholars understand how film redefines the public sphere and the built environment, clinging to a modernist faith in a normative filmic "good" will always obscure the elements of film's moral world that provoke anxiety. To incorporate both points of view it might be useful to look to recent calls to engage with those who might be anathema to the humanities and social

sciences' secular–liberal bases, such as Nusrat Sabina Chowdhury's call to "start rethinking the public sphere . . . from an illiberal perspective." Ali Nobil Ahmad, "Film and Cinephilia in Pakistan: Beyond Life and Death," *BioScope: South Asian Screen Studies* 5, no. 2 (July 2014): 81–98; Salma Siddique, "Book Review: Ali Khan and Ali Nobil Ahmad (Eds), Cinema and Society: Film and Social Change in Pakistan," *BioScope: South Asian Screen Studies* 8, no. 1 (June 2017): 178; Nusrat Sabina Chowdhury, "The Ethics of the Digital: Crowds and Popular Justice in Bangladesh," in *Crowds: Ethnographic Encounters*, ed. Megan Steffen (London: Bloomsbury Press, 2019), 148.

16. Sarah Keller, *Anxious Cinephilia: Pleasure and Peril at the Movies* (New York: Columbia University Press, 2020).

17. Cf. Francesco Casetti, "Why Fears Matter. Cinephobia in Early Film Culture," *Screen* 59, no. 2 (Summer 2018): 145–157.

18. Of this nascent terminology, Canudo listed: "Cinegraphy, cineology, cinemania, cinephilia and cinephobia, cinepoetry and cinoedia, cinematurgy, cinechromism." Ricciotto Canudo, "Reflections on the Seventh Art," trans. Claudia Gorbman, 291–303, in *French Film Theory and Criticism: A History/Anthology, 1907–1939, Volume 1*, ed. Richard Abel (Princeton, NJ: Princeton University Press, 1988), 296–297.

19. Ravi S. Vasudevan, "Introduction," in *Making Meaning in Indian Cinema*, ed. Ravi S. Vasudevan (New Delhi: Oxford University Press, 2000), 15.

20. M. S. S. Pandian, "Tamil Cultural Elites and Cinema: Outline of an Argument," *Economic and Political Weekly* 31, no. 15 (April 1996): 952; S. V. Srinivas, "Gandhian Nationalism and Melodrama in the 30s Telugu Cinema," *Journal of the Moving Image* 1, no. 1 (Fall 1999): 14–36.

21. William Mazzarella, *Censorium: Cinema and the Open Edge of Mass Publicity* (Durham, NC: Duke University Press, 2013), 135.

22. Mazzarella, 137.

23. As Naveeda Khan notes, Pakistan itself is often described as a mosque. This association between film and places of worship became all the more powerful because of this association, as symbolic of a wider act of betraying the national project by mingling these seemingly distinct forces. But as Khan goes on to explain, this simile has a didactic quality, the suggestion being that one has to learn how to comport oneself in the mosque and that such learning can be an ongoing project of becoming a better citizen. Naveeda Khan, *Muslim Becoming: Aspiration and Skepticism in Pakistan* (Durham, NC: Duke University Press, 2012), 21–23.

24. The experience of the built environment is central to recent scholarly work on the aesthetics of atmospheres. In European philosophy, this most often relates to notions of ruination, its uncanniness of presence and feelings of absence, or what Böhme describes as the "modes in which a thing characteristically

steps out of itself" which he calls "ecstasies." This serves as a reminder that "ecstasies" and the Durkheimian "collective effervescence" through which sentiment manifests change do not always signal consent or enthusiasm. Gernot Böhme, *Atmospheric Architectures: The Aesthetics of Felt Spaces*, ed. and trans. A.-Chr. Engels-Schwarzpaul (London: Bloomsbury, 2017), 46.

25. Silpa Mukherjee, "Behind the Green Door: Unpacking the Item Number and Its Ecology," *BioScope: South Asian Screen Studies* 9, no. 2 (December 2018): 208–232.

26. Hortense Powdermaker, *Hollywood, the Dream Factory: An Anthropologist Looks at the Movie-Makers* (London: Secker and Warburg, 1951), 332.

27. Powdermaker, 332.

28. Erich Fromm, *The Fear of Freedom* (London: Routledge, 2001), 4.

29. Fromm, 9.

30. Fromm, 144; Matthew Engelke, *God's Agents: Biblical Publicity in Contemporary England* (Berkeley: University of California Press, 2013), 37.

31. See Fouzia Saeed's study of the anxieties surrounding women's performance during the Zia era. Debashree Mukherjee's work on scandals around women film stars in pre-Partition India film suggests that the moral atmosphere of film was a product of how female actors' professions—their lack of conventionality and routine—were viewed as alien and removed from viewers' everyday lives. Fouzia Saeed, *Taboo! The Hidden Culture of a Red Light Area* (Karachi: Oxford University Press, 2002); Debashree Mukherjee, "Notes on a Scandal: Writing Women's Film History Against an Absent Archive," *BioScope: South Asian Screen Studies* 4, no. 1 (January 2013): 10.

32. The public renunciation of film by former female actors was also a frequent occurrence in 1980s and 1990s Egypt. Lila Abu-Lughod, *Dramas of Nationhood: The Politics of Television in Egypt* (Chicago: University of Chicago Press, 2008); Karin Van Nieuwkerk, "Debating Piety and Performing Arts in the Public Sphere: The 'Caravan' of Veiled Actresses in Egypt," in *Music, Culture, and Identity in the Muslim World: Performance, Politics, and Piety*, ed. Kamal Salhi (London: Routledge, 2013), 80.

33. Tauba can also be seen in this light as an example of the kind of reformist self-discipline that drove the work of Saba Mahmood, Charles Hirschkind, and Talal Asad to build on Michel Foucault's "technologies of the self" as the labor of making sin manifest so as to practice penitence. Michel Foucault, *Technologies of the Self: A Seminar with Michel Foucault* (Amherst: University of Massachusetts Press, 1988), 249.

34. Denzil Ibbetson, *Panjab Castes: Races, Castes, and Tribes of the People of the Panjab* (Lahore: the Superintendent/Government Printing, 1916), 234.

35. Claire Pamment, "Hijraism: Jostling for a Third Space in Pakistani Politics," *TDR/The Drama Review* 54, no. 2 (Summer 2010): 32.

36. Author's translation, S. M. Shahid, *Film Acting Guide* (Lahore: Aleem Publishers, 1994), 27.

37. Melody Jue, *Wild Blue Media: Thinking through Seawater* (Durham, NC: Duke University Press, 2020), 69.

38. Shahid, *Film Acting Guide*, 30.

39. Gwendolyn Kirk, *Uncivilized Language and Aesthetic Exclusion: Language, Power and Film Production in Pakistan* (diss., University of Texas, Austin, 2016).

40. Farida Batool has shown the contradictions at play when cinema hoardings were ubiquitous in the urban milieu while figurative representation in the arts were being clamped down upon by the state and Quranic calligraphy was proffered as official forms of art. Farida Batool, *Figure: The Popular and the Political in Pakistan* (Lahore: ASR, 2004), 10–11. Following Zia's death these requirements were swiftly abandoned or only voluntarily enforced. If division was sown more widely in the 1980s, it was not until the 1990s that their seeds sprouted. Saadia Toor argues that it was only after Zia's death that the effects of his reforms were really felt, particularly with regard to sexualized violence and discrimination against minorities. Saadia Toor, *The State of Islam: Culture and Cold War Politics in Pakistan* (London: Pluto Press, 2011), 159.

41. Fouzia Saeed, *Forgotten Faces: Daring Women of Pakistan's Folk Theatre* (Lahore: Al-Faisal Nashran/Lok Virsa, 2011).

42. Neelam Hussain, "Meaning Makers," in *Re-Inventing Women: Representation of Women in the Media During the Zia Years*, ed. Maha Malik and Neelam Hussain (Lahore: Simorgh Women's Resource and Publication Centre, 1985), 4.

43. Sanjay Srivastava, *Passionate Modernity: Sexuality, Class, and Consumption in India* (New Delhi: Routledge, 2007), 209–219.

44. Fazlur Rahman, "The Concept of Hadd in Islamic Law," *Islamic Studies* 4, no. 3 (September 1965): 237.

45. For the identification of other metaphors and tactics for identifying boundaries in Muslim societies, see Katherine Pratt Ewing, "Crossing Borders and Transgressing Boundaries: Metaphors for Negotiating Multiple Identities," *Ethos* 26, no. 2 (June 1998): 262–267.

46. Rahman, "Concept of Hadd," 245.

47. Asma Jahangir and Hina Jilani, *The Hudood Ordinances: A Divine Sanction?* (Lahore: Sang-e-Meel Publications, 2003).

48. Naveeda Khan, "The Acoustics of Muslim Striving: Loudspeaker Use in Ritual Practice in Pakistan," *Comparative Studies in Society and History* 53, no. 3 (July 2011), 574.

49. Hussein Ali Agrama, "Ethics, Tradition, Authority: Toward an Anthropology of the Fatwa," *American Ethnologist* 37, no. 1 (February 2010): 2–18.

50. For Yasmin Moll, working on Egyptian Islamic television preachers, the interaction between media environments and jurisprudence means tracing "the

social life of theology as a space of critical contestation." It is through this kind of analytical approach that anthropology and theology can learn from one another, Joel Robbins argues, namely from anthropological comparison's acceptance of mutual difference, and the ease with which theology accepts the possibility of the radical and transformative otherness of the divine. Joel Robbins, "Social Thought and Commentary: Anthropology and Theology: An Awkward Relationship?," *Anthropological Quarterly* 79, no. 2 (Spring 2006): 292; Yasmin Moll, "Television Is Not Radio: Theologies of Mediation in the Egyptian Islamic Revival," *Cultural Anthropology* 33, no. 2 (May 2018): 258.

51. *Report of the Indian Cinematograph Committee, 1927–1928* (Calcutta: Government of India Central Publication Branch: 1928), 83.

52. Irfan Ahmad, *Islamism and Democracy in India: The Transformation of Jamaat-e-Islami* (Princeton, NJ: Princeton University Press, 2009), 54.

53. Syed Abul A'la Maududi, *Rasail O Masail Vol. 2* (Lahore: Islamic Publications Private Limited, 2000), 204.

54. André Bazin, "The Ontology of the Photographic Image," trans. Hugh Gray, *Film Quarterly* 13, no. 4 (Summer 1960): 4–9.

55. See Christopher Pinney, "Notes from the Surface of the Image," in *Photography's Other Histories*, ed. Christopher Pinney and Nicolas Peterson (Durham, NC: Duke University Press, 2003), 218. Maududi also drew attention to a broader phenomenon in which charismatic religious authorities call for their followers to engage with what Brian Larkin has called "surfaces, not depths." Brian Larkin, "Islamic Renewal, Radio and the Surface of Things," in *Aesthetic Formations: Media, Religion, Senses*, ed. Birgit Meyer (New York: Palgrave, 2009), 118.

56. Maududi, *Rasail O Masail*, 203.

57. Seyyed Vali Reza Nasr, *Mawdudi and the Making of Islamic Revivalism* (New York and Oxford: Oxford University Press, 1996), 52–53.

58. I do not claim that Maududi's views are representative of Pakistani public culture, but rather they provide an example of how the ontological essence of film can be understood to be key to its moral application. Indeed, even within the Jamaat-e-Islami, there were dissenting opinions to Maududi's views on cinema. Sultan Ahmad Islahi, for example, argued that women should be able to act in films, particularly if their co-actors were male kin, as denying their will to act might cause them to leave Islam. Irfan Ahmad, "Cracks in the 'Mightiest Fortress': Jamaat-e-Islami's Changing Discourse on Women," *Modern Asian Studies* 42, nos. 2–3 (March 2008), 563.

59. Allama Muhammad Iqbal, *The Reconstruction of Muslim Thought in Islam* (London: Oxford University Press, 1934).

60. Allama Muhammad Iqbal, *Bal-e-Jibreel* (Lahore: Taj Company, 1935).

61. Allama Muhammad Iqbal, *Poems from Iqbal*, trans. V. G. Kiernan (London: John Murray, 1955), 7.

62. Sergei Eisenstein, *Eisenstein on Disney*, ed. Jay Leyda (London: Seagull Books, 1986), 64.

63. Pamment calls this bifurcation a "split discourse" and argues that these strategies recall the *anti-nautch* movement of the colonial era, run by British missionaries and "high-caste" Indians in order to abolish certain performance traditions. Claire Pamment, "A Split Discourse: Body Politics in Pakistan's Popular Punjabi Theatre," *TDR/The Drama Review* 56, no. 1 (Spring 2012): 126.

2. Public Demand: Interpreting Atmospheres

1. Mushtaq Gazdar, *Pakistan Cinema, 1947–1997* (Karachi: Oxford University Press, 1997), 78; Iftikhar Dadi, "Registering Crisis: Ethnicity in Pakistani Cinema of the 1960s and 1970s," in *Beyond Crisis: Re-Evaluating Pakistan*, ed. Naveeda Khan (London: Routledge, 2012), 154.

2. Kajri Jain, *Gods in the Bazaar: The Economies of Indian Calendar Art* (Durham, NC: Duke University Press, 2007); Christopher Pinney, *"Photos of the Gods": The Printed Image and Political Struggle in India* (London: Reaktion Books, 2004). Ravi Vasudevan has argued that film production and consumption in South Asia must also be considered part of this story. Ravi S. Vasudevan, "Film Genres, the Muslim Social, and Discourses of Identity c. 1935–1945," *BioScope: South Asian Screen Studies* 6, no. 1 (January 2015): 29.

3. David Gilmartin, *Empire and Islam: Punjab and the Making of Pakistan* (Berkeley: University of California Press, 1988), 228.

4. Akbar S. Ahmed, *Jinnah, Pakistan and Islamic Identity: The Search for Saladin* (London: Psychology Press, 1997), 230.

5. Its economic inverse, what are referred to as the "elite" or *"amir log"* [rich people], is an equally fluid and unstable category that refers less to the actual wealth of people and more to their ability to isolate themselves and create parallel spaces for their enjoyment, such as gated housing communities.

6. Garrett Hardin, "The Tragedy of the Commons," *Science* 162, no. 3859 (December 1968): 1244.

7. Hardin, 1245.

8. Hardin, 1247.

9. Elinor Ostrom, *Governing the Commons: The Evolution of Institutions for Collective Action* (Cambridge: Cambridge University Press, 1990).

10. For more on the Islamic visual culture of South Asia see Yousuf Saeed, *Muslim Devotional Art in India* (London: Routledge, 2012); Jamal J. Elias, *Alef Is for Allah:*

Childhood, Emotion, and Visual Culture in Islamic Societies (Berkeley: University of California Press, 2018); Jürgen Wasim Frembgen, *The Friends of God: Sufi Saints in Islam, Popular Poster Art from Pakistan* (New York: Oxford University Press, 2006).

11. Clifford Geertz, "The Bazaar Economy: Information and Search in Peasant Marketing," *American Economic Review* 68, no. 2 (May 1978): 28.

12. Geertz, 32.

13. Webb Keane, "Freedom, Reflexivity, and the Sheer Everydayness of Ethics," *HAU: Journal of Ethnographic Theory* 4, no. 1 (Summer 2014): 455.

14. Karen Strassler, *Demanding Images: Democracy, Mediation, and the Image-Event in Indonesia* (Durham, NC: Duke University Press, 2020), 9.

15. Aasim Sajjad Akhtar, *The Politics of Common Sense: State, Society, and Culture in Pakistan* (Cambridge: Cambridge University Press, 2018), 2.

16. To paraphrase Lisa Gitelman's work on the materiality of documents. Lisa Gitelman, *Paper Knowledge: Toward a Media History of Documents* (Durham, NC: Duke University Press, 2014), 4.

17. Matthew S. Hull, *Government of Paper: The Materiality of Bureaucracy in Urban Pakistan* (Berkeley: University of California Press, 2012), 116–117.

18. Shaila Bhatti, *Translating Museums: A Counterhistory of South Asian Museology* (Walnut Creek, CA: Left Coast Press, 2012), 143.

19. Yael Navaro-Yashin, *Faces of the State: Secularism and Public Life in Turkey* (Princeton, NJ: Princeton University Press, 2002).

20. Gazdar, *Pakistan Cinema, 1947–1997*, 167.

21. Lotte Hoek, *Cut-Pieces: Celluloid Obscenity and Popular Cinema in Bangladesh* (New York: Columbia University Press, 2013).

22. *Report of the Indian Cinematograph Committee, 1927–1928* (Calcutta: Government of India Central Publication Branch: 1928), 131.

23. Lotte Hoek, "Urdu for Image: Understanding Bangladeshi Cinema Through Its Theatres," in *South Asian Media Cultures: Audiences, Representations, Contexts*, ed. Shakuntala Banaji (London: Anthem Press, 2011), 85.

24. "Abdul Sattar vs. The State," in *Pakistan Law Journal, 1975, Part II* (Lahore: Pakistan Educational Press, 1975), 1138.

25. "Abdul Sattar vs. The State," in *Pakistan Law Journal, 1980, Part I & II* (Lahore: Pakistan Educational Press, 1980), 979–980.

26. "Baho Film Corporation vs. Islamic Republic of Pakistan," *The All Pakistan Legal Decisions, 1981* 33 (1981), 314.

27. Aijaz Gul, "Sex, Bloodbaths and a Pair of Scissors," *Cinemaya* 4 (Summer 1989), 57.

28. Annette Kuhn, *Cinema, Censorship, and Sexuality, 1909–1925* (London: Routledge, 1988).

29. Cinema Commission of Inquiry, *The Cinema: Its Present Position and Future Possibilities* (London: Williams and Norgate, 1917).

30. Cinema Commission of Inquiry, 352. As Robert Spadoni argues, despite the idea that an atmosphere surrounds and clings to film having been deployed from the earliest days of film exhibition by critics, audiences, and trade journals, little work has been done to unpack the implications of its use. Robert Spadoni, "What Is Film Atmosphere?," *Quarterly Review of Film and Video* 37, no.1 (January 2020): 48–75.

31. Twenty-five years later, outdoor cinema would be the subject of one of the first ethnographic studies of film, conducted by John J. Honigmann. This remarkable mission in West Pakistan in 1952, possibly unique in the history of anthropology, was commissioned by the International Motion Picture Service of the U.S. Department of State. Honigmann visited interior Sindh, Khyber Pakhtunkhwa, and Punjab to study the impact of U.S. Information Services (USIS) Films, a propaganda unit whose goal was to project a favorable image of the United States in Pakistan. Honigmann's final report attempted to test the pedagogic effectiveness of the films, and the viewer's ability to apply the lessons learned to their own situation, particularly those relating to hygiene and agriculture. John Joseph Honigmann, *Information for Pakistan: Report of Research on Intercultural Communication through Films* (Chapel Hill: Institute for Research in Social Science, University of North Carolina, 1953); Timothy P. A. Cooper, "The Kaċċā and the Pakkā: Disenchanting the Film Event in Pakistan," *Comparative Studies in Society and History* 62, no. 2 (April 2020): 262–295.

32. *Indian Cinematograph Committee*, 13–14.

33. *Indian Cinematograph Committee*, 20.

34. Abdul Anwar Aziz, *Film Industry in West Pakistan* (Lahore: Board of Economic Inquiry, 1957), 197.

35. Aziz, 199.

36. Constituent Assembly of India (Legislative) Debates, Part 2, Vol. 4, No. 1 (Indian Constituent Assembly, 1949), 2521.

37. More recently, Saim Sadiq's film *Joyland* (2022), about a relationship between a transgender and cis-man, had its certificate revoked after the censor board decided it had violated the 1979 Motion Picture Ordinance's demands to uphold "decency and morality." The same complaints led to Sarmad Khoosat's *Zindagi Tamasha* (2019) suffering the same fate, after the TLP threatened countrywide protests if the film was not banned.

38. Michael T. Taussig, *Defacement: Public Secrecy and the Labor of the Negative* (Stanford, CA: Stanford University Press, 1999), 2.

39. Cf. Saba Imtiaz, "A New Form of Films Emerges," *Express Tribune*, June 23, 2010.

40. Fayyaz Ahmed Ashar, *Pakistani urdu filmi geeton ka safar (1948–1970)* [Journey of Pakistani Urdu Film Songs (1948–1970)] (Lahore: Maqsood Publishers, 2011); Fayyaz Ahmed Ashar, *Pakistani urdu filmi geeton ka safar (1971–1997)* [Journey of Pakistani Urdu Film Songs Part 2 (1971–1997)] (Lahore: Maqsood Publishers, 2018).

41. Ann Laura Stoler, *Along the Archival Grain: Epistemic Anxieties and Colonial Common Sense* (Princeton, NJ: Princeton University Press, 2010), 7–8.

42. Jacques Derrida, *Of Grammatology*, trans. Gayatri Chakravorty Spivak (Baltimore, MD: John Hopkins University Press, 1997), 320.

43. For other instances, see Durriya Kazi, "How Lollywood Lost Lakshmi," in *Arts of People IV: Lollywood! Pakistani Film Posters*, ed. Yuko Yamaki (Fukuoka, Japan: Fukuoka Asian Art Museum, 2006), 2–9; Farida Batool Syeda, *New Media, Masculinity, and Mujra Dance in Pakistan* (Diss., SOAS, University of London, 2015).

44. Finbarr Barry Flood, "Between Cult and Culture: Bamiyan, Islamic Iconoclasm, and the Museum," *Art Bulletin* 84, no. 4 (December 2002): 646.

45. Laura U. Marks, *Touch: Sensuous Theory and Multisensory Media* (Minneapolis: University of Minnesota Press, 2002), xi–xii.

46. Chris Moffat, *India's Revolutionary Inheritance: Politics and the Promise of Bhagat Singh* (Cambridge: Cambridge University Press, 2019).

3. Feeling the Threshold

1. Media ambience usually refers to an anesthetic quality, such as in-flight entertainment designed to distract and sedate, as well as to a sense of ubiquity and omnipresence. See Paul Roquet, *Ambient Media: Japanese Atmospheres of Self* (Minneapolis: University of Minnesota Press, 2016); Stephen Groening, *Cinema beyond Territory: Inflight Entertainment and Atmospheres of Globalization* (London: Bloomsbury, 2014); Anna McCarthy, *Ambient Television: Visual Culture and Public Space* (Durham, NC: Duke University Press, 2001).

2. Brian Larkin, "The Politics and Poetics of Infrastructure," *Annual Review of Anthropology* 42 (October 2013), 336.

3. Marshall Berman, *All That Is Solid Melts into Air: The Experience of Modernity* (London: Verso, 1983).

4. Linda Walbridge, *The Christians of Pakistan: The Passion of Bishop John Joseph* (London: Routledge, 2012); Muhammad Qasim Zaman, *Islam in Pakistan: A History* (Princeton, NJ: Princeton University Press, 2018), 193.

5. Sir Patrick Geddes, *Town Planning in Lahore: A Report to the Municipal Council* (Lahore: Commercial Print Works, 1917), 32.

6. Jamal J. Elias, *On Wings of Diesel: Trucks, Identity and Culture in Pakistan* (Oxford: Oneworld, 2011).

7. Hazrat Inayat Khan, *The Music of Life* (New York: Omega, 1988), 16.

8. Abdul Aziz Anwar, *Film Industry in West Pakistan* (Lahore: Board of Economic Inquiry, 1957), 221.

9. *Report of the Film Fact Finding Committee: Govt. of Pakistan, Ministry of Industries, April 1960–April 1961* (Karachi: Manager of Publications/Government of Pakistan Press, 1962), 255.

10. *Film Fact Finding Committee*, 258.

11. *Film Fact Finding Committee*, 258.

12. *Film Fact Finding Committee*, 258.

13. Italics in original. *Film Fact Finding Committee*, 258; *Film Fact Finding Committee*, 258.

14. *Film Fact Finding Committee*, 95.

15. Mohammad Qadeer, *Pakistan: Social and Cultural Transformations in a Muslim Nation* (Abingdon, UK: Routledge, 2006), 222.

16. Mohsin Hamid, *Moth Smoke* (London: Penguin, 2012).

17. Asma Jahangir and Hina Jilani, *The Hudood Ordinances: A Divine Sanction?* (Lahore: Sang-e-Meel, 2003), 22.

18. Arnold Van Gennep, *The Rites of Passage*, trans. Monika B. Vizedom and Gabrielle L. Caffee (Chicago: University of Chicago Press, 1960), 20.

19. In an essay late in his career, Turner argued that the event of experience—as opposed to "experience" as an unbroken chain of social reproduction—is suffused with experimentation and peril. The disconcerting rupture of such ethical ambiguity acts as the sudden insertion of a catalyst around which existing values, which previously may have had no stable connection, form new clusters and repertoires. For Turner, experience was a matter of moral perception, but also something whose affective debris demands assembling, expressing, and communicating to others, acts which usually take an aesthetic or symbolic form. Victor Witter Turner, *The Ritual Process: Structure and Anti-Structure* (New York: Cornell University Press, 1977); Victor Witter Turner, *Process, Performance, and Pilgrimage: A Study in Comparative Symbology* (New Delhi: Concept, 1979); Victor Witter Turner, "Dewey, Dilthey, and Drama: An Essay in the Anthropology of Experience," in *The Anthropology of Experience*, ed. Victor Witter Turner, Edward M. Bruner, and Clifford Geertz (Chicago: University of Illinois Press, 1986): 33–44.

20. Italics in original. Robert Ranulph Marett, *The Threshold of Religion* (London: Methuen and Co., 1909), 203–204 and 219–220. For Birgit Meyer, Marett's notion of awe understood the constitution of religious experience as sense-making rather than meaning-making that can exist as repeatable statements, cultivated and mediated through procedures of repetition. Birgit Meyer, "How to Capture the 'Wow': R. R. Marett's Notion of Awe and the Study of Religion," *Journal of the Royal Anthropological Institute* 22, no. 1 (March 2016), 17.

21. An exception is Ieva Jusionyte's work which puts to good use the dual meaning of the term as both a spatial boundary and an expression of magnitude and intensity. Ieva Jusionyte, *Threshold: Emergency Responders on the US-Mexico Border* (Berkeley: University of California Press, 2018).

22. Susan Leigh Star, "This Is Not a Boundary Object: Reflections on the Origin of a Concept," *Science, Technology, & Human Values* 35, no. 5 (September 2010): 602.

23. Mary Louise Pratt, "Arts of the Contact Zone," *Profession*, 1991: 34.

24. Gershon foregrounds the role of circulation to show how the dissensus Susan Leigh Star highlights often works in relation to disagreements about value. Ilana Gershon, "Porous Social Orders," *American Ethnologist* 46, no. 4 (November 2019), 411.

25. Through her study of the ocean as a mediatic form, Melody Jue examines phenomena often left out of media theory. One example is how "pressure" makes present the interfaces between phases and forms as a matter of volume and dispersal, rather than in purely material or visual terms, as surface. Melody Jue, *Wild Blue Media: Thinking through Seawater* (Durham, NC: Duke University Press, 2020), 17.

26. Ammara Maqsood and Fizzah Sajjad, "Victim, Broker, Activist, Fixer: Surviving Dispossession in Working Class Lahore," *Environment and Planning D: Society and Space* 39, no. 6 (December 2021): 994–1008.

27. Nikhil Anand, Akhil Gupta, and Hannah Appel, eds. *The Promise of Infrastructure*, (Durham, NC: Duke University Press, 2018).

28. Jurgen Habermas, *The Structural Transformation of the Public Sphere: An Inquiry into a Category of Bourgeois Society* (Cambridge, MA: MIT Press, 1991). Nancy Fraser, while arguing for the utility of Habermas's "public sphere" to understand liberal democracies, instantiates its gaps with regard to gender and race. In its place, parallel arenas emerge in stratified societies in which a single public sphere is not possible, but where competitive spaces of contestation offer multi-layered and often conflicting forms of political participation. Nancy Fraser, "Rethinking the Public Sphere: A Contribution to the Critique of Actually Existing Democracy," *Social Text*, no. 25/26 (1990), 67. See also Michael Warner, "Publics and Counterpublics," *Public Culture* 14, no. 1 (Winter 2002): 49–90.

29. Christopher Pinney, "Introduction: Public, Popular, and Other Cultures," in *Pleasure and the Nation: The History, Politics and Consumption of Public Culture in India*, eds. Rachel Dwyer and Christopher Pinney (Oxford: Oxford University Press, 2002), 2.

30. Rahul Mukherjee, *Radiant Infrastructures: Media, Environment, and Cultures of Uncertainty* (Durham, NC: Duke University Press, 2020), 3.

31. Mukherjee, 12.

32. Max Liboiron, *Pollution Is Colonialism* (Durham, NC: Duke University Press, 2021), 92n46.

33. In the regulation of electromagnetic fields, Mukherjee charts that a threshold refers to the minimum intensity that manifests a sensory change, while saturation refers to the maximum stimulus. Rahul Mukherjee, "Wireless Saturation," in *Saturation: An Elemental Politics*, ed. Melody Jue and Rafico Ruiz (Durham, NC: Duke University Press, 2021), 125.

34. Naveeda Khan, "Flaws in the Flow: Roads and Their Modernity in Pakistan," *Social Text* 24, no. 4 (89) (Winter 2006): 106.

35. Hugh Reginald Haweis, *Music and Morals* (London: Harper & Brothers, 1872), 104.

36. Haweis, 35. Some of Haweis's thoughts on atmosphere resonate closely with those later developed by Inayat Khan, suggesting a likely source of influence. Compare Khan's definition of atmosphere explored in the introduction to this book with Haweis's thoughts on the music of Franz Schubert: "Emotion is the atmosphere in which thought is steeped, —that which lends to thought its tone or temperature, —that to which thought is often indebted for half its power." Haweis, 286.

37. Haweis, 85.

38. Farahnaz Ispahani, *Purifying the Land of the Pure: A History of Pakistan's Religious Minorities* (Oxford: Oxford University Press, 2017), 7.

39. In Jane Bennett's attempts to bring together the study of affect and ethics, she describes the accumulative aspects of affective experience and the palimpsestic ethical surfaces that result. She draws on Gilles Deleuze and Félix Guattari's work on refrains, that posits the idea that accumulative, repetitive series of actions and intensities provide access to the rhythmic nature of being. This resonates closely with the Hall Road repertoire as the accumulative inventory of moral- and value-decisions. The difference I see between a refrain and a repertoire is that the latter can be taken as living inventory which agency renews, while a refrain is the sensation of its recursivity. In this recursive dimension, the refrain is sounded and sensed, and felt as a point of composure in the harmony or dissonance of its onward rhythm. Jane Bennett, *The Enchantment of Modern Life: Attachments, Crossings, and Ethics* (Princeton, NJ: Princeton University Press, 2001), 132. Gilles Deleuze and Félix Guattari, *A Thousand Plateaus: Capitalism and Schizophrenia* (London: Bloomsbury Publishing, 1987). See also Andreas Bandak, "Of Refrains and Rhythms in Contemporary Damascus: Urban Space and Christian-Muslim Coexistence," *Current Anthropology* 55, no. S10 (December 2014): S248–S261.

40. Luke Howard, *Essay on the Modification of Clouds* (London: John Churchill and Sons, 1803), 2.

41. John Ruskin, "The Storm-Cloud of the Nineteenth Century: Two Lectures Delivered at the London Institution, February 4th and 11th, 1884," in *The Complete Works of John Ruskin*, library ed., vol. 34, ed. E. T. Cook and Alexander Wedderburn (London: George Allen, 1903–12), 3–80.

42. My own interest in the air as a mediating form had been shaped by contemporary art-advocacy that examines how military regimes and states weaponize the airborne in order to terrorize or dispossess. In his 2022 work *Air Conditioning* Lawrence Abu Hamdan assembled images and accounts of Israeli military surveillance over Lebanon, creating a composite image made of air pollution, fear, and sonic disturbance. The multidisciplinary research group Forensic Architecture deploy experimental methods to understand how rapidly transforming cloud phenomena borne of aerial bombings, tear gas attacks, and petrochemical emissions might provide evidence to hold those responsible to account. While the material makeup of cloud dust possesses its own architecture, the same cannot be said of mahaul, whose objecthood is dispersed across persons, things, and imagined space. See Cloud Studies 2020/2021, The Bombing of Rafah 2015, among many others. https://forensic-architecture.org.

43. Christopher Pinney, *The Waterless Sea: A Curious History of Mirages* (London: Reaktion, 2018), 16.

44. Pinney, 28.

45. Take, for example, the notion of *parhai ka mahaul*, in which educational outcomes are perceived to be shaped by a social environment, and thereby reproduce social segregation. Roger Jeffery, Patricia Jeffery, and Craig Jeffery, "Parhai ka mahaul? An Educational Environment in Bijnor, Uttar Pradesh," in *The Meaning of the Local: Politics of Place in Urban India*, ed. Henrike Donner and Geert de Neve (London: Routledge, 2006), 116–140.

4. Atmospheres of Moral Exception

1. Golbarg Rekabtalaei, *Iranian Cosmopolitanism: A Cinematic History* (Cambridge: Cambridge University Press, 2019), 77.

2. John Joseph Honigmann, *Three Pakistan Villages* (Chapel Hill: Institute for Research in Social Science, University of North Carolina, 1958), 58.

3. "Documents, December 1978–May 1979," *Pakistan Horizon* 32, no. 1/2 (1979), 278.

4. "December 1978–May 1979," 278.

5. Walter Armbrust, "Synchronizing Watches: The State, the Consumer, and Sacred Time in Ramadan Television," in *Religion, Media, and the Public Sphere*, ed. Birgit Meyer and Annelies Moors (Bloomington: Indiana University Press, 2006), 207–226.

6. Carl Schmitt, *Political Theology: Four Chapters on the Concept of Sovereignty* (Chicago: University of Chicago Press, 2005), 5.

7. Samuli Schielke, "Being Good in Ramadan: Ambivalence, Fragmentation, and the Moral Self in the Lives of Young Egyptians," *Journal of the Royal Anthropological Institute* 15, no. S1 (May 2009): S32.

8. Laura A. Ring, *Zenana: Everyday Peace in a Karachi Apartment Building* (Bloomington: Indiana University Press, 2006), 62.

9. Mariam Abou-Zahab, *Pakistan: A Kaleidoscope of Islam* (London: Oxford University Press, 2020); Ayesha Jalal, *Democracy and Authoritarianism in South Asia: A Comparative and Historical Perspective* (Cambridge: Cambridge University Press, 1995), 239. Conversely, Ali Usman Qasmi argues that sectarian friction should be traced to an increase in similarities rather than differences, through which violence serves to fix the "blurred lines" between one and the other. Muhammad Qasim Zaman, *Islam in Pakistan: A History* (Princeton, NJ: Princeton University Press, 2018), 267; Ali Usman Qasmi, *The Ahmadis and the Politics of Religious Exclusion in Pakistan* (London: Anthem Press, 2015), 226.

10. Mahmoud Ayoub, *Redemptive Suffering in Islam: A Study of the Devotional Aspects of ʿĀshūrāʾ in Twelver Shīʿism* (The Hague, Paris, New York: Mouton Publishers, 1978), 23.

11. For the sake of brevity, I do not go into some aspects of Shiʿi ritual in the kind of depth I would like. For more on tazia and taboot, see Ghulam Abbas, *Tazias of Chiniot* (Lahore: Tarikh, 2007).

12. According to Phillip Auslander, liveness is a category of remediation. This can refer either to a "live recording" as an affective frame that simulates certain environmental qualities of participation, or to live broadcasts in which audiences and the object of viewing are temporally but not spatially co-present. Recent commercial digital technologies provide a third way, in which the possibilities of responding in real time allow participants to engage directly with live events. See Phillip Auslander, *Liveness: Performance in a Mediatized Culture* (London: Routledge, 2008); Phillip Auslander, "Live and Technologically Mediated Performance," in *The Cambridge Companion to Performance Studies*, ed. Tracy C. Davis (New York: Cambridge University Press, 2008), 107–119; Phillip Auslander, "Digital Liveness: A Historico-Philosophical Perspective," *PAJ: A Journal of Performance and Art* 34, no. 3 (September 2012): 3–11.

13. Nida Kirmani, *Questioning the "Muslim Woman": Identity and Insecurity in an Urban Indian Locality* (London: Routledge, 2016), 62.

14. Kirmani, 74.

15. Kirmani, 79.

16. I am inspired here by David Novak's ethnography of the circulation of noise music in Japan. David Novak finds listeners absorbed in the "sonic atmosphere" of live and recorded noise music as an immersive, absorptive experience that

delineates "private thresholds of sensation." David Novak, *Japanoise: Music at the Edge of Circulation* (Durham, NC: Duke University Press, 2013), 43.

17. Hazrat Inayat Khan, *The Music of Life* (New York: Omega, 1988): 18.

18. His assertion also referred to something ontologically purer about his materials. This recalls Ayala Fader's argument that Orthodox Jews, uncertain of the effect the internet might have on their communities, have come to look for "kosher" ways of negotiating media usage. Ayala Fader, "Nonliberal Jewish Women's Audiocassette Lectures in Brooklyn: A Crisis of Faith and the Morality of Media," *American Anthropologist* 115, no. 1 (March 2013): 72–84.

19. Patrick Eisenlohr, *Sounding Islam: Voice, Media, and Sonic Atmospheres in an Indian Ocean World* (Oakland: University of California Press, 2018), 33; Brian Larkin, "Bandiri Music, Globalization, and Urban Experience in Nigeria," *Social Text* 22, no. 4 (Winter 2004): 91–112; Peter Manuel, *Cassette Culture: Popular Music and Technology in North India* (Chicago: University of Chicago Press, 1993), 114–115.

20. Brian Larkin warns of the dangers of reifying the distinctions made by competing groups into an oversimplified vision of a "binary Islam." Brian Larkin, "Binary Islam: Media and Religious Movements in Nigeria," in *New Media and Religious Transformations in Africa*, ed. Rosalind I. J. Hackett and Benjamin F. Soares (Bloomington: Indiana University Press, 2015), 65.

21. Toby Howarth, *The Twelver Shi'a as a Muslim Minority in India: Pulpit of Tears* (London: Routledge, 2005), 59–60.

22. Jim Masselos, "Power in the Bombay 'Moholla,' 1904–1915: An Initial Exploration into the World of the Indian Urban Muslim," *South Asia: Journal of South Asian Studies* 6, no. 1 (1976): 54.

23. Diane D'Souza, "In the Presence of the Martyrs: The Alam in Popular Shi'i Piety," *Muslim World* 88, no. 1 (January 1998), 76.

24. Howarth, *Muslim Minority in India*, 55.

25. Syed Akbar Hyder, *Reliving Karbala: Martyrdom in South Asian Memory* (Oxford: Oxford University Press, 2006), 39.

26. Hyder, 101.

27. Lara Deeb, "Piety Politics and the Role of a Transnational Feminist Analysis," *Journal of the Royal Anthropological Institute* 15, no. S1 (May 2009): S112–S126; Mary Elaine Hegland, "Shi'a Women's Rituals in Northwest Pakistan: The Shortcomings and Significance of Resistance," *Anthropological Quarterly* 76, no. 3 (Summer 2003): 411–442.

28. What is at stake is the communally produced ambiance of public space and collective activity, what Sandria B. Freitag described in colonial Banaras as the increased role of expressions of communal identity in producing a wider public sphere marked by the production of moral authority. Sandria B. Freitag,

"State and Community: Symbolic Popular Protest in Banaras's Public Arenas," in *Culture and Power in Banaras: Community Performance, and Environment*, ed. Sandria B. Freitag (Berkeley: University of California Press, 1992), 228.

29. Recalling the previous chapter, this is the point at which Luke Howard and John Ruskin might have disagreed: the degree to which atmosphere relies on the response of a subjective interlocutor, troubling the extent to which their translation to others becomes merely the experience of their mediation. Tim Flohr Sørensen, "More Than a Feeling: Towards an Archaeology of Atmosphere," *Emotion, Space, and Society* 15 (2015), 64.

30. And recalling the German philosophies of atmospheres, this question raises Böhme's understanding of atmospheres as vulnerable to the dissonant other. Gernot Böhme, *Atmospheric Architectures: The Aesthetics of Felt Spaces*, ed. and trans. A.-Chr. Engels-Schwarzpaul (London: Bloomsbury, 2017), 162.

5. The Absorptive City: Hall Road's Urban Form

1. In Amira Mittermaier's Egyptian ethnography, *khidmas* is the term deployed to describe service, referring not only to the location of service or charitable giving but the act of its distribution. Amira Mittermaier, *Giving to God: Islamic Charity in Revolutionary Times* (Berkeley: University of California Press, 2019), 52.

2. Harvie M. Conn, "Islamic Socialism in Pakistan: An Overview," *Islamic Studies* 15, no. 2 (Summer 1976), 113.

3. Ghulam Ahmed Parwez, *Islam: A Challenge to Religion* (Lahore: Tolu-e-Islam Trust, 2012).

4. Anwar H. Syed, "Z. A. Bhutto's Self-Characterizations and Pakistani Political Culture," *Asian Survey* 18, no. 12 (December 1978): 1261.

5. The term "hybrid regime" was widely used to refer to Pakistani politics, particularly in criticism of Imran Khan's PTI government (2018–2022). It described how thresholds come to characterize a certain kind of political amalgam in the collusion between military and civilian regimes. Policy analysts use the term to refer to a transition to democracy that allowed both genuine elections and military interference, or freedom of speech and enforced disappearances to happen at the same time. On a smaller scale I have evinced this in relation to the inherent contradiction of the coexistence of interdiction and reproduction in film experience that reflects something of the transitional, hybrid regime. Take also the economy of Hall Road, that sits between legitimate and illegal forms of appropriation and exchange.

6. Lawrence Liang, "Porous Legalities and Avenues of Participation," in *Sarai Reader 05: Bare Acts*, ed. Monica Narula, Shuddhabrata Sengupta, Jeebesh Bagchi, Geert Lovink, and Lawrence Liang (Delhi: Sarai Media Lab, 2005), 7.

7. Lawrence Liang, "Beyond Representation: The Figure of the Pirate," in *Access to Knowledge in the Age of Intellectual Property*, ed. Amy Kapczynski and Gaëlle Krikorian (New York: Zone Books, 2010), 353–376; Kamran Asdar Ali, "Cinema and the City: The Ayub Years," *Dawn*, May 5, 2013, http://www.dawn.com/news/1026248/column-cinema-and-the-city-the-ayub-years-by-kamran-asdar-ali.

8. Brian Larkin, "Degraded Images, Distorted Sounds: Nigerian Video and the Infrastructure of Piracy," *Public Culture* 16, no. 2 (Spring 2004): 307; Ravi Sundaram, *Pirate Modernity: Delhi's Media Urbanism* (London: Routledge, 2009), 15.

9. Mohammad A. Qadeer, *Urban Development in the Third World: Internal Dynamics of Lahore, Pakistan* (New York: Praeger, 1983), 6.

10. Arjun Appadurai, "Disjuncture and Difference in the Global Cultural Economy," *Theory, Culture, & Society* 7, no. 2–3 (June 1990): 295–310.

11. Qadeer, *Urban Development*, 10.

12. Benjamin studied Paris not just in texts but through its passages, the covered shopping arcades that so fascinated the Surrealist movement. Benjamin saw the arcades as containers, as boundary objects that demarcate areas for study, like the plotting of an archaeological excavation. Benjamin's study of urban Paris was formed of notes and sketches whose discursive field emanated from the arcades but were not necessarily confined to them. Hall Road's plazas—particularly the unplanned creation of passage-streets—offered a similar threshold through which to explore contemporary Lahore. The arcades of Paris were objects of fascination because—in the case of Louis Aragon's *Paris Peasant* ([1926] 1994) which inspired Benjamin's lifelong project—they were ephemeral; scheduled for demolition to make way for boulevards as part of the urban regeneration of Paris. Rather than objects of nostalgia, Lahore's plazas are themselves the replacement of the past now swept away, a precarious and future-facing affront to the city as palimpsest. Walter Benjamin, *The Arcades Project*, trans. Howard Eiland and Kevin McLaughlin (Cambridge, MA: Harvard University Press, 1999); Louis Aragon, *Paris Peasant*, trans. Simon Watson Taylor (Boston: Exact Change, 1994).

13. Louis Dumont, *Homo Hierarchicus: The Caste System and Its Implications* (Chicago: University of Chicago Press, 1980), 384–385. By beginning with a Brahmanical subject and working downwards it is no surprise that Dumont came to understate the nature of exclusion felt by, say, Dalit communities. Instead, I find Dumont useful to this study in terms of value hierarchy, rather than caste.

Dumont found caste hierarchy, as an order of precedence that ranks certain social values, allowed greater differences to coexist within proscribed limits. The notion of such a system predicated on "the encompassing of the contrary" is one way of understanding the moral contours of atmosphere, particularly in relation to that which lies both immediately within and immediately without the bounds of its operation. Atmospheres of media in Pakistan also operate in parallel with one another, that is laterally, rather than in strict hierarchies.

14. Dumont, 142.

15. Dumont, 142.

16. Keith Hart, "Informal Income Opportunities and Urban Employment in Ghana," *Journal of Modern African Studies* 11, no. 1 (March 1973): 61–89; Jan Breman, *Footloose Labour: Working in India's Informal Economy* (Cambridge: Cambridge University Press, 1996); Barbara Misztal, *Informality: Social Theory and Contemporary Practice* (London: Routledge, 2002); Brian Larkin, *Signal and Noise: Media, Infrastructure, and Urban Culture in Nigeria* (Durham, NC: Duke University Press, 2008); Joe Karaganis, ed., *Media Piracy in Emerging Economies* (New York: Social Science Research Council, 2011); Lawrence Liang, "Cinematic Citizenship and the Illegal City," *Inter-Asia Cultural Studies* 6, no. 3 (September 2005): 366–385; Ramon Lobato, *Shadow Economies of Cinema: Mapping Informal Film Distribution* (London: Bloomsbury, 2012).

17. For example, Amit S. Rai has convincingly separated informality from its reliance on issues of copyright by centralizing the role of recycling and renovation in the circulation of media. Amit S. Rai, *Jugaad: Ecologies of Everyday Hacking in India* (Durham, NC: Duke University Press, 2019).

18. Jeffrey D. Himpele, "Film Distribution as Media: Mapping Difference in the Bolivian Cinemascape," *Visual Anthropology Review* 12, no. 1 (March 1996): 57; Jeffrey D. Himpele, *Circuits of Culture: Media, Politics, and Indigenous Identity in the Andes* (Minneapolis: University of Minnesota Press, 2008).

19. Sundaram, *Pirate Modernity*, 13.

20. William J. Glover, *Making Lahore Modern: Constructing and Imagining a Colonial City* (Minneapolis: University of Minnesota Press, 2008), xiv.

21. Qadeer, *Urban Development*, 19.

22. Qadeer, 22.

23. Matthew S. Hull, *Government of Paper: The Materiality of Bureaucracy in Urban Pakistan* (Berkeley: University of California Press, 2012), 239.

24. William J. Glover, "Translating the Public in Colonial Punjab," in *Punjab Reconsidered: History, Culture, and Practice*, ed. Anshu Malhotra and Farina Mir (Oxford: Oxford University Press, 2012), 370.

25. Naveeda Khan, *Muslim Becoming: Aspiration and Skepticism in Pakistan* (Durham, NC: Duke University Press, 2012), 29.

26. Vazira Fazila-Yacoobali Zamindar, *The Long Partition and the Making of Modern South Asia: Refugees, Boundaries, Histories* (New York: Columbia University Press, 2007).

27. As Carla Bellamy's work shows, this sacred geography held by many South Asian cities suffuses the environment with ambient and elemental ideas around absence, presence, and the ephemeral. Carla Bellamy, *The Powerful Ephemeral: Everyday Healing in an Ambiguously Islamic Place* (Berkeley: University of California Press, 2011).

28. For more on Lahori perceptions of middle-class identity, see Ammara Maqsood, *The New Pakistani Middle Class* (Cambridge, MA: Harvard University Press, 2017).

29. Böhme's language of "tuned spaces" described in the introduction to this book not only deploys a sounded vocabulary to describe atmosphere, but also an object-oriented approach to the ways in which ambient qualities are intimately entangled with the built environment. Gernot Böhme, *Atmospheric Architectures: The Aesthetics of Felt Spaces*, ed. and trans. A.-Chr. Engels-Schwarzpaul (London: Bloomsbury, 2017), 162.

30. Chris Moffat, "Building, Dwelling, Dying: Architecture and History in Pakistan," *Modern Intellectual History* 18, no. 2 (June 2021): 520–546.

31. "Shahbaz Vows to Construct New Heritage Sites Along OLMT Route," *Khabaristan Times*, February 2017.

6. The Master Copy

1. Ahmad Rafay Alam, "The Beginning of the Talibanization of Lahore?," *The News*, October 26, 2008.

2. Salman Masood, "In City of Tolerance, Shadow of the Taliban," *New York Times*, November 2, 2008.

3. Jack Goody, *The Interface Between the Written and the Oral* (Cambridge: Cambridge University Press, 1987), 78.

4. Warda Imran, "Of Consent and Copyrights: Women Lodge 90% Complaints in FIA Cybercrime Circle," *Express Tribune*, April 9, 2018.

5. The face is what Deleuze and Guattari called a "black hole," a kind of affective repository that contrasts with the idea of a "white wall" as the surface upon which such things are projected and refracted. Gilles Deleuze and Félix Guattari, *A Thousand Plateaus: Capitalism and Schizophrenia* (London: Bloomsbury, 1987), 170.

6. Brian Larkin, "Making Equivalence Happen: Commensuration and the Architecture of Circulation," in *Images That Move*, ed. Patricia Spyer and Mary Margaret Steedly (Santa Fe, NM: SAR Press, 2013), 245.

7. Attending to the residual presence of analog media within digital practices is not to look nostalgically at what media were. Instead, to focus on the residual is to understand what Sudhir Mahadevan describes as the "obviation of obsolescence," in which the idea of obsolescence is challenged by events and situations that subvert its economic logic. Sudhir Mahadevan, "Traveling Showmen, Makeshift Cinemas: The Bioscopewallah and Early Cinema History in India," *BioScope: South Asian Screen Studies* 1, no. 1 (January 2010): 40.

8. For many South Asian Muslims, *adab* is a concept that describes the cultivation of moral behavior integral to the formation of a harmonious relationship with Allah and with one's society. Despite being a key medium for respectability, it is a term I heard little among my interlocutors, other than in the negative when traders accused one another of being *beyadabi* [bad-mannered or irreverent]. Perhaps tethered so tightly to a literary elite or a shared repertoire of exemplary figures, in the devotional diversity of Lahore, and due to the scarcity of moral precepts shared among the public at large, atmosphere has taken the place of adab (in the domain of media circulation at least). Barbara Daly Metcalf, "Introduction," in *Moral Conduct and Authority: The Place of Adab in South Asian Islam*, ed. Barbara Daly Metcalf (Berkeley: University of California Press, 1984), 1–20.

9. William Mills Ivins, *Prints and Visual Communication* (Cambridge, MA: MIT Press, 1969), 24.

10. Ivins, 90.

11. Ivins, 40.

12. Ivins, 53.

13. Marshall McLuhan, *The Gutenberg Galaxy: The Making of Typographic Man* (Toronto: University of Toronto Press, 1962), 149.

14. McLuhan, 149.

15. Carlos Alberto Scolari, *Las leyes de la interfaz: Diseño, ecología, evolución, tecnología* (Barcelona: Gedisa, 2018). For the English summation, see Carlos Alberto Scolari, "The Laws of the Interface," UX Collective, Medium, August 25, 2019, https://uxdesign.cc/the-laws-of-the-interface-9bfe09e19e11.

16. Lucy Suchman, *Human-Machine Reconfigurations: Plans and Situated Actions* (New York: Cambridge University Press, 2007), 284.

17. Alexander R. Galloway, *The Interface Effect* (Cambridge: Polity, 2012), 31.

18. André Bazin, "The Ontology of the Photographic Image," *Film Quarterly* 13, no. 4 (Summer 1960): 4–9.

19. Mary Ann Doane, "The Indexical and the Concept of Medium Specificity," *Differences* 18, no. 1 (May 2007), 143.

20. Hito Steyerl, *The Wretched of the Screen* (Berlin: Sternberg Press, 2012), 33.

21. Steyerl, 41.

22. Abdul Aziz Anwar, *Film Industry in West Pakistan* (Lahore: Board of Economic Inquiry, 1957), 115.
23. For an industry and a nation characterized by their bureaucracy and legislation, the only law relating to the archiving of Pakistani films was the requirement of the Film Storage Licences that were issued by the chief inspector of explosives. This law was a remnant of the days when film was made of highly flammable silver nitrate. This did not stop a film "godown," or storage unit, being destroyed by fire in Lahore's Royal Park in 1948. Anwar, 220.
24. Erlend Clouston, "If I Find One Reel, I Must Kill You," *The Guardian*, February 20, 2008, https://www.theguardian.com/film/2008/feb/20/features.afghanistan.
25. Gladys D. Ganley and Oswald Harold Ganley, *Global Political Fallout: The First Decade of the VCR, 1976–1985* (Westport, CT: Praeger, 1987), 46.
26. Blake Atwood, *Underground: The Secret Life of Videocassettes in Iran* (Cambridge, MA: MIT Press, 2021).
27. Rashid Latif Ansari in email communication with author.
28. Nauman Farooqi, "Hawala (Middle East, India and Pakistan)," in *Global Encyclopaedia of Informality, Volume 2: Towards Understanding of Social and Cultural Complexity*, ed. Alena Ledeneva (London: UCL Press, 2018): 143–148.
29. Hassan Javid, "Class, Power, and Patronage: Landowners and Politics in Punjab," *History and Anthropology* 22, no. 3 (2011), 345.
30. As mentioned in chapter 2, while the figurative depiction of the family and the companions of the Prophet Muhammad is anathema to many Muslims, depictions of the Ahl-e Bait and the Twelve Imams are commonly shown in Shi'i places of worship.
31. Roger Silverstone, "Proper Distance," *Digital Media Revisited: Theoretical and Conceptual Innovations in Digital Domains*, ed. Gunnar Liestøl, Andrew Morrison, and Terje Rasmussen (Cambridge, MA: MIT Press, 2004).
32. Silverstone, 477.
33. Silverstone, 475.
34. Similarly challenged by the proliferation of advertisements, self-promotions, and, in their case of Mewati video films, fan cameos, Mukhreejee and Singh argue these inscriptions delineate a public at the same time as addressing them as intimate spectators. For their male Mewati interlocutors, the ability to represent themselves or see traces of themselves onscreen reflects neither on a situation of subalternaeity nor of popular representation, but a politics of aspiration that is closely bound up with media informality. Rahul Mukherjee and Abhigyan Singh, "MicroSD-ing 'Mewati Videos': Circulation and Regulation of a Subaltern-Popular Media Culture," in *Asian Video Cultures: In the Penumbra of the Global*, ed. Joshua Neves and Bhaskar Sarkar (Durham, NC: Duke University Press, 2017): 133–157.

35. Transcending the traditional ontology of the thing in such a way requires close attention to the ways it radiates and goes forth from itself. For Gernot Böhme, between the subject and the object lies atmosphere, where an alert recipient meets what he calls the "ecstasies" of the thing. Gernot Böhme, *Atmospheric Architectures: The Aesthetics of Felt Spaces*, ed. and trans. A.-Chr. Engels-Schwarzpaul, (London: Bloomsbury, 2017), 46.

Epilogue

1. Nida Kirmani, *Questioning the "Muslim Woman": Identity and Insecurity in an Urban Indian Locality* (London: Routledge, 2016), 79.
2. Patrick Eisenlohr, "Atmospheric Citizenship: Sonic Movement and Public Religion in Shi'i Mumbai," *Public Culture* 33, no. 3 (September 2021): 371–392.
3. William Mazzarella, "The Anthropology of Populism: Beyond the Liberal Settlement," *Annual Review of Anthropology* 48 (October 2019): 50.
4. Siegfried Kracauer, "The Mass Ornament," in Siegfried Kracauer, *The Mass Ornament: Weimar Essays*, ed. and trans. Thomas Y. Levin (Cambridge, MA: Harvard University Press, 1995), 79.

Bibliography

Abbas, Ghulam. *Tazias of Chiniot*. Lahore: Tarikh, 2007.

"Abdul Sattar vs. The State." In *Pakistan Law Journal, 1975, Part II*, 1137–1141. Lahore: Pakistan Educational Press, 1975.

"Abdul Sattar vs. The State." In *Pakistan Law Journal, 1980, Part I & II*, 979–981. Lahore: Pakistan Educational Press, 1980.

Abou-Zahab, Mariam. *Pakistan: A Kaleidoscope of Islam*. London: Oxford University Press, 2020.

Abul A'la Maududi, Syed. *Rasail O Masail, Vol. 2*. Lahore: Islamic Publications, 2000.

Abu-Lughod, Lila. *Dramas of Nationhood: The Politics of Television in Egypt*. Chicago: University of Chicago Press, 2008.

Agrama, Hussein Ali. "Ethics, Tradition, Authority: Toward an Anthropology of the Fatwa." *American Ethnologist* 37, no. 1 (February 2010): 2–18.

Ahmad, Ali Nobil. "Film and Cinephilia in Pakistan: Beyond Life and Death." *BioScope: South Asian Screen Studies* 5, no. 2 (July 2014): 81–98.

Ahmad, Ali Nobil, and Ali Khan. "Special Issue: Pakistani Cinema." *BioScope: South Asian Screen Studies* 5, no. 2 (July 2014).

Ahmad, Ali Nobil, and Ali Khan, eds. *Cinema and Society: Film and Social Change in Pakistan*. Karachi: Oxford University Press, 2016.

——. *Film and Cinephilia in Pakistan: Beyond Life and Death*. Oxford: Oxford University Press, 2020.

Ahmad, Irfan. "Cracks in the 'Mightiest Fortress': Jamaat-e-Islami's Changing Discourse on Women." *Modern Asian Studies* 42, nos. 2–3 (March 2008): 549–575.

——. *Islamism and Democracy in India: The Transformation of Jamaat-e-Islami*. Princeton, NJ: Princeton University Press, 2009.

Ahmed, Akbar S. *Jinnah, Pakistan, and Islamic Identity: The Search for Saladin*. Hove, UK: Psychology Press, 1997.

Ahmed, Sara. "Collective Feelings: Or, the Impressions Left by Others." *Theory, Culture, and Society* 21, no. 2 (April 2004): 25–42.

Akhtar, Aasim Sajjad. *The Politics of Common Sense: State, Society, and Culture in Pakistan*. Cambridge: Cambridge University Press, 2018.

Alam, Ahmad Rafay. "The Beginning of the Talibanization of Lahore?" *The News*, October 26, 2008.

Alam, Asiya. *Women, Islam, and Familial Intimacy in Colonial South Asia*. Leiden, NL: Brill, 2021.

Ali Baig, Mariam. "The Pakola Tale." In *Mazaar, Bazaar: Design and Visual Culture in Pakistan*, ed. Saima Zaidi, 157–163. Karachi: Oxford University Press, 2009.

Anand, Nikhil, Akhil Gupta, and Hannah Appel, eds. *The Promise of Infrastructure*. Durham, NC: Duke University Press, 2018.

Anwar, Abdul Aziz. *Film Industry in West Pakistan*. Lahore: Board of Economic Inquiry, 1957.

Appadurai, Arjun. "Disjuncture and Difference in the Global Cultural Economy." *Theory, Culture & Society* 7, no. 2–3 (June 1990): 295–310.

Aragon, Louis. *Paris Peasant*. Trans. Simon Watson-Taylor. Boston: Exact Change, 1994.

Armbrust, Walter. "Synchronizing Watches: The State, the Consumer, and Sacred Time in Ramadan Television." In *Religion, Media, and the Public Sphere*, ed. Birgit Meyer and Annelies Moors, 207–226. Bloomington: Indiana University Press, 2006.

Asad, Talal. *The Idea of an Anthropology of Islam*. Washington, DC: Institute for Contemporary Arab Studies, Georgetown University, 1986.

Asdar Ali, Kamran. *Cinema and the City: The Ayub Years*. Dawn, May 5, 2013, http://Www.Dawn.Com/News/1026248/Column-Cinema-And-The-City -The-Ayub-Years-By-Kamran-Asdar-Ali.

Ashar, Fayyaz Ahmed. *Pakistani Urdu Filmi Geeton Ka Safar (1948–1970)* [Journey of Pakistani Urdu Film Songs (1948–1970)]. Lahore: Maqsood, 2011.

——. *Pakistani Urdu Filmi Geeton Ka Safar (1971–1997)* [Journey of Pakistani Urdu Film Songs, Part 2 (1971–1997)]. Lahore: Maqsood, 2018.

Atwood, Blake. *Underground: The Secret Life of Videocassettes in Iran*. Cambridge, MA: MIT Press, 2021.

Auslander, Phillip. "Digital Liveness: A Historico-Philosophical Perspective." *PAJ: A Journal of Performance and Art* 34, no. 3 (September 2012): 3–11.

——. "Live and Technologically Mediated Performance." In *The Cambridge Companion to Performance Studies*, ed. Tracy C. Davis, 107–119. New York: Cambridge University Press, 2008.

———. *Liveness: Performance in a Mediatized Culture*. London: Routledge, 2008.

Ayoub, Mahmoud. *Redemptive Suffering in Islam: A Study of the Devotional Aspects of 'Āshūrā' in Twelver Shī'ism*. The Hague, NL: Mouton Publishers, 1978.

Aziz, Abdul Anwar. *Film Industry in West Pakistan*. Lahore: Board of Economic Inquiry, 1957.

Bachelard, Gaston. *The Poetics of Space*. Trans. Maria Jolas. Boston: Beacon Press, 1994.

"Baho Film Corporation vs. Islamic Republic of Pakistan." *The All Pakistan Legal Decisions, 1981* 33 (1981), 295–318.

Bandak, Andreas. "Of Refrains and Rhythms in Contemporary Damascus: Urban Space and Christian-Muslim Coexistence." *Current Anthropology* 55, no. S10 (December 2014): S248–S261.

Batool, Farida Syeda. "New Media, Masculinity, and Mujra Dance in Pakistan." PhD diss., SOAS, University of London, 2015.

———. *Figure: The Popular and the Political in Pakistan*. Lahore: ASR, 2004.

Bauer, Thomas. *A Culture of Ambiguity: An Alternative History of Islam*. Trans. Hinrich Biesterfeldt and Tricia Tunstall. New York: Columbia University Press, 2021.

Bazin, André. "The Ontology of the Photographic Image." *Film Quarterly* 13, no. 4 (1960): 4–9.

Bellamy, Carla. *The Powerful Ephemeral: Everyday Healing in an Ambiguously Islamic Place*. Berkeley, CA: University of California Press, 2011.

Benjamin, Walter. *The Arcades Project*. Trans. Howard Eiland and Kevin Mclaughlin. Cambridge, MA: Harvard University Press, 1999.

———. *The Work of Art in the Age of Its Technological Reproducibility, and Other Writings on Media*. Cambridge, MA: Harvard University Press, 2008.

Bennett, Jane. *The Enchantment of Modern Life: Attachments, Crossings, and Ethics*. Princeton, NJ: Princeton University Press, 2001.

Berlant, Lauren. *Cruel Optimism*. Durham, NC: Duke University Press, 2011.

Berman, Marshall. *All That Is Solid Melts into Air: The Experience of Modernity*. London: Verso, 1983.

Bhatti, Shaila. *Translating Museums: A Counterhistory of South Asian Museology*. Walnut Creek, CA: Left Coast Press, 2012.

Bhaumik, Kaushik. "Cinematograph to Cinema: Bombay, 1896–1928." *BioScope: South Asian Screen Studies* 2, no. 1 (January 2011): 41–67.

Bille, Mikkel. *Homely Atmospheres and Lighting Technologies in Denmark: Living with Light*. London: Routledge, 2020.

Böhme, Gernot. *Atmospheric Architectures: The Aesthetics of Felt Spaces*. Ed. and trans. A.-Chr. Engels-Schwarzpaul. London: Bloomsbury, 2017.

———. "A Matter of Taste? On the Significance of Aesthetic Judgement for Morality." *Senses and Society* 16, no. 3 (2021): 351–355.

——. "Atmosphere as the Fundamental Concept of a New Aesthetics." *Thesis Eleven* 36, no. 1 (August 1993): 113–126.

Bowen, John R. *Islam, Law, and Equality in Indonesia: An Anthropology of Public Reasoning.* Cambridge: Cambridge University Press, 2003.

Boyer, Dominic. "Digital Expertise in Online Journalism (and Anthropology)." *Anthropological Quarterly* 83, no. 1 (Winter 2010): 73–95.

Breman, Jan. *Footloose Labour: Working in India's Informal Economy.* Cambridge: Cambridge University Press, 1996.

Brennan, Teresa. *The Transmission of Affect.* Ithaca, NY: Cornell University Press, 2004.

Canudo, Ricciotto. "Reflections on the Seventh Art." Trans. Claudia Gorbman. In *French Film Theory and Criticism: A History/Anthology, 1907–1939, Volume 1,* ed. Richard Abel, 291–303. Princeton, NJ: Princeton University Press, 1988.

Casetti, Francesco. "Why Fears Matter: Cinephobia in Early Film Culture." *Screen* 59, no. 2 (Summer 2018): 145–157.

Chowdhury, Nusrat Sabina. "The Ethics of the Digital: Crowds and Popular Justice in Bangladesh." In *Crowds: Ethnographic Encounters,* ed. Megan Steffen, 133–150. London: Bloomsbury, 2019.

Cinema Commission of Inquiry. *The Cinema: Its Present Position and Future Possibilities.* London: Williams and Norgate, 1917.

Clarke, Morgan. *Islam and New Kinship: Reproductive Technology and the Shariah in Lebanon.* London: Berghahn Books, 2009.

Clouston, Erlend. "If I Find One Reel, I Must Kill You." *The Guardian,* February 20, 2008.

Conn, Harvie M. "Islamic Socialism in Pakistan: An Overview." *Islamic Studies* 15, no. 2 (Summer 1976): 111–121.

Constituent Assembly of India (Legislative) Debates. Part 2, Vol. 4, No. 1. Indian Constituent Assembly: 1949.

Cooper, Timothy P. A. "The Kaččā and the Pakkā: Disenchanting the Film Event in Pakistan." *Comparative Studies in Society and History* 62, no. 2 (April 2020): 262–295.

Dadi, Iftikhar. "Bioscopic and Screen Studies of Pakistan, and of Contemporary Art." *BioScope: South Asian Screen Studies* 1, no.1 (January 2010): 11–15.

——. *Lahore Cinema: Between Realism and Fable.* Seattle: University of Washington Press, 2022.

——. "Registering Crisis: Ethnicity in Pakistani Cinema of the 1960s and 1970s." In *Beyond Crisis: Re-Evaluating Pakistan,* ed. Naveeda Khan, 167–198. London: Routledge, 2012.

Das, Veena. "Moral and Spiritual Striving in the Everyday: To Be a Muslim in Contemporary India." In *Ethical Life in South Asia,* ed. Anand Pandian and Daud Ali, 232–252. Bloomington: Indiana University Press, 2010.

———. "What Does Ordinary Ethics Look Like?" In *Four Lectures on Ethics*, ed. Michael Lambek, Veena Das, Webb Keane, and Didier Fassin, 53–126. Chicago: HAU Books. 2015.

Dass, Manishita. *Outside the Lettered City: Cinema, Modernity, and the Public Sphere in Late Colonial India*. Oxford: Oxford University Press, 2016.

Deeb, Lara. "Piety Politics and the Role of a Transnational Feminist Analysis." *Journal of the Royal Anthropological Institute* 15, no. S1 (May 2009): S112–S126.

Deleuze, Gilles, and Félix Guattari. *A Thousand Plateaus: Capitalism and Schizophrenia*. London: Bloomsbury, 1987.

Dennis, Simone. *Smokefree: A Social, Moral, and Political Atmosphere*. London: Bloomsbury, 2016.

Derrida, Jacques. *Of Grammatology*. Trans. Gayatri Chakravorty Spivak. Baltimore, MD: Johns Hopkins University Press, 1997.

Doane, Mary Ann. "The Indexical and the Concept of Medium Specificity." *Differences* 18, no. 1 (May 2007): 128–152.

"Documents, December 1978–May 1979." *Pakistan Horizon* 32, no. 1/2 (1979): 277–337.

D'Souza, Diane, "In the Presence of the Martyrs: The Alam in Popular Shi'i Piety." *The Muslim World* 88, no. 1 (January 1998): 67–80.

Dumont, Louis. *Homo Hierarchicus: The Caste System and Its Implications*. Chicago: University of Chicago Press, 1980.

Durkheim, Émile. *The Elementary Forms of the Religious Life*. Trans. Joseph Ward Swain. London: George Allen and Unwin, 1964.

Eisenlohr, Patrick. "Atmospheric Citizenship: Sonic Movement and Public Religion in Shi'i Mumbai." *Public Culture* 33, no. 3 (September 2021): 371–392.

———. "Atmospheric Resonance: Sonic Motion and the Question of Religious Mediation." *Journal of the Royal Anthropological Institute* 28, no. 2 (June 2022): 613–631.

———. *Sounding Islam: Voice, Media, and Sonic Atmospheres in an Indian Ocean World*. Berkeley: University of California Press, 2018.

Elias, Jamal J. *Alef Is for Allah: Childhood, Emotion, and Visual Culture in Islamic Societies*. Berkeley: University of California Press, 2018.

———. *On Wings of Diesel: Trucks, Identity, and Culture in Pakistan*. Oxford: Oneworld, 2011.

Engelke, Matthew. *God's Agents: Biblical Publicity in Contemporary England*. Berkeley: University of California Press, 2013.

Ewing, Katherine Pratt. *Arguing Sainthood: Modernity, Psychoanalysis, and Islam*. Durham, NC: Duke University Press, 1997.

———. "Crossing Borders and Transgressing Boundaries: Metaphors for Negotiating Multiple Identities." *Ethos* 26, no. 2 (June 1998): 262–267.

——. "The Illusion of Wholeness: Culture, Self, and the Experience of Inconsistency." *Ethos* 18, no. 3 (September 1990): 251–278.

——. "Introduction: Ambiguity and *Shariʿat*—A Perspective on the Problem of Moral Principles in Tension." In *Shariʿat and Ambiguity in South Asian Islam*, ed. Katherine Pratt Ewing, 1–22. Berkeley: University of California Press, 1988.

Ewing, Katherine Pratt, and Rosemary R. Corbett, eds. *Modern Sufis and the State: The Politics of Islam in South Asia and Beyond*. New York: Columbia University Press, 2020.

Fader, Ayala. "Nonliberal Jewish Women's Audiocassette Lectures in Brooklyn: A Crisis of Faith and the Morality of Media." *American Anthropologist* 115, no. 1 (March 2013): 72–84.

Fadil, Nadia, and Mayanthi Fernando. "Rediscovering the 'Everyday' Muslim: Notes on an Anthropological Divide." *HAU: Journal of Ethnographic Theory* 5, no. 2 (Fall 2015): 59–88.

Faiz, Faiz Ahmad. "What Would You Have?" In Faiz Ahmed Faiz, *Culture and Identity: Selected English Writings of Faiz*, ed. Sheema Majeed, 120–121. Oxford: Oxford University Press, 2005.

Farooqi, Nauman. "Hawala (Middle East, India, and Pakistan)." In *Global Encyclopaedia of Informality, Volume 2: Towards Understanding of Social and Cultural Complexity*, ed. Alena Ledeneva, 143–148. London: UCL Press, 2018.

Flood, Finbarr Barry. "Between Cult and Culture: Bamiyan, Islamic Iconoclasm, and the Museum." *The Art Bulletin* 84, no. 4 (December 2002): 641–659.

Foucault, Michel. *The Archaeology of Knowledge*. Trans. A. M. Sheridan Smith. New York: Pantheon, 1972.

——. *Technologies of the Self: A Seminar with Michel Foucault*. Amherst: University of Massachusetts Press, 1988.

Fraser, Nancy. "Rethinking the Public Sphere: A Contribution to the Critique of Actually Existing Democracy." *Social Text*, no. 25/26 (1990): 56–80.

Frazer, James George. *Taboo and the Perils of the Soul*. London: Macmillan, 1911.

Freitag, Sandria B. "State and Community: Symbolic Popular Protest in Banaras's Public Arenas." In *Culture and Power in Banaras: Community, Performance, and Environment*, ed. Sandria B. Freitag, 203–228. Berkeley: University of California Press, 1992.

Frembgen, Jürgen Wasim. *The Friends of God: Sufi Saints in Islam, Popular Poster Art from Pakistan*. Oxford: Oxford University Press, 2006.

Fromm, Erich, *The Fear of Freedom*. London: Routledge, 2001.

Galatsanos, Nick, and Aggelos Konstantinos Katsaggelos, eds. *Signal Recovery Techniques for Image and Video Compression and Transmission*. Amsterdam: Kluwer Academic Publishers, 1998.

Galloway, Alexander R. *The Interface Effect*. Cambridge: Polity, 2012.

Ganley, Gladys D., and Oswald Harold Ganley. *Global Political Fallout: The First Decade of the VCR, 1976–1985*. Westport, CT: Praeger, 1987.

Gazdar, Mushtaq. *Pakistan Cinema, 1947–1997*. Karachi: Oxford University Press, 1997.

Geddes, Sir Patrick. *Town Planning in Lahore: A Report to the Municipal Council*. Lahore: Commercial Print Works, 1917.

Geertz, Clifford. "The Bazaar Economy: Information and Search in Peasant Marketing." *American Economic Review* 68, no. 2 (May 1978): 28–32.

Gennep, Arnold Van. *The Rites of Passage*. Trans. Monika B. Vizedom and Gabrielle L. Caffee. Chicago: University of Chicago Press, 1960.

Gershon, Ilana. "Porous Social Orders." *American Ethnologist* 46, no. 4 (November 2019): 404–416.

Gilmartin, David. *Empire and Islam: Punjab and the Making of Pakistan*. Berkeley: University of California Press, 1988.

Gitelman, Lisa. *Paper Knowledge: Toward a Media History of Documents*. Durham, NC: Duke University Press, 2014.

Glover, William J. *Making Lahore Modern: Constructing and Imagining a Colonial City*. Minneapolis: University of Minnesota Press, 2008.

——. "Translating the Public in Colonial Punjab." In *Punjab Reconsidered: History, Culture, and Practice*, ed. Anshu Malhotra and Farina Mir, 356–374. Oxford: Oxford University Press, 2012.

Golbarg, Rekabtalaei. *Iranian Cosmopolitanism: A Cinematic History*. Cambridge: Cambridge University Press, 2019.

Goody, Jack. *The Interface between the Written and the Oral*. Cambridge: Cambridge University Press, 1987.

Gopalan, Lalitha. *Cinema of Interruptions: Action Genres in Contemporary Indian Cinema*. London: British Film Institute, 2002.

Groening, Stephen. *Cinema beyond Territory: Inflight Entertainment and Atmospheres of Globalization*. London: Bloomsbury, 2014.

Gul, Aijaz. "Sex, Bloodbaths, and a Pair of Scissors." *Cinemaya* 4 (1989): 56–57.

Habermas, Jurgen. *The Structural Transformation of the Public Sphere: An Inquiry into a Category of Bourgeois Society*. Cambridge, MA: MIT Press, 1991.

Hamid, Mohsin. *Moth Smoke*. London: Penguin, 2012.

Hardin, Garrett. "The Tragedy of the Commons." *Science* 162, no. 3859 (December 1968): 1243–1248.

Hart, Keith. "Informal Income Opportunities and Urban Employment in Ghana." *Journal of Modern African Studies* 11, no. 1 (March 1973): 61–89.

Haweis, Hugh Reginald. *Music and Morals*. London: Harper & Brothers, 1872.

Hegland, Mary Elaine. "Shi'a Women's Rituals in Northwest Pakistan: The Shortcomings and Significance of Resistance." *Anthropological Quarterly* 76, no. 3 (Summer 2003): 411–442.

Himpele, Jeffrey D. *Circuits of Culture: Media, Politics, and Indigenous Identity in the Andes.* Minneapolis: University of Minnesota Press, 2008.

——. "Film Distribution as Media: Mapping Difference in the Bolivian Cinemascape." *Visual Anthropology Review* 12, no. 1 (March 1996): 47–66.

Hirschkind, Charles. *The Ethical Soundscape: Cassette Sermons and Islamic Counterpublics.* New York: Columbia University Press, 2006.

Hoek, Lotte. *Cut-Pieces: Celluloid Obscenity and Popular Cinema in Bangladesh.* New York: Columbia University Press, 2013.

——. "Urdu for Image: Understanding Bangladeshi Cinema Through Its Theatres." In *South Asian Media Cultures: Audiences, Representations, Contexts,* ed. Shakuntala Banaji, 73–89. London: Anthem Press, 2011.

Honigmann, John Joseph. *Information for Pakistan: Report of Research on Intercultural Communication through Films.* Chapel Hill: Institute for Research in Social Science, University of North Carolina, 1953.

——. *Three Pakistan Villages.* Chapel Hill: Institute for Research in Social Science, University of North Carolina, 1958.

Howard, Luke. *Essay on the Modification of Clouds.* London: John Churchill and Sons, 1803.

Howarth, Toby. *The Twelver Shīʿa as a Muslim Minority in India: Pulpit of Tears.* London: Routledge, 2005.

Hughes, Stephen Putnam. "Music in the Age of Mechanical Reproduction: Drama, Gramophone, and the Beginnings of Tamil Cinema." *Journal of Asian Studies* 66, no. 1 (February 2007): 3–34.

Hull, Matthew S. *Government of Paper: The Materiality of Bureaucracy in Urban Pakistan.* Berkeley: University of California Press, 2012.

Hussain, Neelam. "Meaning Makers." In *Re-Inventing Women: Representation of Women in the Media During the Zia Years,* ed. Maha Malik and Neelam Hussain, 1–10. Lahore: Simorgh Women's Resource and Publication Centre, 1985.

Hyder, Syed Akbar. *Reliving Karbala: Martyrdom in South Asian Memory.* Oxford: Oxford University Press, 2006.

Ibbetson, Denzil. *Panjab Castes: Races, Castes, and Tribes of the People of the Panjab.* Lahore: the Superintendent/Government Printing, 1916.

Imran, Warda. "Of Consent and Copyrights: Women Lodge 90% Complaints in FIA Cybercrime Circle," *Express Tribune,* April 9, 2018.

Imtiaz, Saba. "A New Form of Films Emerges." *Express Tribune,* June 23, 2010.

Iqbal, Muhammad. *Bal-E-Jibreel.* Lahore: Taj, 1935.

——. *Poems From Iqbal.* Trans V. G. Kiernan. London: John Murray, 1955.

——. *The Reconstruction of Muslim Thought in Islam.* London: Oxford University Press, 1934.

Ispahani, Farahnaz. *Purifying the Land of the Pure: A History of Pakistan's Religious Minorities*. Oxford: Oxford University Press, 2017.

Ivins, William Mills. *Prints and Visual Communication*. Cambridge, MA: MIT Press, 1969.

Jabbar, Javed. "Passion in the Pakistani Cinema." In *Snapshots: Reflections in a Pakistani Eye*, ed. Javed Jabbar, 149–151. Lahore: Wazidalis, 1982.

Jahangir, Asma, and Hina Jilani. *The Hudood Ordinances: A Divine Sanction?* Lahore: Sang-E-Meel, 2003.

Jain, Kajri. *Gods in the Bazaar: The Economies of Indian Calendar Art*. Durham, NC: Duke University Press, 2007.

Jalal, Ayesha. *Democracy and Authoritarianism in South Asia: A Comparative and Historical Perspective*. Cambridge: Cambridge University Press, 1995.

Javid, Hassan. "Class, Power, and Patronage: Landowners and Politics in Punjab." *History and Anthropology* 22, no. 3 (2011): 337–369.

Jeffery, Roger, Craig Jeffery, and Patricia Jeffery. "Parhai Ka Mahaul. An Educational Environment in Bijnor, Uttar Pradesh." In *The Meaning of the Local: Politics of Place in Urban India*, ed. Henrike Donner and Geert De Neve, 116–140. London: Routledge, 2006.

Jervis-Read, Cressida. "Frontier Town: Marking Boundaries in a Delhi Resettlement Colony 30 Years On." In *Sarai Reader 07: Frontiers*, ed. Monica Nerula, Shuddhabrata Sengupta, Jeebesh Bagchi, and Ravi Sundaram, 516–526. Delhi: Sarai Media Lab, 2007.

Jue, Melody. *Wild Blue Media: Thinking through Seawater*. Durham, NC: Duke University Press, 2020.

Jue, Melody, and Rafico Ruiz. "Introduction." In *Saturation: An Elemental Politics*, ed. Melody Jue and Rafico Ruiz, 1–28. Durham, NC: Duke University Press, 2021.

Jusionyte, Ieva. *Threshold: Emergency Responders on the US-Mexico Border*. Berkeley: University of California Press, 2018.

Kabir, Alamgir. *The Cinema in Pakistan*. Dhaka: Sandhani, 1969.

Karaganis, Joe, ed. *Media Piracy in Emerging Economies*. New York: Social Science Research Council, 2011.

Kazi, Durriya. "How Lollywood Lost Lakshmi." In *Arts of People IV: Lollywood! Pakistani Film Posters*, ed. Yuko Yamaki, 2–9. Fukuoka, JP: Fukuoka Asian Art Museum, 2006.

Kazi, Taha. *Religious Television and Pious Authority in Pakistan*. Bloomington: Indiana University Press, 2021.

Keane, Webb. "Freedom, Reflexivity, and the Sheer Everydayness of Ethics." *HAU: Journal of Ethnographic Theory* 4, no. 1 (Summer 2014): 443–457.

Keller, Sarah. *Anxious Cinephilia: Pleasure and Peril at the Movies*. New York: Columbia University Press, 2020.

Khan, Hazrat Inayat. *The Music of Life*. New York: Omega, 1988.

Khan, Naveeda. "The Acoustics of Muslim Striving: Loudspeaker Use in Ritual Practice in Pakistan." *Comparative Studies in Society and History* 53, no. 3 (July 2011): 571–594.

——. "Flaws in the Flow: Roads and Their Modernity in Pakistan." *Social Text* 24, no. 4 (Winter 2006): 87–113.

——. *Muslim Becoming: Aspiration and Skepticism in Pakistan*. Durham, NC: Duke University Press, 2012.

Kierkegaard, Søren. *Either/Or: A Fragment of Life*. Abridged ed. Trans. Alastair Hannay. London: Penguin, 1992.

Kirk, Gwendolyn. "Uncivilized Language and Aesthetic Exclusion: Language, Power, and Film Production in Pakistan." PhD diss., University of Texas, 2016.

Kirmani, Nida. *Questioning the "Muslim Woman": Identity and Insecurity in an Urban Indian Locality*. London: Routledge, 2016.

Kracauer, Siegfried. "The Mass Ornament." In *The Mass Ornament: Weimar Essays*, trans. Thomas Y. Levin, 75–88. Cambridge, MA: Harvard University Press, 1995.

Kuhn, Annette. *Cinema, Censorship, and Sexuality, 1909–1925*. London: Routledge, 1988.

Laidlaw, James. *The Subject of Virtue: An Anthropology of Ethics and Freedom*. Cambridge: Cambridge University Press, 2013.

Larkin, Brian. "Bandiri Music, Globalization, and Urban Experience in Nigeria." *Social Text* 22, no. 4 (Summer 2004): 91–112.

——. "Binary Islam: Media and Religious Movements in Nigeria." In *New Media and Religious Transformations in Africa*, ed. Rosalind I. J. Hackett and Benjamin F. Soares, 63–81. Bloomington: Indiana University Press, 2015.

——. "Degraded Images, Distorted Sounds: Nigerian Video and the Infrastructure of Piracy." *Public Culture* 16, no. 2 (Spring 2004): 289–314.

——. "Islamic Renewal, Radio, and the Surface of Things." In *Aesthetic Formations: Media, Religion, Senses*, ed. Birgit Meyer, 117–136. New York: Palgrave, 2009.

——. " 'Making Equivalence Happen': Commensuration and the Architecture of Circulation." In *Images That Move*, ed. Patricia Spyer and Mary Margaret Steedly, 237–256. Santa Fe, NM: SAR Press, 2013.

——. "The Politics and Poetics of Infrastructure." *Annual Review of Anthropology* 42 (October 2013): 327–343.

——. *Signal and Noise: Media, Infrastructure, and Urban Culture in Nigeria*. Durham, NC: Duke University Press, 2008.

Latour, Bruno. *Pandora's Hope: Essays on the Reality of Science Studies*. Cambridge, MA: Harvard University Press, 1999.

Lempert, Michael. "No Ordinary Ethics." *Anthropological Theory* 13, no. 4 (December 2013): 370–393.

Liang, Lawrence. "Beyond Representation: The Figure of the Pirate." In *Access to Knowledge in the Age of Intellectual Property*, ed. Amy Kapczynski and Gaëlle Krikorian, 353–376. New York: Zone Books, 2010.

———. "Cinematic Citizenship and the Illegal City." *Inter-Asia Cultural Studies* 6, no. 3 (September 2005): 366–385.

———. "Porous Legalities and Avenues of Participation." In *Sarai Reader 05: Bare Acts*, ed. Monica Narula, Shuddhabrata Sengupta, Jeebesh Bagchi, Geert Lovink, and Lawrence Liang, 6–17. Delhi: Sarai Media Lab, 2005.

Liboiron, Max. *Pollution Is Colonialism*. Durham, NC: Duke University Press, 2021.

Lobato, Ramon. *Shadow Economies of Cinema: Mapping Informal Film Distribution*. London: Bloomsbury, 2012.

MacDougall, David. *The Corporeal Image: Film, Ethnography, and the Senses*. Princeton, NJ: Princeton University Press, 2005.

Mahadevan, Sudhir. "Traveling Showmen, Makeshift Cinemas: The Bioscopewallah and Early Cinema History in India." *BioScope: South Asian Screen Studies* 1, no. 1 (January 2010): 27–47.

———. *A Very Old Machine: The Many Origins of the Cinema in India*. Albany: State University of New York Press, 2015.

Mahmood, Saba. *Politics of Piety: The Islamic Revival and the Feminist Subject*. Princeton, NJ: Princeton University Press, 2011.

Manuel, Peter. *Cassette Culture: Popular Music and Technology in North India*. Chicago: University of Chicago Press, 1993.

Maqsood, Ammara. *The New Pakistani Middle Class*. Cambridge, MA: Harvard University Press, 2017.

Maqsood, Ammara, and Fizzah Sajjad. "Victim, Broker, Activist, Fixer: Surviving Dispossession in Working Class Lahore." *Environment and Planning D: Society and Space* 39, no. 6 (December 2021): 994–1008.

Marett, Robert Ranulph. *The Threshold of Religion*. London: Methuen, 1909.

Marks, Laura U. *Touch: Sensuous Theory and Multisensory Media*. Minneapolis: University of Minnesota Press, 2002.

Masood, Salman. "In City of Tolerance, Shadow of the Taliban." *New York Times*, November 2, 2008.

Masselos, Jim. "Power in the Bombay 'Moholla,' 1904–1915: An Initial Exploration into the World of the Indian Urban Muslim." *South Asia: Journal of South Asian Studies* 6, no. 1 (1976): 75–95.

Mazzarella, William. "The Anthropology of Populism: Beyond the Liberal Settlement." *Annual Review of Anthropology* 48 (October 2019): 45–60.

———. *Censorium: Cinema and the Open Edge of Mass Publicity*. Durham, NC: Duke University Press, 2013.

——. *The Mana of Mass Society*. Chicago: University of Chicago Press, 2017.

McCarthy, Anna. *Ambient Television: Visual Culture and Public Space*. Durham, NC: Duke University Press, 2001.

McLuhan, Marshall. *The Gutenberg Galaxy: The Making of Typographic Man*. Toronto: University of Toronto Press, 1962.

Messick, Brinkley. *Shariʿa Scripts: A Historical Anthropology*. New York: Columbia University Press, 2018.

Metcalf, Barbara Daly. "Introduction." In *Moral Conduct and Authority: The Place of Adab in South Asian Islam*, ed. Barbara Daly Metcalf, 1–20. Berkeley: University of California Press, 1984.

Meyer, Birgit. "An Author Meets Her Critics: Around Birgit Meyer's 'Mediation and the Genesis of Presence'—Toward a Material Approach to Religion." *Religion and Society: Advances in Research* 5, no. 1 (September 2014): 205–254.

——. "How to Capture the 'Wow': R. R. Marett's Notion of Awe and the Study of Religion." *Journal of the Royal Anthropological Institute* 22, no. 1 (March 2016): 7–26.

——. *Sensational Movies: Video, Vision, and Christianity in Ghana*. Berkeley: University of California Press, 2015.

Mir, Farina. "Urdu Ethics Literature and the Diversity of Muslim Thought in Colonial India." *American Historical Review* 127, no. 3 (September 2022): 1162–1189.

Misztal, Barbara. *Informality: Social Theory and Contemporary Practice*. London: Routledge, 2002.

Mittermaier, Amira. "Dreams from Elsewhere: Muslim Subjectivities Beyond the Trope of Self-Cultivation." *Journal of the Royal Anthropological Institute* 18, no. 2 (June 2012): 247–265.

——. *Dreams That Matter: Egyptian Landscapes of the Imagination*. Berkeley: University of California Press, 2010.

——. *Giving to God: Islamic Charity in Revolutionary Times*. Berkeley: University of California Press, 2019.

Moffat, Chris. "Building, Dwelling, Dying: Architecture and History in Pakistan." *Modern Intellectual History* 18, no. 2 (June 2021): 520–546.

——. *India's Revolutionary Inheritance: Politics and the Promise of Bhagat Singh*. Cambridge: Cambridge University Press, 2019.

Moll, Yasmin. "Television Is Not Radio: Theologies of Mediation in the Egyptian Islamic Revival." *Cultural Anthropology* 33, no. 2 (May 2018): 233–265.

Mukherjee, Debashree. "Notes on a Scandal: Writing Women's Film History Against an Absent Archive." *BioScope: South Asian Screen Studies* 4, no. 1 (January 2013): 9–30.

Mukherjee, Rahul. *Radiant Infrastructures: Media, Environment, and Cultures of Uncertainty.* Durham, NC: Duke University Press, 2020.

———. "Wireless Saturation." In *Saturation: An Elemental Politics*, ed. Melody Jue and Rafico Ruiz, 123–143. Durham, NC: Duke University Press, 2021.

Mukherjee, Rahul, and Abhigyan Singh. "MicroSD-ing 'Mewati Videos': Circulation and Regulation of a Subaltern-Popular Media Culture." *Asian Video Cultures: In the Penumbra of the Global,* ed. Joshua Neves and Bhaskar Sarkar, 133–157. Durham, NC: Duke University Press, 2017.

Mukherjee, Silpa. "Behind the Green Door: Unpacking the Item Number and Its Ecology." *BioScope: South Asian Screen Studies* 9, no. 2 (December 2018): 208–232.

Nakassis, Constantine V. *Doing Style: Youth and Mass Mediation in South India.* Chicago: University of Chicago Press, 2016.

Nasr, Seyyed Vali Reza. *Mawdudi and the Making of Islamic Revivalism.* Oxford: Oxford University Press, 1996.

Navaro-Yashin, Yael. *Faces of the State: Secularism and Public Life in Turkey.* Princeton, NJ: Princeton University Press, 2002.

———. *The Make-Believe Space: Affective Geography in a Postwar Polity.* Durham, NC: Duke University Press, 2012.

Neves, Joshua, and Bhaskar Sarkar. "Introduction." In *Asian Video Cultures: In the Penumbra of the Global,* ed. Joshua Neves and Bhaskar Sarkar, 1–34. Durham, NC: Duke University Press, 2017.

Novak, David. *Japanoise: Music at the Edge of Circulation.* Durham, NC: Duke University Press, 2013.

Omer, Shahab. "One of Pakistan's Oldest Cinemas in a State of Shambles, Plays Vulgar Films All Year Round." *Daily Times,* August 12, 2018.

Ostrom, Elinor. *Governing the Commons: The Evolution of Institutions for Collective Action.* Cambridge: Cambridge University Press, 1990.

Pamment, Claire. "Hijraism: Jostling for a Third Space in Pakistani Politics." *TDR/The Drama Review* 54, no. 2 (Summer 2010): 29–50.

———. "A Split Discourse: Body Politics in Pakistan's Popular Punjabi Theatre." *TDR/The Drama Review* 56, no. 1 (Spring 2012): 114–127.

Pandian, Anand. *Reel World: An Anthropology of Creation.* Durham, NC: Duke University Press, 2015.

Pandian, M. S. S. "Tamil Cultural Elites and Cinema: Outline of an Argument." *Economic and Political Weekly* 31, no. 15 (April 1996): 950–955.

Pernau, Margrit. "Introduction: Concepts of Emotions in Indian Languages." *Contributions to the History of Concepts* 11, no. 1 (June 2016): 24–37.

Parwez, Ghulam Ahmed. *Islam: A Challenge to Religion.* Lahore: Tolu-e-Islam Trust, 2012.

Peters, John Durham. *The Marvelous Clouds: Toward a Philosophy of Elemental Media*. Chicago: University of Chicago Press, 2015.

——. *Speaking in the Air: A History of the Idea of Communication*. Chicago: University of Chicago Press, 1999.

Pinney, Christopher. "Introduction: Public, Popular, and Other Cultures." In *Pleasure and the Nation: The History, Politics, and Consumption of Public Culture in India*, ed. Rachel Dwyer and Christopher Pinney, 1–34. Oxford: Oxford University Press, 2002.

——. "Notes from the Surface of the Image." In *Photography's Other Histories*, ed. Christopher Pinney and Nicolas Peterson, 202–220. Durham, NC: Duke University Press, 2003.

——. *"Photos of the Gods": The Printed Image and Political Struggle in India*. London: Reaktion Books, 2004.

——. *The Waterless Sea: A Curious History of Mirages*. London: Reaktion Books, 2018.

Powdermaker, Hortense. *Hollywood, the Dream Factory: An Anthropologist Looks at the Movie-Makers*. London: Secker and Warburg, 1951.

Pratt, Mary Louise. "Arts of the Contact Zone." *Profession* (1991): 33–40.

Qadeer, Mohammad. *Pakistan: Social and Cultural Transformations in a Muslim Nation*. London: Routledge, 2006.

——. *Urban Development in the Third World: Internal Dynamics of Lahore, Pakistan*. New York: Praeger, 1983.

Qasmi, Ali Usman. *The Ahmadis and the Politics of Religious Exclusion in Pakistan*. London: Anthem Press, 2015.

Rahman, Fazlur. "The Concept of Ḥadd in Islamic Law." *Islamic Studies* 4, no. 3 (September 1965): 237–251.

Rai, Amit S. *Jugaad: Ecologies of Everyday Hacking in India*. Durham, NC: Duke University Press, 2019.

Raqs Media Collective. *Seepage*. Berlin: Sternberg Press, 2010.

Reinhardt, Bruno. "Atmospheric Presence: Reflections on 'Mediation' in the Anthropology of Religion and Technology." *Anthropological Quarterly* 93, no. 1 (Winter 2020): 1523–1553.

Report of the Film Fact Finding Committee: Govt. of Pakistan, Ministry of Industries, April 1960–April 1961. Karachi: the Manager of Publications/Government of Pakistan Press, 1962.

Report of the Indian Cinematograph Committee, 1927–1928. Calcutta: Government of India Central Publication Branch, 1928.

Ring, Laura A. *Zenana: Everyday Peace in a Karachi Apartment Building*. Bloomington: Indiana University Press, 2006.

Robbins, Joel. "Dumont's Hierarchical Dynamism: Christianity and Individualism Revisited." *HAU: Journal of Ethnographic Theory* 5, no. 1 (Spring 2015): 173–195.

———. "What Is the Matter with Transcendence? On the Place of Religion in the New Anthropology of Ethics." *Journal of the Royal Anthropological Institute* 22, no. 4 (December 2016): 767–781.

Roquet, Paul. *Ambient Media: Japanese Atmospheres of Self.* Minneapolis: University of Minnesota Press, 2016.

Ruskin, John. "The Storm-Cloud of the Nineteenth Century: Two Lectures Delivered at the London Institution, February 4th and 11th, 1884." In *The Complete Works of John Ruskin*, library ed., vol. 34, ed. E. T. Cook and Alexander Wedderburn, 3–80. London: George Allen, 1903–12.

Saeed, Fouzia. *Forgotten Faces: Daring Women of Pakistan's Folk Theatre.* Lahore: Al-Faisal Nashran/Lok Virsa, 2011.

———. *Taboo!: The Hidden Culture of a Red Light Area.* Karachi: Oxford University Press, 2002.

Saeed, Yousuf. *Muslim Devotional Art in India.* London: Routledge, 2012.

Schielke, Samuli. "Being Good in Ramadan: Ambivalence, Fragmentation, and the Moral Self in the Lives of Young Egyptians." *Journal of the Royal Anthropological Institute* 15, no. S1 (May 2009): S24–S40.

Schmitt, Carl. *Political Theology: Four Chapters on the Concept of Sovereignty.* Chicago: University of Chicago Press, 2005.

Schmitz, Hermann, Rudolf Owen Müllan, and Jan Slaby. "Emotions Outside the Box: The New Phenomenology of Feeling and Corporeality." *Phenomenology and the Cognitive Sciences* 10, no. 2 (June 2011): 241–259.

Scolari, Carlos Alberto. *Las leyes de la interfaz: Diseño, ecología, evolución, tecnología.* Barcelona: Gedisa, 2018. For the English summation, see Carlos Alberto Scolari, "The Laws of the Interface," UX Collective, posted August 25, 2019. https://Uxdesign.Cc/The-Laws-Of-The-Interface-9bfe09e19e11.

Sevea, Iqbal. "'Kharaak Kita Oi!' Masculinity, Caste, and Gender in Punjabi Films." *BioScope: South Asian Screen Studies* 5, no. 2 (July 2014): 129–140.

Shafi, Maulana Mufti Muhammad. *Alat-E Jadida Ke Shari'i Ahkam* (The Orders of the Shari'a on Modern Inventions). Karachi: Idarat-Ul Maruf, 1996.

Shahid, S. M. *Film Acting Guide.* Lahore: Aleem, 1994.

Siddique, Salma. "Book Review: Ali Khan and Ali Nobil Ahmad (Eds), Cinema and Society: Film and Social Change in Pakistan." *BioScope: South Asian Screen Studies* 8, no 1. (June 2017): 176–180.

Silverstein, Brian. "Disciplines of Presence in Modern Turkey: Discourse, Companionship, and the Mass Mediation of Islamic Practice." *Cultural Anthropology* 23, no. 1 (February 2008): 118–153.

Silverstone, Roger. "Proper Distance: Toward an Ethics for Cyberspace." In *Digital Media Revisited: Theoretical and Conceptual Innovations in Digital Domains*, ed. Gunnar Liestøl, Andrew Morrison, and Terje Rasmussen, 469–490. Cambridge, MA: MIT Press, 2004.

Singh, Bhrigupati. "The Headless Horseman of Central India: Sovereignty at Varying Thresholds of Life." *Cultural Anthropology* 27, no. 2 (May 2012): 383–407.

Škof, Lenart, and Petri Berndtson. "Introduction." In *Atmospheres of Breathing*, ed. Lenart Škof and Petri Berndtson, iv–xxvii. New York: State University of New York Press, 2018.

Sørensen, Tim Flohr. "More Than a Feeling: Towards an Archaeology of Atmosphere." *Emotion, Space, and Society* 15 (May 2015): 64–67.

Spadoni, Robert. "What Is Film Atmosphere?" *Quarterly Review of Film and Video* 37, no. 1 (January 2020): 48–75.

Spitzer, Leo. "Milieu and Ambiance: An Essay in Historical Semantics, Part I." *Philosophy and Phenomenological Research* 3, no. 2 (December 1942): 169–218.

Sreberny, Annabelle, and Ali Mohammadi. *Small Media, Big Revolution: Communication, Culture, and the Iranian Revolution.* Minneapolis: University of Minnesota Press, 1994.

Srinivas, Lakshmi. *House Full: Indian Cinema and the Active Audience.* Chicago: University of Chicago Press, 2016.

Srinivas, S. V. "Gandhian Nationalism and Melodrama in the 30's Telugu Cinema." *Journal of the Moving Image* 1 (Fall 1999): 14–36.

Srivastava, Sanjay. *Passionate Modernity: Sexuality, Class, and Consumption in India.* New Delhi: Routledge, 2007.

Star, Susan Leigh. "This Is Not a Boundary Object: Reflections on the Origin of a Concept." *Science, Technology, & Human Values* 35, no. 5 (September 2010): 601–617.

Stasch, Rupert. *Society of Others: Kinship and Mourning in a West Papuan Place.* Berkeley: University of California Press, 2009.

Steyerl, Hito. *The Wretched of the Screen.* Berlin: Sternberg Press, 2012.

Stoler, Ann Laura. *Along the Archival Grain: Epistemic Anxieties and Colonial Common Sense.* Princeton, NJ: Princeton University Press, 2010.

Strassler, Karen. *Demanding Images: Democracy, Mediation, and the Image-Event in Indonesia.* Durham, NC: Duke University Press, 2020.

Suchman, Lucy. *Human-Machine Reconfigurations: Plans and Situated Actions.* New York: Cambridge University Press, 2007.

Sundaram, Ravi. "Uncanny Networks: Pirate, Urban and New Globalisation." *Economic and Political Weekly* 39, no. 1 (January 2004): 64–71.

——. *Pirate Modernity: Delhi's Media Urbanism.* London: Routledge, 2009.

Syed, Anwar H. "Z. A. Bhutto's Self-Characterizations and Pakistani Political Culture." *Asian Survey* 18, no. 12 (December 1978): 1250–1266.

Tanvir, Kuhu. "Pirate Histories: Rethinking the Indian Film Archive." *BioScope: South Asian Screen Studies* 4, no. 2 (July 2013): 115–136.

Taussig, Michael T. *Defacement: Public Secrecy and the Labor of the Negative.* Stanford, CA: Stanford University Press, 1999.

Taylor, Diana. *The Archive and the Repertoire: Performing Cultural Memory in the Americas*. Durham, NC: Duke University Press, 2003.

Throop, C. Jason. "Moral Moods." *Ethos* 42, no. 1 (March 2014): 65–83.

——. "Moral Sentiments." In *A Companion to Moral Anthropology*, ed. Didier Fassin, 150–168. London: Wiley-Blackwell, 2012.

Toor, Saadia. *The State of Islam: Culture and Cold War Politics in Pakistan*. London: Pluto Press, 2011.

Turner, Victor Witter. "Dewey, Dilthey, and Drama: An Essay in the Anthropology of Experience." In *The Anthropology of Experience*, ed. Victor Witter Turner, Edward M. Bruner, and Clifford Geertz, 33–44. Chicago: University of Illinois Press, 1986.

——. *Process, Performance, and Pilgrimage: A Study in Comparative Symbology*. New Delhi: Concept, 1979.

——. *The Ritual Process: Structure and Anti-Structure*. Ithaca, NY: Cornell University Press, 1977.

Usai, Paolo Cherchi. *The Death of Cinema: History, Cultural Memory, and the Digital Dark Age*. London: Bloomsbury, 2001.

van Nieuwkerk, Karin. "Debating Piety and Performing Arts in the Public Sphere: The 'Caravan' of Veiled Actresses in Egypt." In *Music, Culture, and Identity in the Muslim World: Performance, Politics, and Piety*, ed. Kamal Salhi, 80–102. London: Routledge, 2013.

Vasudevan, Ravi S. "Film Genres, the Muslim Social, and Discourses of Identity, c. 1935–1945." *BioScope: South Asian Screen Studies* 6, no. 1 (January 2015): 27–43.

——. "In the Centrifuge of History." *Cinema Journal* 50, no. 1 (Fall 2010): 135–140.

——. "Introduction." In *Making Meaning in Indian Cinema*, ed. Ravi Vasudevan, 1–36. New Delhi: Oxford University Press, 2000.

Walbridge, Linda. *The Christians of Pakistan: The Passion of Bishop John Joseph*. London: Routledge, 2012.

Warner, Michael. "Publics and Counterpublics." *Public Culture* 14, no. 1 (Winter 2002): 49–90.

Weiss, Anita. *Walls within Walls: Life Histories of Working Women in the Old City of Lahore*. Boulder, CO: Westview Press, 1992.

Zaman, Muhammad Qasim. *Islam in Pakistan: A History*. Princeton, NJ: Princeton University Press, 2018.

Zamindar, Vazira Fazila-Yacoobali. *The Long Partition and the Making of Modern South Asia: Refugees, Boundaries, Histories*. New York: Columbia University Press, 2007.

Zamindar, Vazira Fazila-Yacoobali, and Asad Ali, eds. *Love, War, and Other Longings: Essays on Cinema in Pakistan*. London: Oxford University Press, 2020.

Zigon, Jarrett. "Moral and Ethical Assemblages." *Anthropological Theory* 10, no. 1–2 (March 2010): 3–15.

Index

absorption, 34, 159–161, 164–167

actors, 8, 13, 16, 53–55, 63–64, 86, 88, 92–93, 131

aesthetics, 3, 10–13, 25, 42–43, 121–122, 221n24

Afghanistan, 41, 191

Ahl–e Bait, 22–24, 53, 72, 126, 130, 134–135, 137, 148

Ahmadiyya, 21, 38, 96, 155

Ali, Imam, 72, 130, 132–133

air conditioning, 101–102, 109–112, 117, 120

Allah: closeness to, xv, xvii; limits of, 57; will of, 96

ambience: ambient media, 101–102; and authority, 53; in relation to atmosphere, 10–11, 120–122

ambiguity, 103, 115, 149

amplification, xv, 105

architecture. *See also* plazas

archives: damage to, 112; deaccessioning of, 89; Guddu's Film Archive, 85–87; and repertoires, 30. *See also* Pakistani film: and absence of national archive

Ashura (religious day), 23, 115, 125, 131, 148, 186

atmosphere: and alterity, 24–25, 203, 208, 215n44, 217n56; and ambience, 10–11; and anthropology, xix, 19; atmospheric citizenship, 9–10, 203–204; and censorship, 55, 70, 82–83, 142; and film, 81–83, 115, 227n30; and hierarchy, 237n13; and music, 120–122; philosophy of, 3, 8–10, 18, 109, 121, 136, 221n24, 213n20; and pollution, 3, 11, 81, 117, 119–121; and social class, 111–112, 170–174. *See also* mahaul

awaam, xvii, 35, 68–69, 74, 87, 146, 169, 172 205

awe, 113–114, 147–148, 229n20

Ayub Khan, 5, 66–67

azadari, 23–24, 132, 134–135, 138, 147, 150

Bangladesh, 66, 79, 191

Barelvi (Sunni Islam), 23–24, 116, 130, 177, 217n55

Bhutto, Zulfiqar Ali, 41–42, 55, 155, 191
blasphemy, 38–39, 45, 94–97, 103, 219n1
bureaucracy, 76–78, 84, 206

camera-print, 36, 178–180, 183–186, 189,
    193, 200
caste, 54, 162
celluloid, 19, 79, 85, 89–92, 181, 193
censorship: incisions and excisions,
    89–93; in marketplace film trade,
    84–85, 93; Pakistan Boards, 79, 82; of
    poster art, 70, 90–92, 97; Punjab
    Censor Board, 14, 78, 83; vigilante,
    92–93, 97; Motion Picture
    Ordinance (1979), 55, 80. *See also*
    Central Board of Film Censors
Central Board of Film Censors, 14, 79,
    83–84
Christianity, 21, 51–54, 103–105,
    118–120, 124
cinemas: air–conditioning, 109, 111–112;
    attacks on, 45–48, 176; during
    Muharram, 127–128, 234n28; during
    Ramadan, 128–130; multiplexes, 50,
    63–64; Pakistan Talkies, 14, 19; Plaza
    Cinema, 39, 112; repertory, 89–92;
    Tarannum Cinema, 14, 159; and
    urban space, 50–51
CinePax chain court case, 48–50, 63
cinephilia, 3, 44, 220n15
cinephobia, 13, 44–45, 65, 220n15
circulation: of currency, 180; and
    originality, 146–147; and patina, 199;
    and value, 189–190
citizenship. *See* atmospheric citizenship
class, 111–112, 185–186
collectors, 85–89, 180–181
colonialism: and film, 16, 42, 58–59,
    80–83; and urban form, 39, 50, 63,
    163–165, 169–171
commons, 69–70, 206

common sense, 74
cosmopolitanism, xvi–xvii, 157–158
currency, 139, 143, 181, 199

data, 97, 101–102, 145, 158, 180, 184, 186
demand, 29, 35, 66–74, 89, 98, 126,
    143–144, 176, 181
Deobandi (Sunni Islam), 23
digital: and analog, 185–186; glitches, 19,
    28, 159
digital economy, 51
digital storage media, 180
drama: serials, 197; stage drama, 52,
    55–56, 197
DVDwalla, 7–8, 66–67, 84
Dubai, xvi–xvii, 42, 93, 158. *See also*
    Gulf migration

electronic media: adoption of, 4, 192–193,
    207; destruction ceremonies of, 7, 36,
    45, 175–177, 207; and obsolescence,
    xvii, 105–107, 111, 185, 212n9, 239n7
encroachment. *See* Qabza
ethics: and aesthetics, 12–13; and the
    airborne, 112; *akhlaq* literature,
    42–43; anthropology of, 15–19, 31,
    33, 129–130; and atmosphere, 1, 10;
    and mediation, 190, 208; "ordinary
    ethics," 16–17, 214n39, 215n41; and
    transcendence, 215n42
evacuee property, 6, 166, 172
Evernew Studio, 17–18, 131

Facebook, 134, 138, 147
Faiz Ahmed Faiz, 41–42
film: absence of, 127–131; analog-to-
    digital, 185; extras, 85–86; labor, 16,
    51, 53–58, 59; ontology of image,
    58–63; and permissibility, xviii–xix, 21,
    21, 29, 39–43, 52, 58–67; propaganda,
    227n31; and public morality, xviii, 1, 8,

13–15, 22, 26, 42, 47, 51–52, 80–85, 92, 176, 203–205; studios, 1, 16–20, 53, 131; trade policies, 4–5; unions, 64
film music, xv, xvii, 8, 88–89, 151

guardianship, 142, 146–147, 190
Gulf migration, 6, 99, 134, 148–149, 158, 161, 191–192, 195–196, 202

Hall Road: Durrani Electronics, 26–28, 99–102, 175, 182–183, 195, 202; film trade, 3–8, 159, 186–190, 193–199; history of, 104–105, 168–69, 175; and piracy, 5, 36, 180; and pornography, 80, 175–176, 207; repertoire, 29–31, 66–67, 70, 76, 78, 190, 196, 204–207, 231n39; and technological change, xvii, 100–101, 180–181, 202–203; trade unions, 23, 152–153, 164–166, 175, 182; urban form, 36, 174; and Yaseen Street, 105–112
Hawala/Hundi, 193–194
heritage, 172–174
Hinduism, in Pakistan, 21, 168, 170, 198
Hudood Ordinances, 25, 57, 112–113, 169
Hussain, Imam, 22–23, 132–134, 139–141, 198

image quality, 26, 36, 179–184, 186, 193, 205
India: and electronics markets, 6; Indo–Pakistani War (1965), 5
Indian Cinematograph Committee Report (1927–1928), 16, 58–59, 81–82
Indian film, 5–6, 31–32, 42, 45–46, 78–79, 84, 156, 192–193, 197
informality, 84, 156–157, 161–167, 192–194, 206–207
infrastructure: and ambience, 102; breakdown and intermittence,

102–103, 107–108, 117–118; new provision of, 100; and politics, 115–118
interface, 33–34, 36–37, 55, 76, 177, 179–180, 184–186, 200–201, 205–206
internet shutdown, 102, 129
Iqbal, Muhammad, 58, 61–63, 99
Iran, xviii, 41, 133, 192
Islam: and ambiguity, 216n54; anthropology of, 31; and media technologies, xviii–xix, 30, 58–63. See also Islamic jurisprudence; Islamic socialism
Islamic cultural center, 48–50
Islamic jurisprudence, xviii–xix, 21, 25, 30, 57, 155, 223n50
Islamic posters, 70–73
Islamic socialism, 154–155
item numbers, xvii, 52–54, 64, 80

"Jaal Agitation," 4–5

Karbala, Battle of, 22, 104, 115, 125, 130–131, 133, 139
Karachi, 6, 45, 48–50, 64, 80, 87, 167, 178, 189, 191
Khan, Imran, 68, 155–156, 235n5
khidmat, 152–156
Khidmat Group (professional union), 152–156, 164–167
kinship, 194

Lahore: demographics of, 21–22; ethnographies of, 33; film industry of (see Lollywood); liberalism of, 175–176; microcosm of, 77; migration to, 51, 54–55, 170–172; population growth of, 100; urban form, 107, 159, 164–175; Walled City of Lahore, 13–14, 94, 133, 136, 141, 148; zoo, 151, 158

liberalization, of media, 99–100
liveness, 135–136, 147–150
loadshedding, 107–108, 116,
    118–120
Lollywood: aesthetics of, xvii, 7, 189;
    film distribution, 5; studio
    production of, 17–18

mahaul: and airborne phenomena, 3,
    232n42; and cinema halls, 13–15; and
    economic activity, 177, 199–200; and
    interiority, 114–115; and Islam, 2; and
    manners, 234n8; and mirages, 123;
    positive attributes of, 24, 135–139,
    149–150; and public demand, 67, 74,
    97–98; and social class, 170–174,
    232n45; and sound, xv–xvii; and
    technology, 3, 8; and terror, 1–2; and
    virtual reality, 109
mahauliyat, xix, 31, 109, 206
master copies, xvii, 28, 36, 141, 176–177,
    179–189, 193–195, 200, 202
Maududi, Syed Abul A'la, 58–63, 224n58
mazhab, xvii, 72, 125
mediation, 12, 32–33, 198–201
mirage, 123
modernity, 111–112, 119
mohalla, 148–150
Motion Picture Ordinance (1979),
    55, 80
mourning, 22–24, 35–36, 72, 125–127,
    130–140, 148–150, 181–182. *See also*
    azadari
Muharram: and figurative depiction,
    132–133; on Hall Road, 126–127,
    134–135, 186; and moral exception,
    22, 35, 125–131, 149–150, 207
Muhammad, Prophet, xv, xviii, 22–23,
    38, 45, 71–72, 104,
Musharraf, Pervez, 5, 99–100

music, during Muharram, 22, 104, 115,
    125–134, 207

na'at, xv, 8, 23, 130, 136
National Council of Public Morals
    Report (1917), 16, 81–82
National Film Development
    Corporation (NAFDEC), 41–42, 191
nazar, 109

obscenity, 43, 82–83, 197, 203
open culture, 69
Orange Line Metro Train, 169–174

Pakistan Telecommunication Authority,
    46–47, 173
Pakistani film: and absence of national
    archive, 28, 69, 98, 190–193; decline
    and rebirth narrative in, 21, 40–42,
    55–56; new wave, 13, 19, 40;
    Pashto-language, 46, 55, 92, 192;
    Punjabi-language, 19, 42, 46, 55–56,
    80, 86, 90–92, 115, 151; study of, 13,
    30–31; Urdu-language, 64, 192.
    See also Lollywood
Pakistan Television Corporation (PTV),
    64, 127, 145, 191–192, 197
partition, 4, 50–51, 166–173
patriarchy, 52–53, 203–204
performance, 13, 30–31, 45, 56, 64
permissibility, 39–43, 52, 56–57, 74,
    220n14
photography, 61, 93–94, 152–153,
    178–179, 186, 198–199
piracy, 5, 163, 180, 185, 190, 195,
    206–207
plagiarism, 5
plazas, 6–7, 66, 105–107, 151, 154,
    159–161, 164, 167, 175, 186,
    195–196

politics: and elections, 100, 117, 153, 219n2; hybridity in, 235n5; and protest, 38, 51, 151–153

populism, 68, 155, 205

pornography, 79–80, 189

pressure, 114–115, 230n25

printmaking, 183–184

PTV. *See* Pakistan Television Corporation

public. *See* awaam

public affect, 22–24, 153, 205–207

public service. *See* khidmat

purity, xvi, xviii, 11, 121, 162

qabza, 154, 164–168, 202–203

Quran, 61, 99, 105, 154, 196

radio, 4, 9, 88, 112, 127, 165, 168, 188

Ramadan, 128–130, 149–150

recitation, xv, xviii, 24–25, 34–35, 57, 130–131, 137, 178

renunciation. *See* tauba

reproduction, 30, 32, 35–36, 67, 179, 183–185, 205

reputation, 12, 18, 26, 36, 177, 181–182, 193, 197–198

Romanticism, 3, 120

saints, 22–24, 70–71, 104–105, 110, 115, 168.

Salafism, 104

saturation, 26, 55, 102, 115, 205.

Saudi Arabia, 63, 71, 148, 192, 196–197

Shalimar Recording Company, 87, 181, 183, 191–193, 197

Sharif, Nawaz, 119, 166, 170

smartphones, xvii, 7, 105, 107–109, 140–141, 144, 198

smog, 100–102, 118–124,

social media, 21, 47–48, 52, 134, 147–148, 173, 202, 207. *See also* Facebook; TikTok; WhatsApp; YouTube

sound: and atmosphere, 8–11, 112, 120–122, 150, 231n36, 233n16; and Islam, 31

tauba, 53–54, 63, 86, 222n33

taste, 12–13, 41–43, 46, 111, 120

Tehreek-e-Labbaik Pakistan (TLP), 38–40, 43, 51, 65, 96, 116–117, 219n2, 227n37

television, 7, 21, 28, 38, 88, 92, 100, 123, 125, 127, 129, 131, 141, 220n14

terrorism, 36, 175–176, 191

theology, 15, 21, 46, 56–63, 223n50

thresholds: in anthropological theory, 25, 113; between faiths, 21–22, 105, 110, 131; in ecology and elemental media studies, 25, 117; in Francophone philosophy, 218n71; *hadd/hudood*, 24, 56–57, 112–113; of image decay, 19–20, 186; and infrastructure, 102–103, 110–112, 118–120; interdiction and reproduction, 32, 43, 204–205; as interface, 26, 199; moral, 22, 126, 130–131, 204–207; in music, xviii, 8, 130–131, 136–137; and pollution, 117, 122–124; in Shi'ism, 137–138, 149–150; and tauba, 53–54

TikTok, 47

totay, 79–80, 87, 93

transgender, 14, 54, 188

transcendence, 15, 17, 60, 112, 198, 215n42

Twelver Shi'a: Alid piety, 72, 130, 135; and cinema, xviii, 125; Imambargah, 102; Majlis, 139–140, 148; media repertoire of, 36, 126–127, 134–135, 198; orators in, 146; in Pakistan, 21–24; posters, 71–73; religious media stores of, 24, 35, 134–150; and tauba, 53–54; violence against, 23, 126

Printed and bound by CPI Group (UK) Ltd, Croydon, CR0 4YY

10/06/2024

14513085-0001